# COMPANION INTO KENT

*Spurbooks Companion Reprints*

COMPANION INTO BUCKINGHAMSHIRE
by Maxwell Fraser

COMPANION INTO BERKSHIRE
by R. P. Beckinsale

COMPANION INTO SUSSEX
by Norman Wymer

COMPANION INTO SURREY
by L. Collison Morley

COMPANION INTO LAKELAND
by Maxwell Fraser

# COMPANION INTO
# KENT

*By* DOROTHY GARDINER

*WITH FIFTEEN PLATES AND
ENDPAPER MAP*

SPURBOOKS LIMITED

First published by Methuen Ltd., 2nd edition 1946

This edition with new photographs and map by
SPURBOOKS LIMITED
1 Station Road, Bourne End, Buckinghamshire
1973

SBN 0 902875 30 2

Printed offset litho by
Biddles Ltd., Guildford, Surrey

## PREFACE TO SECOND EDITION

THE first edition of this book had for background the Kent of 1934, remaining substantially unaltered till 1939.

Since then War has worked many changes, not only by the ruin of towns like Canterbury and Dover, the destruction, wholly or in part, of ancient buildings like Little Chart Church, but also by a transformation of the landscape. The felling of thousands of great trees; the veil of growing corn on downlands once green with turf; the erection, too, of camps and war-factories, hideous, though often but temporary, blots on the country-side; all these factors play their part.

By and by there will be repair, reconstruction, after the lapse of years in some cases. To bring the *Companion* ' up to date ' is plainly futile. Where it falls behind let its pictures become part of the story of our county in days gone by.

D. G.

COGAN HOUSE
  CANTERBURY
    *September 1946*

# CONTENTS

# ILLUSTRATIONS

# INTRODUCTION

READER, you have here no guide-book, but something much more incomplete : merely a companion into Kent, a friend to walk with you some of the way, to tell you a little of those things in particular which have taken his fancy on the country-side. It may be that you require a lead, a suggestion, as to where to settle down for good; or only as to where to make holiday for a few crowded weeks. All undecided, you have looked England up and down, from the Scottish heather to the Surrey pines, from a fishing-stream on Bodmin Moor to some village under hanging woods, among the Downs. So be it; there is still Kent, the most alluring of counties. Its past can show you patterns incomparably various; its present, every phase of modern life, from an aerodrome to a coal-mine; and the setting for past and present is an England like a happy girl, an England rich in healthful beauty and in simple things, blossoming orchards, wide, unfenced cornfields, meadow-lands by a gentle stream, river estuaries crowded with trafficking ships, church and cathedral, holy places of our people, villages where one cottage is framed of forest oak, another of yellow mud-bricks from the seaward marshes.

Nor shall our wanderings be confined to the range of my eyes or yours, or to the society of Kent men and women of to-day. We will re-people ancient dwellings, question the dead and gone about their love for Kent, their lives passed on its soil; we will read their thoughts in old books and new, their epitaphs on marble tombs or on some gravestone under a churchyard yew. You shall breathe the air of Kent, of marsh and upland or bracing sea-coast; you shall look out to her pearl-grey horizons, smell the cherry-blossom, the hops, the ripe apples; the cement works too and the petrol fumes on by-pass roads, and the Sittingbourne brickfields. You shall hear the nightingale in bluebell woods; the rooks high on cathedral limes; the roundabout's music across Margate sands. And when the last page is turned you will know a mere fraction of all there is to know : yet perhaps enough to move you to try, or it may be to remind you, how it feels to be a Kentish man; to join a band of lovers, the jealous keepers of an ancient inheritance. What companion could ask a better reward?

D. G.

PRECINCTS
CANTERBURY
*April 1934*

## Chapter I: CANTERBURY

*The Precincts—The City—Of Ingoldsby and Dickens in Canterbury*

### THE PRECINCTS

IF you should decide to live in Canterbury, a house in the Precincts is my suggestion. It is a heart of peace in an over-crowded, noisy little city. The Precincts are crowded too for a few be-touristed months, and crowded the year round with memories. Think of it: these dozen acres have been inhabited without a break since the mid-sixth century, when King Ethelbert of the hill-side became a town-dweller. Even then he settled where, before the unchronicled years of sword and fire, Roman buildings had stood. After Bertha and her maids ceased to pass daily through Queningate to their prayers, the monks, who took possession, must have sat more closely to the Precincts than any dwellers there before or since. Evidence is not lacking how much they cared for the place: it is hard to live there long without striking root deeply. Their lives centred round the cathedral. When fire consumed their choir they were inconsolable; in the nave, which stood unharmed, they 'howled, rather than sung, matins and vespers', abandoned to grief for all that had dropped to ashes. In their dreams they pictured the beloved building, during the hours empty of prayer, peopled with angels in their places, reading, singing, treading the stairs into lofty triforium and clerestory.

Corners of the Precincts were hallowed by immemorial custom. John Stone writes, almost on every page of his chronicle, about the pavement slab of the infirmary chapel.

I

There each brother, dying of plague or asthma or old age, lay a while, with uncovered face, on a sprinkling of ashes.

Not that our Benedictines were immured in the Precincts. Brother John again—so vividly picturing his companions; the huge granary-keeper, taller than any other religious of his day; the humble monk who had once moved among the great, pronotary to Henry IV, chancellor to the Lady Joan, ambassador overseas; Cellarer Stephen, a jocund man, well-loved of all; Thomas Selmiston, fair of face, fairer of faith, who broidered a golden chasuble for Brother Thomas Herne—John Stone remembers many a procession, when the monks, wearing green copes, or white or red, passed through Burgate to St. Augustine's Abbey, or by All Hallows into the Friars Preachers' Church, and so back again through the garden gate. The chronicler himself, fifty years a monk, saw the bells blessed in the vanished belfry of St. George's Church.

Visitors came not seldom, sometimes from afar. Queen Margaret of Anjou heard the boys sing mass before Our Lady's altar of the Undercroft; the Abbess of Shaftesbury stood in choir on the prior's right hand; the Patriarch of Antioch brought strange beasts in his train—four dromedaries and two camels, 'the like of which had not before been seen in England'.

The superintendence of outlying estates took officers of the monastery riding into the country. You and I shall meet them in the lanes, in the darkness of huge barns, in many a village street : for the monkish farmer is a personage of Kent in the Middle Ages.

Soon after the ' Plunder ', lay folk, unconnected officially with the great Church, began to live in the Precincts. By Cranmer's time the common garden of the monks, south and east of the Corona, had been ' made plain, all hedges . . . being taken away, and the place made handsome . . . for a common walking-place of the prebendaries, and for the children to play

EFFIGY OF THE BLACK PRINCE, CANTERBURY CATHEDRAL

in, at all times as it shall seem good to the schoolmaster to license them to go further for their pastime '.

And so along the eastern walk, still called the Oaks (but the sheltering trees are all limes), venerable canons sunned themselves in the bygone leisured days; until compelled to hurry out through the postern gate on multifarious errands. And so for at least 400 years, King's School boys and choristers have obediently played on the grass plots and city babies rolled among the unofficial daisies which grow here so very thick and fine.

One little house you know already, Flemish gable-ended, canopied with an Adams' shell over the narrow front door, amply bow-windowed by the Georges, disfigured by some Victorian vandal with a frightful bay of ' mathematical tiles ' : Albrecht Barbier roses try to conceal the blemish under a cloak of cream-white buds and glossy leaves. This, ' the new-bricke house in the Covent Garden ', was built under Charles I and let on lease. A cherry-orchard flourished on its south side, and the old King's Schoolhouse afforded it stable room. The house is a bungalow compared with the oldest canonical residence; that having a Norman kitchen and chambers called Heaven and Paradise : it is a mushroom beside Meister Omer's, where lived in the thirteenth century the lay officer who supervised monastic affairs. Nowadays should you come here you would join a company of unclerical tenants, ' precinctified ' as the ribald say, for the Dean and Chapter have divided some rambling houses into flats, and converted into dwellings the stables of coaching days. The charm of the place is unique : the living cathedral; the beautiful shell of the monks' home; these incomparable things stand among great trees, some two centuries old, and flowering shrubs, chosen with forethought. The lime-blossom winds up a procession of blossoms, headed by the shivering almond and the golden wall-flower, which crowns our ruins in their hoary age.

When Elizabeth Carter came to our Precincts 200 years ago

TOWER VAULTING, CANTERBURY CATHEDRAL

(dismounting from the London coach to pay her visits of ceremony and walking sixteen solid miles home to Deal), although no poetess she was stirred to metrical effusion because one of the prebends purposed 'cutting down a shady walk'. Thus she addressed him :

> In plaintive notes that tun'd to woe
>   The sadly sighing breeze
> A weeping Hamadryad mourn'd
>   Her fate-devoted trees.
> Ah ! stop thy sacrilegious hand
>   Nor violate the shade
> Where Nature forms a silent haunt
>   For Contemplation's aid.

To-day the axe is more judiciously wielded; our dread is of a fierce sou'-wester when the old limes are heavy with leafage; fortunately their roots strike deep and wide.

Not all dwellers in the Precincts have been inspired by their charm or awed by their dignity. A dancing assembly was held in 1718, at the house of one Mr. Hardres, when the returning guests—titled guests too—at the unreasonable hour of one a.m. disturbed the Dean's slumbers. The host, called before the outraged Chapter, 'put off' the blame upon his wife; she, spirited soul, summoned in her turn, entreated leave to arrange yet one more assembly, the very, very last. One scarcely doubts but that the invitations had been dispatched long since. Stern permission was given her 'for this time only, upon condition that the Assembly break up by Ten at Night' (amended to eleven—oh, the wiles of woman !), 'and that no more Meetings be held'. Then, again, when Miss Robinson of Mount Morris, afterwards the celebrated Mrs. Elizabeth Montagu, was driven from home by smallpox at the lodge, her papa 'and very good and tender mamma' insisted that she took refuge in the Precincts with a prebend's wife. She did not much appreciate clerical society : 'We have met with a great deal of civility,' she scribbled in her youthful vein, 'and have nothing but visits from prebends, deacons and the rest of the church militant here on earth. In short, the whole town takes to me so much that I am sure they would choose me member of parliament if I would offer myself as a candidate.'

The other blue-stockings here among the shades are more sedate : the child Elizabeth Elstob, orphaned from the north country, living in the stern society of her canonical uncle and Aunt Matilda at the eighth prebend's house; Catherine Talbot, Miss Carter's bosom friend, and sweet Mrs. Hester Chapone. The best prose pictures of the Precincts were made by a woman. The letters of Sibylla Holland (wife of an honoured treasurer of the cathedral) are too little known to country-lovers, and now indeed out of print; their tone of profound melancholy has perhaps been their undoing. No other has crystallized as she did the impression which the cathedral surroundings make upon a spirit sensitive to great beauty framed in little space. She was mystic as well as poet; when a girl of fifteen, staying with her kinsman Dean Lyall, she crept out with his stolen key, let herself into the dark, empty, vast, and mysterious church and passed much of the night prostrate before the altar.

' Bell Harry Tower ', she wrote, ' holds me as with a spell. I understand what keeps the rooks and jackdaws in their ever-circling flight.'

Most of her Precincts' sketches were made in winter : in summer she moved up to live among the Harbledown woods. Here are two from June and December.

' The nightingales have sung in the Precincts this year. . . . Last night, just as the bell practice began, a sudden storm from the sea, preceded by a thick mist, swept over Canterbury, great claps of thunder and streaming lightning. It was like an assault on Bell Harry, the lightning played all round him. " The bells kep' on," as an old verger observed, " and come right through; and when all was said and done, there they was." '

And next : ' At 2 a.m. I looked out of my window and saw Bell Harry rearing himself against a clear sky, and the moon riding high in the south-east pouring a flood of silver light on the great Church from the clock tower to Becket's Crown. Below, the soft south breeze was lifting white masses of mist and tilting them across the Missioner's garden and over the city wall. Not the faintest sound was audible in earth or sky, and silently I long watched the wondrous operation, while I felt the imprisoned fog escaping over my head from the house into the open air—to join its kind.'

Excepting for the nightingale's song, of which we are envious but not convinced, how characteristic all this is! Those still moonlit nights when passing footsteps echo the length of Becket's church and there is a pale sparkle in the dark windows so jewel-like by day. The mists also; it is a drawback which may be minimized but cannot be gainsaid, that our lovely buildings are rooted in the Stour marshes. We lie low, some say unkindly ' below sea-level ', and evening enwraps us with a chilly cloak. Mrs. Holland's writing communicates the spirit of the place in a degree to which Hugh Walpole's *Cathedral* (a novelist's picture of composite origin) nowhere attains. After all, he was a schoolboy here and she a grown woman of sentiment. In the *Cathedral* are little touches that recall Canterbury; the tourists who whisper together as the archdeacon crosses to the lectern; the humble worshipper at the daily office ' lost between the huge arms of her seat '; the asphalt paths which have replaced the ancient cobbles. There are good pictures of the building's vastness; but too often it is felt to be ' intolerably inhuman '. Its majesty brings terror, ruin even, rather than joy, to dwellers in its courts.

As a Precincts' poet once wrote about our rocks and choughs :

> Those there are whom God hath set to dwell
> In and beside old buildings, and doth teach
> With the near soughing of his watered trees.

But so to dwell is not the chosen lot of all; it may not be your choice. Yet it is from the gabled house under the cathedral shadow that I shall companion you into Kent.

## THE CITY OF CANTERBURY

I

*Punch* published a delightful poem to celebrate the one hundred and twentieth anniversary of John Stow's death. It described the tailors of London at the bench, snipping, sewing, and dreaming of fortunes yet to be made. The happiest of them all, old John Stow, the antiquary, throws down his needle when the bells chime, and goes into the street to conjure up visions of his bygone fellow-citizens :

> He beholds o'er Cornhill's mud,
> The spears and chariots of King Lud,
> And all along
> The clattering street
> Hears Roman feet
> And Saxon song,
> And dwelleth in a city wrought
> Of old by hands, but now by thought.

The stones of cities like London or Canterbury invite many such resurrections. One may begin by living at the tailor's bench of everyday. That is satisfying enough; although just as a human has his 'moments', so in Canterbury the spell wakes afresh at certain corners, certain seasons, or times of day. From the doorstep of the Sidney Cooper School of Art, in St. Peter Street, a pastoral of green meadows opposite meets the eye at a narrow lane's end, along a telescope of greyish houses. Most Canterbury streets look away to river, hill-side, or orchard. The green slopes, alas! are less virginal than a few years ago; yet the new houses have gardens and little plantations massed pleasantly together. Canterbury's enchanted hour falls at spring and autumn when lamps are lit before daylight fades. There is a bluish veil blurring hard outlines, as it were the mist of the city's antiquity; the softest veiled sky, with a few diamond star-points; on the eye-level a twinkling parade of lights which ray out towards ancient West Gate or sparkle along Mercery

Lane. And Canterbury's season is when the cherry-blossom
from some secret town-garden sends fragrance into the old
streets; when white petals are blown along the pavement from
a double cherry-tree, a princess captive in St. Mary Breadman's
churchyard. The tourist is wisest who comes to us in the
pilgrims' season :

> Whan that Aprille with his shoures sote
> The droghte of Marche hath perced to the rote;

or at latest in May or June. So to avoid August languors,
crowds, and charabancs.

Here one must make exception of Cricket Week. Then the
High Street is wreathed in flags and Mercery Lane hung with
baskets of flowers. Then the morning traffic draws one way
to St. Lawrence Ground, and comes triumphing back when
stumps are drawn.

II

Cherry-orchards cover the hill-slopes which hold Canterbury
in a green cup; they stretch up to its confines, and here and
there find an inlet still nearer the red roofs.

Close to Martyrs' Field, the hollow where Queen Mary lit
her torturing fires, and men and women, dragged in from
quiet Kent villages, passed to liberty through the flame, cherry-
trees white and fragrant hang garlands against the sky. Climbing to steeper meadows one sees the cathedral tower, a flower
of the ages, rise over the transient blossom.

In an early season, before March is out, the bud-clusters at the
tip of every bough have separated, and are at the delicious stage
of unwrapping; their trim security is loosened, and from a dis-
order of green scales and brown, many pearl-white buds and
pointed leaflets—a flower or two even—have shaken out. In
the lanes they are contemporaries of stitchwort and dandelions;
on the hedgerow, of the stiff twin leaflets which clasp a dog-
wood flower between their wrinkled fingers. In the hop-
gardens skylarks rise exultantly from the clods, but the vines

push out no more than tiny reddish shoots, spraying above coronella and trailing weeds. The traditional background for flowering cherries is a stainless sky; but on overcast evenings one can study the effects of shifting cloud-groups. Now the blossom shows delicately against a sudden patch of blue; now opaque against fleecy cumuli; now behind the orchards is a rift of orange under a storm-curtain; its rays dazzle in the flowery mazes, and the grass, uncanny as a witch's green cloak, is only less bright-painted upon the low-lying cloud than the sapling plum-tree's vivid leafage.

In these Canterbury orchards avenues of trees—each one wearing a glutinous girdle against foes creeping insidiously up from the ground—slant over the hill-brow into a blossomed distance. When the clusters are full-blown, they drape black stem and bough in a veil fine-patterned as lace. So lightly is this veil tossed over the tree that next moment surely it must slip to the ground and leave an ebony skeleton, disenchanted.

Fruit-gardens close at hand become a feature of the city's social life, the scene of lovers' meetings and of Sunday walks. Old pilgrim-paths, now bordered with pleached hedges of privet or hawthorn, cross many Canterbury orchards. Since cherries came into England with the Romans Chaucer's company might have lingered here among the trees,

Of which many on fayn is.

Then they would turn to look past the blossoms to the pilgrims' city, within stout walls and grey embattled gateways, a crowded city of many spires.

And so back by the well-worn track from April's fairyland into the homely streets.

III

The modern pilgrim should notice our street-names and look curiously into their origins. A 'Lover of Canterbury' once provoked correspondence in the local press by asking, 'Where do the absurd names of some Canterbury lanes come from?'

He had heard 'many tourists joke about Iron Bar, White Horse, Beer Cart, Duck and Love Lanes', embarrassing (so he said!) the residents and making them wish for addresses more stylish and unremarkable. Yet every name has its scrap of history. The Iron Bar at the end of its lane for centuries kept out intruding sheep and oxen, now driven in their motor-cars to our 'Rither-cheap'. Duck Lane is a corruption of Dog Lane, if that is any improvement. The neighbouring street, rather squalidly, remembers a certain holy well named after St. Radigund. She was that Princess of France, once a German captive, afterwards Abbess of Poitiers, for whose nuns Bishop Fortunatus wrote 'The Royal Banners Forward Go'; while for Radigund herself, 'with violets', he made lyrics a modern poet has translated:

> Yea, though the flowers of Paradise are sweet,
> These fain would lie
> Where thou wert passing by.

White Horse Lane was once part of Jewry Lane; in bygone days the White Horse, the county emblem, pranced over a hostelry near by; some have fancied the name was originally 'White House', embodying a tradition of the Roman 'Guildhall', ruins of which lie under the County Hotel. Beer Cart Lane continues Watling Street to the Stour ford; but the brewers' drays which crowded there usurped the legacy of Rome. Love Lane is named after a local family; it was never winding enough for a lovers' walk, and was earlier called Lodere's Lane, from another property-owner. The street-markets were god-parents to Mercery Lane and Win (Wine) cheap, and, far, far earlier, to the Staplegate of St. Augustine's followers.

Butchery Lane, meaning the Butchers' Lane, was once more elegantly called Angel Lane. *Cathedrall Newes from Canterburie*, written in 1644, tells its story as Richard Culmer, the image-breaker, knew it. In those days of mad destruction 'a great Idoll of stone, which stood on the top of the roofe of that Cathedrall over the South dore under Bell Harry steeple, was pulled down by 100 men with a rope; in the fall it buried itselfe in the ground, it was so heavy and fell so high. This image held a great brazen Crosse in his hand; it was the Statue of Michael the Arch-Angel, looking straight to a lane right over against it, in Canterburie, called Angell-Lane.'

The northward view along the lane of soaring Bell Harry remains such an ' angelic vision ' that one could wish for a re-christening in the forsaken name; and better inspiration for the meagre signs in front of the shops. Some Canterbury streets their churches have adopted—St. Gregory, St. Margaret, St. George, St. Peter, and St. Paul; some, the city gates—West-gate and vanished Northgate, Burgate, and Worthgate; one, the banished friars; others, some inn, the ' Black Griffin ' or the ' Prince of Orange ', shortened to Orange Street.

St. Dunstan's Street leads to ancient St. Dunstan's Church, where a marble slab, placed in 1932, commemorates Sir Thomas More. There, in a vault below the south-eastern Chapel of St. Nicholas, Margaret Roper hid her father's severed head. Per-haps she intended to be buried near it herself, although her grave is believed to be in Chelsea Old Church. The brick-gabled gateway of the Ropers' house, now electrical works, is just across the street. With what abandonment of grief Margaret brought secretly home that mournful relic of her best of fathers : a father bound to his children by ties of the spirit ' more straitly than by nearness of blood '.


**IV**


There is no Chaucer Street in Canterbury, as might be ex-pected. Some day there will surely be a Chaucer monument; one that shall become him better than the languorous dancing-girl under the Dane John trees befits Marlowe's stately muse. Not that Chaucer ever brought his pilgrims to the Shrine, or stayed them on Harbledown Hill to watch the towers which

rise in majesty from clustering houses, first gilded by the sunset
and after quenched in marsh mist. It was left for a fustian verse-
maker, the author of the 'Tale of Beryn', to convoy the party
through the West Gate and lodge them at the 'Cheker of the
Hope', which still, in massive outline, fills the west side of
Mercery Lane. He makes, you will remember, the Wife of
Bath, tired with her journey, lead the Prioress to the inn
garden, where the trim alleys are planted with pot-herbs. A
fragment of that garden remained till recently, open to the sky,
at the heart of the building which, after a disastrous fire,
replaced the old courtyard and pilgrims' sleeping-chambers.
Then development in the drapery business demanded passage-
way, and the little ghostly garden was swallowed up in a
smart modern establishment. I fancy sometimes the long-ago
figures standing bewildered on that new staircase, when the
need of a pair of gloves takes me where sage and hyssop once
grew in the sun.

Beryn's pilgrims had none too good manners; they quarrelled
over some object in a stained-glass window which one took for
a quarter-staff, another for a spear, until Herry Bailly, mine
host of the 'Tabard', called them to order. The Miller and the
Pardoner too, having just knelt in penitence at the Shrine, stole
a handful of 'Canterbury brooches' to carry home. It was
Herry who addressed 'mury words' to an absent-minded poet,
staring on the ground :

> He semeth elvish by his contenaunce
> For unto no wight dooth he daliaunce.

The *Tales* bring us no nearer than this to making a pilgrim
of the pilgrims' poet. Yet he was well acquainted with the
county, and not improbably owned property in Kent. He
became a Kent J.P. in August 1385, an office usually bestowed
on members of landed families. His fellow-justices in the
commission were all qualified in this way, except William
Topclif, the archbishop's land-steward. Then, too, Chaucer
represented Kent in Parliament, and witnessed transfers of

land near Greenwich and Chislehurst. Yet if indeed he was a Kent landowner, his holding has not as yet been discovered: the Woolwich neighbourhood is a favourite suggestion.

Would that one could bring his ancestry nearer to Canterbury and to Boughton-under-Blean of the *Tales*. It pleases me to remember that while Topclif, J.P., was supervising the repair of Canterbury Castle by the royal master-mason Henry Yevele, about 1398, Chaucer was clerk of the works to Richard II; this may well have brought him to Canterbury from Westminster. . . . Chaucer's pilgrims never came to our city; their prototypes, as modern research avers, were not men of Kent: yet in a sense they haunt our streets for ever, and for ever ride, as Lydgate said,

> Throughout Kent, by hilles or by vales.

Ironically enough the *Tales of Caunterbury*—

> Some of knighthod, some of gentlenesse
> And some of love and some of perfitnes—

had their bewitching title made into a proverb for any wild story. Since Chaucer's day, wrote old Fuller, *Canterbury Tales* are parallel to *Milesian Fables*, neither true nor like to be true, but ' meerely made to marre precious time and please fanciful people '.

v

Your Canterburian has an ineradicable affection for his ' Jerusalem ', bred in him through generations cradled to the sound of cathedral bells. He may at times destroy; he will not concur in others' destruction of his city. When Elizabeth's thrifty Cecil was building Salisbury House he bethought himself of the stoneheaps of St. Augustine's Abbey, and his agents bargained for the demolition of certain buildings because Caen stone of Canterbury ruins, seaborne to London, ' came cheaper ' than new stone from Caen. One of them indeed ' took down the inner part of the gate at Canterbury, which will yield sixty or seventy loads of stone fit for London ', but he refrained from meddling with the outer part ' because the townsmen keep so much ado '.

The townsman is your true aristocrat : his surname is met with perhaps in civic records of the Wars of the Roses, or was carried into Kent by some French or Flemish ancestor, flying from cruel persecution.

The young people of a town with no industry but tourists and prosperous markets need the spur of ambition to seek elsewhere more varied employment; yet it is not easy, with that subconscious magnetism of Bell Harry Tower, to cajole them into a larger world.

Before the motor era Mrs. Holland wrote of our streets ' full of children; every girl skips and every boy drives a top. This invariable custom comes into play on Candlemas Day.' Her words are true, I think, of the by-ways, though I cannot be so precise as to date : do these which follow still hold good? ' No one,' she declares, ' ever reproves a child in Canterbury. . . . Perhaps the children if scolded would not go out hopping or fruiting with their mammas.'

Alas, our days are more nerve-racked than her calm eighties. (Though indeed Canterbury owes its St. Augustine to certain yellow-haired Angles, and so may be to all children a debt of loving kindness.) In 1934 even the little mamma in short petticoats has an adventure in the pilotage of her perambulator across the High Street. Fortunately there is a better provision of public gardens; although our old ' Dane John ' (once the burial-place of some Roman grandee, a gallows-ground, a plague-pit) remains first favourite. There, under the huge mound, the youngest citizens tumble on their grass plot, and the elders sit on a sun-bathed terrace above the walls.

One ' poetic childhood ' belongs to our city. After Marlowe left the King's School the memories of him in his native place are very scanty; has notice enough been taken, I wonder, of the formative power of its tradition upon a sensitive mind? The Canterbury of Marlowe's boyhood was no ill nursery for a

dramatic child. The plunder of the monasteries, the horrors of Mary's reign, had given place to comparative tranquillity; but for the boy's parents they were unforgettable experiences. John Marlowe, his father, belonged to that City Guild of 'Shoe- makers, Coriours, and Cobblers' which offered yearly in the Church of the Friars Eremite, Chaplains to the Guild, a wax candle to Saints Crispin and Crispian on their memorable day. Yet Marlowe wrote—from what memory of paternal admonitions—

> The prayers
> Of Holy Fryers having mony for their paines
> Are wondrous, and indeed doe no man good.

The destruction of medieval buildings was still going on; at St. Augustine's Abbey,

> the monastery
> Which standeth as an outhouse to the town,

time and weather, and greed, were compelling :

> Papal towers to kiss the lowlie ground.

Or, again, as elsewhere I have written; 'When Marlowe was ten the waggons of French and Flemish exiles creaked down St. Martin's Hill, and their looms began to stir. From boy- hood the poet must have known the tragic story of the Massacre of Paris. He might even have heard it from onlookers. Had not Cardinal Odet de Châtillon, brother of Coligny, died mysteriously, rumour said of a poisoned apple, at Meister Omer's house, and the shadow of Black Bartholomew drawn very near?'

Then, too, in that pageant-loving city, was still much to stir the imagination. 'In Marlowe's eleventh year Elizabeth her- self descended on Canterbury; childish eyes saw " the townes- men maske in silke and cloath of gold "; the Virgin Queen, glamorous and magnificent, ride, to the music of flute and drum, along the High Street, to the Cathedral.'

There are phrases in the plays which it is tempting to relate to childish memories; from

> The golden stature of their feathered bird
> That spreads her wings upon the citie wals,

as did the winged Michael on the cathedral roof, to the glimpses of a country-side, like Kent:

> The Meads, the Orchards and the Primrose lanes,

or Dido's

Orchard that hath store of plums; . . . a garden where are beehives full of honey.

The medieval city had its 'running streams and common channels', and one might go

> Walking the back lanes through the gardens.

And was it at Canterbury or

Once at Jerusalem . . . the pilgrims kneeled . . . upon the marble stones,

and afterwards limped away on their crutches.

### VI

After Chaucer, standing beside the Norman castle, and Marlowe, conning his book in the old King's School, our literary horizon is, in the seventeenth century, a blank. It was a disturbed time of sordid civil conflict which perhaps has scarcely aroused the interest it deserves.

The last pilgrim to the Shrine has vanished over the hills; but the influx of sufferers from the King's evil 'in sometime' has to be checked. The time-honoured custom which made Canterbury a passage-way of kings and their careless banqueting-hall persists until the crown itself topples to the dust.

Still the city revels in pageantry; there is a new king, Charles I; a queenly bride, Henrietta Maria; her 'little army of 4,000 attendants' crowd the streets with French faces; diamonds glitter in the monks' old guest-chamber over St. Augustine's Gate; the crown jewels have arrived there, under strict guard, from the Tower of London.

Yet the background of intolerance while the century was

yet young is worth recalling as the shadows of civil strife deepen. For the destruction which then dogged the city arose from the renewal of old dread and hatred as well as from a new fanaticism. New and old conspiring together proved more fatal to the cathedral than the ' Plunder ' itself had been.

In 1539 royal cupidity sacrificed the Shrine. A century later artistry stood at the judgement bar, and ignorance pronounced sentence. Richard Culmer was of course the arch-iconoclast. His fury was rooted in personal grievances as much as religious conviction. ' I have had very ungracious dealeing from the Lambeth Patriarch,' he wrote from Harbledown to Sir Edward Dering in 1640, ' by whom I have bene deprived of my Ministry and all the profitts of my Liveing [of Minster] three yeares and seaven monthes, haveing myselfe, my wife and 7 children to provide for; such is the Prelate's tyranny for not consenting to morris dauncing uppon the Lord's day.' His *Cathedrall Newes from Canterburie* is melancholy reading. He complained against the Dean and Chapter, ' these Prelaticall successours of the Idolatrous Monks ', for encouraging the ordination of their singing men, and providing them with benefices. This after all was in accordance with the spirit of Cranmer's Regulations for the King's School : ' If the gentleman's son be apt to learning let him be admitted; if not apt let the poor man's child apt enter his room.' He objected to a sermon in the cold choir, whereas the chapter-house hitherto in use was ' large, warme and wel-seated ', and to the provision of ' a most idolatrous costly Glory-Cloth ' for the high altar. One suspects that Culmer felt an involuntary admiration for this masterpiece, such as Prynne's for the stained-glass windows in Lambeth Chapel, which he at once denounced and glowingly described. ' The Glory,' Culmer writes, ' which is the shame of their Cathedrall, is made of very rich Imbroydery of Gold and Silver; the name Jehovah on the top, in Gold, upon a cloth of Silver, and below it a semi-circle of Gold, and from thence glorious rayes and clouds and gleames and points of rayes

streame downewards upon the Altar, as if Jehovah (God him-
selfe) were there present in glory.' If one were to stop there—
but Culmer recollected himself; 'All this . . . thereby to
usher in the breaden god of Rome and Idolatry.'

It is from him we learn how the Glory was made, by John
Rowell, a London embroiderer, how the paper pattern came
down from London and the prebendaries, particularly one
' W. B.' (Canon William Bray of the First Stall), consulted over
it; ' We conceive this Ovall-forme would doe better in a semi-
circle and extend the Glory more on either side. These Clouds
well shadowed and well wrought and pierced with raies will
be most proper. We conceive also that the Field should be more
Azure than Silver which will soone tarnish.' These remarks
were carefully copied by the arch-enemy from John Rowell's
evidence, when the Glory-cloth was on trial before Sir Robert
Harvey and ' appointed to the fire '. The Commissioners,
Culmer included, began on December 13th, 1642 ' demolishing
the Monuments of Idolatry '. The east window of St. Thomas's
Chapel was first attacked, the image of Austin the Monk first
destroyed. ' Many pictures in glasse were demolished that
day, and many Idolls of stone; thirteen representing Christ and
his twelve Apostles standing over the West doore of the Quire
[that is, in the choir screen] were all hewed down, and more
at the North dore of the Quire.'

One brave protest was made. While the evil work was going
on, ' in comes a Prebend's wife and pleaded for the Images
there. . . . When she saw a picture of Christ demolished she
skreekt out and ran to her husband.' He too came to ask the
authority for these doings; ' being answered that there was the
Ordinance of the King and Parliament, he replyed, not of
the King, but of the Parliament if you wil '. Culmer's smash-
ing of King Edward the Fourth's glorious window, how from
a ladder he rattled down ' proud Becket's glassy bones ', and
how (but this he omits to tell) he was near being stoned on his
perch by a zealous supporter from the town; these are oft-

quoted episodes in a grievous tale. Wharton, the church historian, wrote Culmer's epitaph from contemporary evidence: 'Upon the whole one of the greatest villains in the kingdom.'

VII

If Culmer changed the aspect of the cathedral (the fabric miraculously escaped, although the 'Store powder of the County') the City's iconoclasts were among its dignitaries of the eighteenth century. Five out of six medieval city gates and the black flint archway which crossed 'the Friars' next St. Peter's Street wholly or partially disappeared between 1781 and 1791. The legend, oft repeated, of the West Gate, Sanger's elephants, and the Mayor's casting vote, has no documentary support.

The Commission for Paving, Lighting, and Watching within the walls held its first meeting in 1787; M.P.s for county and city, the mayor, recorder and justices, dean and vice-dean, and a hundred citizens composed that zealous but unimaginative body. They tilted like Quixotes against the projecting storey, the bay-windows of ancient houses, against inn signs, porches, and forecourts; from street to street they roved, abolishing, reforming, standardizing. Luckily many old roofs and gables escaped them, as he may judge who overlooks the city to-day from the West Gate tower. Our revolution ended as another began, and in 1789 the Burghmote thanked the honourable Commissioners for their 'steady and unremitted attention to the Important Business of paving, watching and lighting this ancient and respectable City, and for the very judicious and satisfactory manner in which they have compleated the same'.

About this time the west side of Watling Street was built up through the garden of the Mans' dwelling-house; their stately mansion, partitioned into offices, still stands opposite its grounds on the east side. The oldest houses of the western range are numbered nowadays up to 30, and some of them

figure in Defoe's tale of the Apparition of Mrs. Veal.  Mrs.
Bargrave, who received that ghostly visitor, lived for many
years in a house on the site of No. 29, reconstructed some half
a century ago.  When the spectral Mrs. Veal ' got without the
door in the street '—our Watling Street—she turned north,
past the house-fronts we pass day by day, and afterwards—
who can say?  Now that we know Defoe's material to have
been no invention of his fancy but a local incident, very real
to a real Mrs. Bargrave, deeply interesting to her neighbours,
how vivid it all becomes.  Barbara Bargrave was not a happy
woman.  Widowed before her twenty-sixth birthday, her second
marriage to Richard Smith, or possibly her adult baptism just
before it, so offended her father, a Bekesbourne yeoman, that
he cut her off with ' the sume of twelve pence '.  Once more a
widow, she again remarried, one Richard Bargrave of Bridge,
a maltster and a drunkard.  He used her brutally, and evidently
compelled her to send her little five-year-old girl away from
home.  To this lonely soul there came, in some strange renewal
of confidence, an old friend from the shades.

'This Gentlewoman ', says the letter, recently discovered,
which told the story for the first time, ' was much overjoyed
at the sight of Mrs. Veal, and went to salute her; but she
rushed by her and sat herself down in a great armed chair, and
fell into discourse of severall things that had hapned when they
lived together at Dover. . . . Mrs. B. sayes that she had the
strangest Blackness about her Eyes she ever saw.  She stayd
two hours and at last seemed uneasy to be gone.'

Surely the most circumstantial visit ghost ever paid : was it
only the creation of a melancholy mind?  Defoe in his *Tour
Through the Whole Island of Great Britain*, writes of the
royal effigies in Canterbury Cathedral, and notes the ' Antient '
houses and ruins, so numerous that they made the place look
' like a general Ruin a little recovered '.  The social changes
then in progress interested him; the varying fortunes of the
broad silks weavers, the surprising increase of hop gardens in

the vicinity. 'They may say without boasting there is at Canterbury the greatest Plantation of Hops in the whole Island, something near six thousand acres within a very few miles.'

About that period the city was full of movement. The 'military' were one great source of excitement. On May 23rd 1756 Lieut.-General Wolfe's Regiment of Foot marched out, to make room for 1,500 Hanoverians newly landed at Chatham. The 'Bands of Musick' sometimes gave concerts in the local Vauxhall Gardens, weather permitting; shilling tickets to be had at the three Grand Taverns. One January day General Hawley's Regiment of Foot held a sham fight in the Old Park. The Duke of Marlborough attended, and 'a new and peculiar method' was tried out; 'in a very agreeable Manner, which gave entire Satisfaction to the Generals and to a great Number of Spectators. Two pieces of Artillery were made use of.'

How alluring to the nose-flattener must the shops have been in Georgian days. Here is a Huguenot milliner's stock-in-trade from the *Kentish Gazette* of December 1st 1753 :

### 'ELIZABETH DEBART
#### ' Milliner from London

'At the Corner Shop facing the Green Court Gates in the Borough of Staple-gate.

'Sells all sorts of Ribbons as cheap as any Weavers in London. Women's Fans at 9*d.* and 12*d.* a Piece; fine open-arm'd Cotton Gloves for Women; Velvet Pelerines and all sorts of Velvet Caps for Men, Women and Children. French Mirtins, Velvet Capuchin Cloaks, very good Velvet at 12*s.* the Yard. Choice of Horsehair Hats, black and white; likewise French Chip Hats; Ear-rings of several sorts, the best London Pins, silk Garters, silk Purses, black Lace for Hoods, Paris Nets, Artificial Flowers, silver Ribbons, long Lawns, silk Laces three Yards long at 6*d.* each; Leather Gloves, Hoop-Petticoats and other things too tedious to mention.

'N.B. If any Ladies please to look on these Goods, they

are to be sold very cheap, she going to leave the Country. The House and Shop to be Lett.'

But the nineteenth century knocks at the door. It is time perforce, wrapped warmly in a Velvet Capuchin Cloak, to clamber into the New Four Wheel Chaise Machine, on its four Steel Springs, and so to rumble on our way.

### OF INGOLDSBY AND DICKENS AT CANTERBURY

I

A tall, dark house in Burgate—a street which keeps its old-world vista unspoilt—has had of late secured to its dignified front wall, rather out of view, a bust of Richard Harris Barham. ' Ingoldsby ' was born at No. 61, at the corner of Canterbury Lane, in 1788, in the fourth generation of Barhams connected with the house. His great-grandfather, John Barham, having married the only daughter of Thomas Harris of Canterbury, heiress to a fortune made in hops, settled himself here as a tenant of the Dean and Chapter. Ingoldsby's father, also Richard Harris, a portentous alderman who weighed, can it be credited, ' seven-and-twenty stone before he was forty-eight ', died when his only son was seven. He left him the residue of the fortune in hops, a small encumbered estate which included the Manor of Tappington Everard in Barham. Richard Barham was baptized in St. Mary Magdalene's (close to the old Fishmarket), of which since 1871 only a picturesque tower remains. The names of his forbears are, or were, inscribed on some of the decaying tablets under the tower. Barham did not proceed to the King's School, but ' took learning ' at St. Paul's, and passed on to a congenially hilarious spot, Brasenose College, Oxford. The principal of the moment ' hated a college of paupers '; Barham tried to live up to his standard, played high and lost heavily. His guardian, Lord Rokeby, of Mount Morris, Ingoldsby's ' Matthew Robinson too, with his beard, from Monks' Horton ', refused to pay gambling debts, but gave as a friend the money he would not lend, a generous quibble which so impressed the culprit that it made a turning-point in his career. Back he comes, his own master, to No. 61 Burgate. And what goings-on enlivened that little town garden, hid behind its brick wall. Picture it; a gathering of the Wig Club founded by our genial Richard. Here they come, descending the old stair with its twisted balusters. Some are boisterous enough; some choked with laughter; some sheepishly conscious of their headgear, the more absurd the better; a parson's or a lawyer's wig, a wig full-bottomed, or scratch, or a 'brown George'. Once the fun drew near to tragedy. 'The raillery running higher than common the temper of one of the party gave way; swords as well as wigs formed part of the club costume, and the angry disputant drew his weapon. A grand mêlée ensued and the president narrowly escaped being run through the body in his own garden.' The Wig Club were patrons of all local merry-making. A light comedian, a penniless Mr. Harley, came with a travelling company to the city, destitute of any ward-robe but a tarnished laced 'frock', relic of the *Beggars' Opera*, and a pair of jack-boots sizes too large. Barham fitted him out as 'Goldfinch' in the *Road to Ruin*, with a buck's costume, his own 'green coat with gilt buttons, crimson waistcoat trimmed with fur, buff buckskin breeches, top-boots and silver spurs'. Burgate must have been a gayer place when it could see any day young Barham and his friends thus attired turn out of No. 61 and swagger along the pavement.

But Richard the Jester had another more serious side. In 1813 he was ordained, became curate of Westwell near Ashford and served other cures in the smuggler-haunted neighbourhood of Romney Marsh. His personal connexion with Kent ceased when he was beneficed in London, but the *Ingoldsby Legends* are full of local colour. Tappington, or Tapton Everard, that 'antiquated but commodious' manor-house which Thomas Marsh of Brandred built about 1628, is Barham's background

for many an irresponsible adventure. It stands a little out of
Denton village, at the junction of two wooded valleys beneath
steep escarpments of the North Downs; a picturesque place,
with ivied gables and thatched barns and a tree-shaded duck-
pond in attendance on it. Barham provided Tapton with a
spectre, a Bad Sir Giles, who murders his guest, the nameless
stranger, and ' in a neighbouring copse hides his victim's trunk-
hose, the pockets stuffed with inconvenient title-deeds '. The
tale hints at an ' ineradicable bloodstain on the oaken stair ', at
a dark tradition with which some have conjoined the solemn
word ' historical '. But the Marshes' ownership, lasting for
two or three generations, affords no hint of romantic mystery.

In the Snuggery at Tapton Grandpapa, in his high-backed
chair twiddling his thumbs, made the Witches Frolic for little
boy Ned, the Family Hope so tiresomely addicted to martial
music on tin trumpet and sixpenny drum. And there, Hugh
the page-boy, through the keyhole, saw the old miser murdered
as he counted his good red gold.

Barham enjoyed planting elderly heroes in high-backed chairs
before blazing fires. So sat Mr. John Ingoldsby, in his house
in the Precincts, to hear in comfort the tale of Nell Cook con-
cocted by Master Tom, the King's Scholar.

That ' legend ' of the portly, merry-eyed canon, of his ' niece '
and the pretty jealous serving-maid, judiciously located in the
days of Bluff King Harry, is in Barham's least decorous vein.
It ends, as everybody knows, with two deaths by poison secreted
in a Warden Pie and the disappearance of Nell. A century
goes by. Dean Bargrave's masons unearth, beneath a loose
paving-stone, in the Dark Entry—where, by the way, no canon
ever lived—a fleshless skeleton; beside it a small pitcher and a
bit of ' kissing crust '. Released from her living prison :

Though two hundred years have flown, Nell Cook doth still pursue
Her weary walk, and they who cross her path the deed may rue. . . .
And whoso, in that Entry Dark, doth feel that fatal breath,
He ever dies within the year some dire untimely death. . . .

The entry is less dark now by the removal of an overhead chamber than it was when Master Tom—a bandanna round his throat—manœuvred so artfully to delay his return to school:

> Now nay, dear Uncle Ingoldsby, now send me not, I pray,
> Back by that Entry Dark, for that you know's the nearest way:
> I dread that Entry Dark, with Jane alone, at such an hour;
> It fears me quite—it's Friday night! and then Nell Cook hath
>   pow'r. . . .

Another legend, ' The Ghost ', immortalized Barham's birth-place:

> There stands a City, neither large nor small,
>   Its air and situation sweet and pretty:
> It matters very little—if at all—
>   Whether its denizens are dull or witty,
> Whether the ladies there are short or tall. . . .

And the city has a castle

> Resembling (to compare great things with smaller,)
> A well-scooped mouldy Stilton cheese, but taller.

The stately keep is stuffed

> With leaden pipes and coke and coal and bellows;
> In short, so great a change has come to pass
> 'Tis now a manufactory of Gas. . . .

But that reproach was wiped out when the Corporation, in 1928, bought back the noble ruin into the city's keeping. And the Cathedral—well, from Richard the Jester, what should one expect but some such jumble as this; of the pilgrim and the Black Prince, of the pseudo-ancestor Fitz-Urse, First Bear of Bearham and the snores of the stout, paternal alderman:

> A fair Cathedral too, the story goes,
>   And kings and heroes lie entombed within her;
> There pious saints in marble pomp repose,
>   Whose shrines are worn by knees of many a sinner;
> There, too, full many an Aldermanic nose
>   Roll'd its loud diapason after dinner:
> And there stood high the holy sconce of Becket,
>   Till four assassins came from France to crack it. . . .

## II

At two crises of his life came David Copperfield into Canterbury; the first time was on a summer's day when the old street 'dozed in the hot light' and rooks sailed round Bell Harry. He was a boy then, a fugitive from Murdstone and Grinly's warehouse; a 'romantic innocent boy' making his way to his aunt, Miss Betsy Trotwood, who lived near Dover, but whether at Hythe, Sandgate, or Folkestone he knew not for sure. Years later, twenty years perhaps, he went again on a softer errand; went to learn at last the secret of Agnes Wickfield's constant heart: 'How well I recollect the wintry ride. The frozen particles of ice, brushed from the blades of grass by the wind and borne across my face; the hard clatter of the horse's hoofs, beating a tune upon the ground; the stiff-tilled soil; the snow-drift, lightly eddying in the chalk-pit as the breeze ruffled it . . . the whitened slopes and sweeps of Down-land lying against the dark sky, as if they were drawn on a huge slate!'

At the end of his ride: 'I found Agnes alone. The little girls' [her scholars] 'had gone to their homes now and she was alone by the fire reading.'

Canterbury identifies the window where she sat with the pretty old casements, diamond-paned, of the so-called 'House of Agnes'. No. 71 St. Dunstan's some years ago adopted this attractive name and painted it up conveniently on the wall. Canterbury has tried its utmost to cultivate a Dickens tradition, with, if truth be told, scanty material, beyond the immortal exception of *David Copperfield*. Dickens's biography and letters give but meagre help; he cannot have stayed long or often in our city or he would surely have recorded more than his one visit at the Fountain Inn, when he lectured to a Canterbury audience and found it responsive 'as the touch of a beautiful instrument', a perfect compliment to any audience.

He must often have passed along St. Dunstan's on his way to the Thanet towns, about which he is so much more expansive. Then the house of Agnes might well attract his attention; it is outstanding among the many old houses cheek by jowl. Still to some extent it bulges out over the road, and the wide upper windows try ' to see what is passing on the pavement below '. There is still an ' old-fashioned brass knocker, ornamented with carved garlands of fruit and flowers (which) twinkles like a star '. Inside the ' wonderful old staircase, with a balustrade so broad that we might have gone up that almost as easily ', leads still into the old room lighted by those quaint windows visible from the street. The house faces north and south, as it should to ' catch the early sun edgewise on its gables and windows '. One could not expect Dickens to describe No. 71 in every detail, but to-day no trace remains of the important ' little round tower which formed one side ' of Mr. Wickfield's house; nor of the turret office which Mr. Micawber occupied, nor the round window through which David saw Uriah's cadaverous face. The arched doorway approached by two descending steps is gone, and under the projecting storey the grotesque beasts' heads, which David could see sideways out of his window, are replaced by less interesting scrolls. But the present owner assures me the house has been modernized in various ways. Mr. Wickfield lived nearer the cathedral as I read it, and David walked from his house out of the town along the Ramsgate road; but why press such small discrepancies when quite convincingly one can imagine Agnes's sweet face behind the diamond panes of No. 71? The ' Sun Inn ', close to Christchurch Gate, stores among its memories the sojourn of Mr. Wilkins Micawber in ' a little room partitioned off from the commercial room and strongly flavoured with tobacco smoke ', and it remembers also Little Dorrit; while the author asserts that St. Alphege Church witnessed Dr. Strong's marriage with Annie Markleham.

The historians of the King's School mention a visit of Dickens to Canterbury to collect materials for *David Copperfield*, when he learned from local gossip of a domestic tragedy connected

with a former head master. This incident, they tell us,
Dickens worked up (and incidentally transformed) into the
story of Dr. Strong's marriage. They had no doubt access to
local information unknown to Dickens's biographer. The
grounds for identifying David's seminary with the King's
School are, one must suppose, the fact that as a Canterbury
schoolboy he went every Sunday to the Cathedral, ' assembling
first at school for that purpose '; while his dream-like recollection of ' the earthy smell, the sunless air . . . the resounding
of the organ through the black and white arched galleries and
aisles ', Dickensians relate to the glory of Canterbury. They
remind us too that Master Micawber's remarkable head-voice
was at the service of the ' Cathedral corps '. They have indeed
for the moment forgotten Uriah Heep's present address. He
used to reside in North Lane, but his house has been pulled
down and he has moved more than once to other quarters in
the city.

Dickens's grave is at Westminster; Barham's in St. Gregory's
Church in the City. On the north side of the garden-cemetery
at Canterbury, sheltered by tall firs and copper-beeches, stands
a block of rough-hewn Cornish granite. A patch of its surface
has been smoothed for the chisel, and there a stranger's name
is inscribed, ' Joseph Teador Konrad Korzeniowski '. A
strange name, yet two words of it are known wherever English
is spoken—Joseph Conrad—the sea-lover whose genius made
our language his instrument.

Hugh Walpole once told a Canterbury audience what, as
he believed, intimacy with our Kent country-side had meant to
Conrad's storm-tossed spirit. How, leading him up to the last
peace of all, it made apposite those lines of Spenser engraved
under his name :

> Sleep after Toyle, Port after stormie seas,
> Ease after Warre, Death after Life doth greatly please.

Canterbury rejoices that so illustrious a pilgrim lies at rest in
the pilgrims' city.

*The Approach to Thanet—Thanet in later days*

### THE APPROACH TO THANET

I

CANTERBURY for centuries past has been a Sabbath-keeping place. Nowadays, while summer-time lasts, it is a matter of circumspection on a Sunday to cross the streets leading to the coast towns.

A procession scarcely broken; the charabanc that houses a jolly, shouting, paper-capped crew; the mouse-like baby-car, conveying to Elysium its pair of lovers; dragonish ' motor-bikes', carrying knights errant whose password is ' Speed'; nowadays these folk break in on our Sunday's rest, bell-voices, and drowsy sunshine. With strangled cries and screeches off they go, past St. Augustine's stately gate, and the stretch of wall and bastion; past the stepped gables of Broad street; past those old-world refuges, the Hospitals of Jesus and of St. John, guardians of an end-of-life quietude to which it is un-thinkable these people of new England should ever submit. ' A short day but a merry one,' one might call after them, but hardly, hardly except in mockery, ' Peace upon your way.'

Yet one would like the younger folk to recall what road they are taking to the sea-side: who, on horse and foot, have followed it before them.

The Thanet road, though its beauty is stark and spacious, worn chiefly when the unhedged fields ripen their harvest, is one of the most fascinating of English roads. It deserves better than to be bordered with petrol pumps, tin barns painted scarlet, hotel signs foretelling creature comforts five miles ahead.

Let us go leisurely along it, even turn up a by-lane to let the traffic grind past. No need to halt before the black mill and the white mill at Sturry corner come in sight, except to hear how old John Somner, brother of Canterbury's historian, found out that the sea once swept up an estuary, a branch of the Wantsum channel, between the flat-topped hills where Stour now winds. How, too, the tides once brought salt airs to Canterbury, and even beyond it, to where Chartham's great tower now stands, swinging its bells to meet the voices of Bell Harry among the water-meadows. Somner wrote down the story so shortly before his death that some one has added a note begging that nothing imperfect in the record may be imputed to him who ' by such unavoidable necessity ' went his unreturning journey before the writing was corrected. Mr. John Somner, then, ' in September, 1668, sinking a well at Chartham . . . and digging for that purpose about seventeen foot deep . . . turned up, a parcel of strange and monstrous Bones, some whole, some broken, together with four Teeth, perfect and sound, but in a manner turned into Stone; weighing (each Tooth) something above half a pound, and almost as big . . . as a man's fist. . . . Some that have seen them . . . are of opinion that they are the Bones of an Hippopotamus . . . that is a River-horse. . . . The mould wherein it lay was altogether miry, like to that " oase " on many parts of the sea-coast.' From this ' Parcel of strange Teeth and Bones ' Somner guessed that the sea had once ' insinuated itself ' to the threshold of his new house, and that Canterbury stood upon ground swept together by the tides of ages. The Stour valley nowadays is flat and pastoral; no flotsam casts up on its shores except little brick dwellings which narrowly escape the winter floods; the river has shrunk and silted; barges come no more beside the quay at Fordwich.

## II

Fordwich lies away to the right of the Sturry mills; you turn by the picturesque manor-house of John Foche, last Abbot of St. Augustine's. This was Lord Milner's well-loved home, given in his memory to the Junior King's School, Canterbury.

Fordwich has civic records miniature in all but their extreme length. Before *Domesday* even it was an organized 'little burgh', of but seventy-three dwellings, and small in size it remained, although Canterbury's port of access to the Want-sum seaway. There toll-gatherers of the kings of Kent collected revenue from water-borne goods; dues upon casks of wine and honey, sacks of resin and of wool, baskets of raisins, ginger jars, silk and saffron, the pelt of foxes, sable, marten and wild cat.

The Confessor appropriated the town to St. Augustine's Abbey, and by 1110 it all belonged to 'God and St. Peter, and to St. Augustine, Apostle of the English, and the Abbot Hugh'. More important to the burgesses were Henry the Second's charter and grant of a merchant guild. In another century or so our burgh became the smallest 'limb' of Sand-wich, paying its quota of a quarter mark to the purse of the Cinque Ports, its fraction of a ship to their combined fleet. Always a 'poor relation', the wealthy brethren made undue demands upon its loyalty, to find sometimes the worm could protrude a serpent's tooth. One reads of forty pounds wrung out in excess of right, which Sandwich was compelled to drop back into Fordwich coffers. Year by year a solemn deputation, the mayor, two jurats, a freeman, with the town sergeant, rode to the Court of Shepway at the cross-roads below Lympne Hill. At the Court they took precedence of Folkestone, Faversham, Lydd and Deal, and if least were not lowest among their brethren. So it went on until in 1861, at Lord Palmerston's installation as Lord Warden, when the clerk of the Court called three times for Commission from Fordwich 'there was no voice nor any that regarded'.

Fordwich had a mayor nearly two centuries before Canterbury; often he was a man of substance, of some old county
family. His salary began at a quarter of a mark, and by 1700
had reached the handsome total of £6 13s. 4d. Then Admiral
John Graydon, a retired commander of Benbow's fleet settled
at Fordwich, accepted office, but declined the emoluments:
'The Mayor', wrote some wag in the Corporation Minute-
book, 'to have no salary but much punch.'

Fordwich barges disappeared towards the close of the nineteenth century, when the dues had dropped to thirty shillings.
The Corporation was extinguished in 1886; the civic privileges,
which once allowed of capital punishment by drowning at
Thief's Well or hanging at Little Gallows, were withdrawn;
the ancient Court Hall was given over to seven trustees and the
curious tripper. The building is not impressive; its lower story
of unwrought stone is patched with brickwork, and the upper
projecting one is plastered. The Council Chamber measures
only 31 ft. by 23 ft. 8 in., and its windows have oak mullions
and latticed casements, while the prison cell is but 8 ft. 3 in. by
7 ft. 9 in. The seal of ' the Barons of Fordwich ' preserved here
displays a lion regardant, companioned by a salmon trout on a
dish, such as Fordwich could once offer to a guest. The scolds'
ducking-chair, to be plunged from the Court Hall gable into
the Stour, is renowned; perhaps the milder alternative, which
drove the sharp-tongued hussy through the streets, a mortar on
her head, a minstrel with mocking pipe going before, was more
often administered.

There are old residences in Fordwich, should you be attracted
by the charming vista from the bridge, the green marshes and
river reach where the King's School boys have boats. Between
the wooden bridge and the brick bridge (called ' the stone
bridge ' in memory of its predecessor) is Tancrey House on the
right hand; it has a long roll of tenancy from the noble family
of Maregny to Sir Bertram de Tancrey, the Beverleys, Nortons,
Jenningses, until in 1830 it begins to pass on by purchase. The

walls of 'batten and rubble' were set up about 1200, but the timber-work is hidden by tiles and the interior modernized. Tancrey owns a river-side terrace above a Tudor wall, looped for defence—it is said against the Christchurch monks. The walk is on springy turf with a prospect of unpollarded willows, grey and leafy, marshalled in the Stour meadows. The estate occupies an island site, one branch of the stream going to the black mill, the other to the white mill—a site so water-bound that damp fogs would seem inevitable; but no, the mists stop at the gate, because the girdling stream runs swiftly and mists only hang about the stagnant dike. In July Tancrey has flowers everywhere, gay beyond words—cosmea, syringa, 'crimson pillar' roses like huge bunches of scarlet grapes. Certainly a lovely garden may bless those who settle hereabouts. They may pray o' Sundays in Our Lady of Fordwich, with its Chapels of St. John and St. Katherine, where votive candles once twinkled, and the font cover was fastened with bar and staple against witches' spells.

III

In summer it must be a nightmare to live in Sturry Street, a narrow, serpentine street, with only a frail wall between you and torrential motor traffic, dreading lest your child should step out heedlessly, as children will, or your limbs not carry you quickly enough across to the shop for a pinch of tea. What a blessed relief from noise and anxiety that long-promised by-pass through Hackington and Broadoak will bring.

One fastens on passages of the old topographers which suggest the shifts of scene that time has brought about. So in my turn I record the signs of immense changes coming over East Kent, inevitable, of course, but grievous to those who love the green ways. Take the roadside factories which strew our meadows with gigantic drain-pipes and every object cement can serve under- or above-ground. At first the vigorous spring grasses, buttercups, and moon-daisies strain up between the intruders and try to carry on the expected hay crop; soon they will give over and a scrap more of open country pass out of being. A favourite vista here at Westbere Butts, only a few months ago, down a rutted lane, over a broom-gilded hill-side, towards the grove sheltering Westbere Church, is gone to-day; a light railway has been laid; there is an air of desolation, a sense that nothing is let to live except drain-pipes and cement products. A little farther, to the right of the road, are tall shafts, belonging to one of the vaunted Kent coal-mines, an ever-extending ash-heap, and one of the new mining-villages. Hersden was begun during the Great War, when a few skimpy cottages, of concrete over a wall of lath, with eaveless slate roofs and metal-framed windows, were put up at war-time prices. With peace came more liberal ideas, backed by an immense resolve that the new mining-village shall be the antithesis of the old, that Abertillery and Dowlais shall never be transplanted from the black hills of Wales into the garden of England.

The new cottages are in warm brick and tile, set crescent-wise, so that monotony is avoided. When the creeping roses and gay shrubs grow up, and village life takes firmer root, there is everything to make it a lovable place. What do the inhabitants feel about it? In a sense they are in exile, for the county is seeing a miniature migration of the tribes, workless-ness driving the dour son of the North, the Welshman, the Midlander to take refuge among our men of Kent. How soon will they become at one, making our country-side population as varied in origin as persecution made Canterbury's generations ago? Already little Eiryns and Myfanwys are coming into the schools, and sound Yorkshire sense lends a hand in local administration.

Beyond Hersden the Roman road drives along a rib, straight as an arrow, between the Stour valley and the Nethergone folded deep on the left hand. As the sea-ward hills rise again, beyond bleak marshes where the wind tortures the grey reed-grass, the queer clumsy steeple of Chislet Church stands out on the ridge. So the road drives on, through the bric-à-brac hamlet of Upstreet, past Grove Ferry among its lavender gardens, sloping at last to the edge of England.

## IV

History and topography in Thanet are bound up with the vanished Wantsum channel, the waterway which once made it an island.

In the prehistoric age the mouth of the channel extended for eight miles, a huge gap eaten out of the coast-line from Ramsgate cliffs to Deal. The waters thrust westward from their entrance back into the land as far as Sarre, and then took a northward trend to emerge between Reculver and Birchington at the Northmouth. The long strip of beach extending from Ebbsfleet to Sandwich toll-bar was laboriously flung together by strong ocean currents which flowed continually north to south. Later came some commotion in the Channel between Dover and Calais, and, lo and behold, the currents' flow was reversed; sands from Deal were now swept northward to begin by slow degrees the silting of the ample Wantsum entrance.

Through that entrance rode the Roman triremes at their second invasion, and on an island in that channel they established their fortress of Richborough. Away at the Northmouth, where the gaunt twin towers of Saxon St. Mary's still afford a beacon for passing ships, stood the sister-fortress of Reculver. Stonar, a forgotten name until the Great War, was founded upon that piled-up strip of beach, probably before the Roman withdrawal; as the encroaching sands restricted Richborough Harbour, Stonar rivalled it in size and importance, flourishing until the Danes set it afire, rebuilt by the Conqueror, wiped out by the French in 1385; yet not before its day also had gone by. For as it had ousted Richborough, so the sand-shoals made at length sufficient grounding for its own successful rival. Sandwich gained foothold for men and houses first in the sixth or seventh century, and took over by degrees the harbourage that had made Stonar's fame.

So much for those far-off times. Come nearer our own; see how the villages sprang up along the Wantsum shore; they stand there still, although nothing is left but the white mists of autumn sometimes to make a ghostly channel at their feet and to show they once were seaboard places.

v

The stories of Minster and Monckton on the Wantsum and of Reculver by Northmouth belong to monastic history. The Thanet acres, enriched by careful tillage, were royal demesne. Ostensibly because they had been hallowed by St. Augustine's landing, perhaps also because they were inaccessible and 'oversea', the Saxon kings gave them readily to endow the royal foundations. Acre was laid to acre over a term of years, until the eastern half of the island, the Manor of Minster, roughly speaking belonged to St. Augustine's Abbey; and the western to Christchurch, lords of Monckton Manor. For a century or so the religious on Minster sea-shore were holy women, the first foundress and abbess, Earmenburga ('Domneva'); her daughter St. Mildred; Eadburga, who rebuilt on a fresh site church and nunnery, and translated, 'with immense thanksgiving', the relics of her predecessor; Sigeburga, in whose sad times the Danes descended on Thanet; and Selethritha, under whom the nunnery was finally destroyed. Selethritha probably escaped the flames in which chroniclers have immolated her and her nuns, and reigned on a while at Lyminge Abbey. Domneva's deer, and those ten thousand acres of the best Thanet land over which its feet flew to redeem each acre from royal to church ownership, that so the murder of Domneva's brothers might be expiated; this famous story is nowadays regarded as a monkish fable. The broken boundary-line, still in places traceable by its lynch, though doubtless due to the haphazard assemblage of manorial property, suggested to some imaginative monk the wayward course a driven stag would take. And he might well have seen his superiors hunting over those very lands. Did not Prior Goldstone, granting leases in the island, reserve the hunting and fishing to his convent's use? While on a Monckton lease now in the Cathedral library some monkish hand has sketched a huntsman blowing his horn, a greyhound in full chase after a hare.

## VI

The chief relics of monkish lordship in Thanet are the churches. The ground-plan of Eadburga's second church has lately been uncovered, and parts of the abbey-house and the huge barns of Augustinian days are close beside it. The Norman Church of Minster, built by Eadburga's male successors, a cathedral of the marshes, is there in its glory; the little southwest tower may be a last upstanding fragment of the nunnery buildings, made to contain a beacon light. The Church of St. Mary Magdalene at Monckton the Christchurch brethren once served; Queen Ediva, 'Ediva Felix' as she called herself, 'Mother of the whole English nation', gave it to Canterbury, 'the monks there to feed'. The brethren's stalls, the fragments of glass with heads of the priors, the quaint verses written on the west nave wall, by some island-lover—

Insula rotunda, tanetos quam circuit unda
Fertilis et munda, nulla est in orbe secunda

—these relics have all vanished since Hasted saw and described them. The priors sometimes made their *villegiatura* at Monckton Court, and not without their little comforts; my lord prior's pillow of snow-white linen bore a tassel of white silk; his coverlet broidered with lions had a bordering of clouds; a branch candle-stick, double-nozzled, lit him nightly to bed. The

Abbot of St. Augustine's rested at Salmeston Grange; not that his stay there was all holiday, for he took clerks with him, and there received the homage of tenants-in-chief. The buildings at Salmeston, as one infers from their ruins, which are not far from Manston Aerodrome, were ample in extent, including a well-lighted hall and chapel of some architectural beauty.

In early days monastic lands were ploughed by the tenants, supervised by lay brothers; later on they were let to tenant-farmers. Half a century before the Peasants' Revolt the tenantry attacked Salmeston, armed with their implements and with fire-brands, and the two resident monks, William Biholte and William de Middleton, were grimly besieged for fifteen days. What were the special discontents of the men of Thanet one hardly knows. The convent was liberal to the poor in their own fashion, with dishes of peas for the wayfarer and doles of loaves and herrings. But the land-services were oppressive to some awakening spirit of independence, though, alas! unrelieved by this outbreak; only in 1441 were they commuted for ordinary rentals. This embryo revolution is the one event of Salmeston history; it impressed the local imagination forcibly. To-day as one clambers over modern implements housed in the chapel-barn, or climbs precarious ladders to trace a trefoiled light, or as one follows some stooping passage into a tiny deserted courtyard, where are a crypt and mouldering steps; the spirit of the men who dominated the island for nearly a thousand years still defies the reign of villadom, though it creeps up to the Grange boundaries and encroaches fast upon the ancient plough.

### THANET IN LATER DAYS

#### I

On either side of the road as it crosses the Wantsum channel, green marshes, dotted with grazing cattle, stretch to the horizon.

Here and there a thorn bush breaks the level; dikes, shining to the sky, pattern the green plain with lines of silver. Yet within hail of Elizabeth's subjects—'in the memory of my ancestors' says John Twyne—what a noise of wind and wave was here. In the mile-wide passage, opposite Sarre, there clashed 'the greatest Recourse of the Stream and Reverberation from the Reflux of the Sandwich Shore; here the Tides opposed one another with . . . a mutual Vicissitude, that the Western Ebb gave way to the Eastern Flood, and again the Eastern Ebb gave place to the Western Flood, but not with equal Force, nor at the like Hours. . . .' So he wrote, picturing with ease the daily drama because the waters in his time had not entirely given place to green pastures. Sarre then looked out on a frequented waterway; ships anchored at its quay, on their way from Thames waters to the English Channel at Sandwich. The Deal coast entrance of the Wantsum was the first to close, although the loam from the cliffs which swept in at the North-mouth was part cause of the silting. From the Northmouth water continued to flow across the marshes until, in the eighteenth century, two walls or dams parallel to the coast— the 'Sarre wall', over which the Thanet road passes, and 'Chambers' wall', more to seaward—were constructed, and the old channel bed was brought under pasture. The Want-sum stream and the Nethergone, flowing in their new courses, meet at 'Sarre Bent', near the bridge by the entrance to the village. St. Giles's Church at Sarre, which stood by the chalk pit under the old windmill on the Ramsgate road, was ruinous before the fourteenth century closed. This marks, it may be, the ebb of the seafaring population; for the ebb of the tides had left them workless.

There were lay-owners in the Thanet uplands side by side with the monks; a group of old manors along the north of the island, the names of which appear on the most ancient and on the newest maps of Thanet, names such as Hale and Frost, Bartlett's, Down-Barton, and Shuart, were never monastic property. Shuart (Somner speaks of a wood called Shoorth, part of Blean Forest, perhaps the same word) stands on an old creek of the Wantsum. The mistress of Shuart took me out to see a certain chain hanging on an old decrepit willow.

'I always think,' she said, 'it may have been used to fasten up the barges as they came into the creek to unlade.'

'Which is the willow?' I asked, full of interest. 'Oh, this, the one that overleans the most. Why! why! I saw that chain there a day or two ago, where it has always hung! Now it is gone!'

'Who can have taken it; or has it rusted off from sheer old age?'

'No, there is no sign of it on the ground. It has been broken off and carried away. Oh, what a pity!'

'And with it goes one of the last memories of the creek,' I said; 'but, after all, I am not sure that a pollard willow is such a very long-lived tree. . . .'

Back we went to the glorious old barn.

'No vandal hand here,' I remarked, as we looked up into the ample roof-spaces, which house such deep shadows; 'these timbers must be older than the present dwelling-house?'

'That has been plastered over, and the gable concreted, which takes off the look of age.'

'That companion block, just the same style of building except for the little round-house at the south end, suggests to me that the old mansion had, originally, two wings, which remain, while the connecting range has been pulled down?'

'It may be so; I know nothing of its past history. You realize that second block is now a row of cottages, facing west, away from the dwelling-house?'

'Their ancient brickwork and that unspoilt Dutch gable are charming; the round-house may have been the dovecote at one time.'

'I wish one knew who built and cared for the place in days gone by.'

' The earliest tenant I can hear of, about Henry the Seventh's day, was John Wigmore, though there had been others before him; then Corpus Christi College, Oxford, came in as owners, and later purchasers were some Kempes, younger sons probably of the Kempes of Olantigh. I think the most likely builder of the present house was Sir Roger Manwood, who owned the property under Elizabeth. It reminds me of his almshouses at St. Stephen's, Hackington.'

' Shall I show you the sea-path before you go? '

' The sea-path; do you still call it " Pope's Gate ", as Lewis called it two centuries ago? And does the old watch-tower still stand hard by? '

But no, alas! no one nowadays has ever heard of the Pope or the tower, unless it may be those dumb things a few hoary stones in the cowyard wall. Shuart is so distinctive, so modestly withdrawn into its sheltering grove, one could pray that the plague of pink-roofed bungalows already at St. Nicholas-at-Wade might not advance along its quiet lane.

Nearer the village, St. Nicholas' Court has but one fragment of history: an old Lady St. Nicholas obtained a dispensation to hear mass at home in the winter when the church lane was blocked with mire. Lacking a history the Court has its mystery: a chamber of hewn stone at the end of a subterranean passage and steep descending steps. It lies under the lawn before the house. Of its origin, or purpose, no record remains, nor is it known where the blocked passage leading from one end of it might land a bold explorer.

As late as 1906 the ' Hooden Horse ' still pranced in Thanet; Sarre or St. Nicholas-at-Wade on occasions kept Christmas with this Kent form of mumming. Here is a description of Christmas Eve in a Thanet farm-house by Mr. Maylam, the historian by pen and camera of the famous steed: ' Seated round the fire we hear the banging of gates, trampling of feet on the gravel paths . . . and loud clapping. Every one springs up; " The hoodeners have come, let us go and see

the fun." The front door is flung open, there they all are outside; the "Waggoner" cracking a whip and leading the restive
"Horse" . . . champing his teeth, rearing and plunging, and
doing his best to unseat the "Rider" . . . while the "Waggoner" shouts whoa! and snatches at the bridle. "Mollie" is
there also. She is a lad in woman's clothes and vigorously
sweeps the ground behind the "Horse" with a birch broom!'

Once there was 'hoodening' all through Kent east of Godmersham. Some writers believe the custom to be as ancient as
Woden-worship; others, like our author, associate it with the
Robin Hood games. And the unlearned regret that it is now
only a memory.

II

After the break-up of the monastic estates the landed gentry
of Thanet became more numerous. Yet we know all too little
of them; only the old church monuments sum up their virtues
with the first and last of their mortal careers. There were
Paramores at St. Nicholas, one of whom built the village school;
Bridges, too, ancestors of the Poet Laureate, whose family still
owns the north chapel. The Norwoods dwelt at Nash Court;
the Pettits succeeded the Dandelions at Dentdelyon. Captain
Henry Pettit one could wish to have known if his epitaph tells
the truth about him: 'He was just and devout and of so
knowen integrity as to have the title of Honest commonly
given him, which made him to live beloved and honoured and
to die lamented. The righteous shall be had in everlasting
remembrance.'

There is more substance about the Crispe family of Quex. A
Crispe married the heiress of the Queakes, who left their un-
usual name to the family seat, under Henry VII. They had
been Crispes of Stanlake, who intermarried with Harcourts of
Stanton Harcourt, all belonging to the history of Oxfordshire.
By the date of the Queakes' match they had adopted Kent, and

soon rose to eminence in their new county. Two Crispes were high sheriffs; Henry VIII knighted the second, his own name-sake. He should rather have crowned him, according to John Twyne, who dubbed him ' totius insulae Thanati regulus '. With the Crispes, father to son, Quex remained till near the end of Charles II; then Thomas Crispe left four daughters, co-heiresses : the house fell to the share of the eldest, Maria Adriana, and was promptly sold by her husband, Richard Breton.

' Quex is a large commodious old building,' wrote the his-torian of Thanet in 1723, ' partly of Timber and partly of Brick, and is the only Gentleman's Seat in this island, besides that of Nash Court, which is not converted into a Farm-house. It is pleasantly situated among a Toll of Trees, which defends it from the Winds. There are handsome Gardens about it, walled in, with a pretty Vineyard and good Fruit.'

This is the house known to present-day visitors by Major Powell Cotton's splendid collection of hunting-trophies, gathered in lands of which the old home-keeping squires never so much as dreamed.

Between these successive families are apportioned the monu-ments in the crowded north chapel of Birchington Church. The most grandiose of them all was compiled by a Sir Henry Crispe, who died under the Commonwealth. It holds six busts, and is decked with coats of arms, festoons of fruit, a skull laurel-crowned.

Some day when the story of the great Denne lawsuit is told two other Crispes modestly remembered on stone slabs in the floor, Sir Nicholas and his wife, Thomasine Denne, may come alive again. Then there is good Anna Gertrude, the orderly maiden sister of Maria Adriana. Secured upon a bleak-looking Crispe Farm in the valley between Acol and the high road, she left twenty shillings to the parish clerk ' to keep clean the Isle and Monuments ' belonging to her numerous relations. She provided wearing apparel in which five widows of Birchington and Acol should go tidily to church, and found schooling, under dame or master, for twelve boys and girls. Poor, good Anna, how she must have detested her brother-in-law who left her nothing of her girlhood's home but to dust the family monuments!

The clergy also, who took over the Thanet churches when the monks departed—one would like to know more of them, of their griefs especially when they too were driven away under the Commonwealth. Meric Casaubon of Minster and Monckton figures in history, no less than Richard Culmer of Canterbury ill-fame, who ousted Meric and drove his poor wife almost to starvation.

Another vicar, Nicholas Chewney, who moved across the island from St. Nicholas-by-the-Ford to Margate to die, wrote polemic works with terrific titles like *Hell with the Everlasting Torments thereof Asserted*. He is more lovable, less pitiable even, when, in his desolate home, he pens a last message to his young wife, Katharine, and her little ones, still to be read on her gravestone:

> Pignus $\left.\begin{array}{l}\text{Am} \\ \text{Dol}\end{array}\right\}$ oris
>
> A loyal loving wife, a mother dear,
> Twixt her two babes doth lye interred here,
> Whose souls sit crownèd in that Heavenly Quire
> Of endless joy, filled with Celestial fire.
> And yet my tears, even in their passion, would
> Recall you from that Kingdom if they could.
> Pardon, my dear, this my distracted zeale
> And you, my Babes, to whom I do appeale.
> My loss being great, my grief must needs be soe,
> The more I strive 'gainst tears, the more they flow;
> Till I approach your blisse, O who can tell
> Your happy welcome, or my sad farewell.

The majestic tower of St. Nicholas-at-Wade and the shingled spire of Birchington have always been serviceable to ships at sea, which steer by them on the way from the Thames to the North Foreland.

III

To walk along the Margate front from end to end, from the old sea-bathing infirmary to the Jubilee clock by the harbour; through public gardens, some of great beauty; through hotel-dom, past thermal baths and tennis courts, variety shows and photographers' booths, band-stands and bathing-machines; and so to Cliftonville on the far side—this is to marvel at the paraphernalia which enables the English family to endure a fortnight, or even twelve hours, of sea air. And how has it all come about? What was Margate doing when the few little old-world houses still lurking round odd corners were put up?

One must go by stages : first behind the era of the charabanc, and then of the excursion train. I happened by chance on a dusty little tract called the *Epistle from Master Cockney at Margate to his Friend in London*, written in 1791, which preserves delightfully the atmosphere of those far-off days.

Master Cockney, a ' bright ' schoolboy, the ' son of a cit ', rides down to Margate with father, mother and sister in ' a ship called a Hoy ', and comes to anchor at the pier.

> So soon as we landed on this pretty spot,
> As t'were a fresh dainty from town, piping hot,
> There came all about us, with bows to the ground,
> From all the Hotels in the neighbourhood round,
> A set of such waiters, so frizzëd and flour'd,
> We seemed with civility quite overpower'd.
> One snatch't up the saddle-bags, bearing my best coat,
> My yard and half buckskins and fur-collared waistcoat;
> Another my father's portmanteau, and many
> The pile of band-boxes of Mother and Nanny,
> The maid followed after, and carried her own
> Little bundle, containing a clean linen gown.
> As thus in procession we went up the beach,
> I thought it but proper to make a short speech.
> Said I, ' Gentlemen—be so good as to say
> If you're all going one, or a different way,
> Because you see, Father and Mother and I
> Would go to one House, as we came in one Hoy.'[1]

[1] Is this a Cockney rhyme slyly slipped in, or in contemporary parlance, was Hoy pronounced High?

Mama is dressed for the seaside in ' a stand-alone silk with a sash on '; Papa wears crimson and a large flowing wig, his best; the schoolboy displays boots and spurs, ' which I lashed with my whip '. This charming family party wander about the streets, till they espy on a window the legend ' a login to lete ', which Papa aptly translates ' Apartments for hire '. It proves to be :

> A neat little place of two rooms on a floor,
> And snug in a roof, without ceiling, two more,

the whole quite inexpensive at two guineas a week.

They amuse themselves with bathing, among the fashionable folk, even ' my honoured Mama rolling largely about '; they go to plays and make excursions in the neighbourhood, and naughty Master Cockney is initiated in the ways of the world :

> I have been to the place which they call Dandelion,
> And all other places of ton it cries fie on,
> Where you get a cold roll and a nice cup of tea
> For only two shillings and sixpence per die,
> And there you may dance in your boots on the green,
> And see such a prospect as never was seen,
> A great fleet of fishing boats all out at sea,
> And a fine face of country that yields not a tree . . .
>
> . . . . . . .
>
> To Margate returned and the evening advancing,
> You pull off your boots and prepare for more Dancing.
>
> . . . . . . .
>
> Besides if you like it, and understand play,
> There is hazard all night for you, billiards all day.
> For me, I knew nothing at all how to throw
> Or tumble a ball, till some folk taught me how.
> To be sure I have lost me some guineas in learning,
> But what would not one give to get more discerning?
>
> . . . . . . .
>
> But Mother and Sister have spent such a deal,
> You can't think, my friend, how unhappy I feel,
> When I tell you my Father is quite in a rage,
> And has taken their places in this evening's stage,
> And swears that as soon as they're gone, he and I
> Will pack up our duds and return by the Hoy.

IV

The development must have come about the mid-century,
for Lewis's *History* in 1723 makes no mention of Margate as
a watering-place. ' It is a small fishing town,' he says,
' irregularly built and the Houses generally old and low,
and has formerly been of good Repute for the fishing and
coast trade. . . . On that part of the Town next the Sea
is a Pier of Timber, built East and West, in the Form
of a Half Moon, to defend the Bay from the main Sea, and
make a small Harbour for . . . the Corn Hoys, and Fishing Craft.' It seems that the natural creek was widened to
such an extent by the greater force of the sea after the Wantsum
channel had closed that the inhabitants were compelled to build,
and then continually to enlarge, their pier, to prevent Margate
being inundated. The harbour was the pulse of the place :
beating firmly when harvests were abundant; growing feeble if
there was little cargo for the hoys. The Lord Warden of the
Cinque Ports made its laws, and ordered the choice, every May
Day, of Pier-Wardens to collect the ' Droits '. These tolls were
elaborately calculated; thus the schedule ran : ' For every
voyage beyond the Seas, viz. into the Netherlands, the East
Country, or the Kingdom of France, for the great vessels  5  0
                                   for small vessels  .  4  0
For every voyage to Spain or further to the Southward 10  0 '
What a sense of country-side industry the cargoes present; the
barrels of Ale or Sweet Oil, the Weighs of Essex and Suffolk ·
and Holland Cheese, the Bushels of Apples and Pears, the
Wash of Oysters, the Cards of Red Herrings. There were Pan
Tyles too for stout roofs, loads of Oak boarding, wrought
Pewter for the cottage dresser. But trade diminished as ships
were bigger built—too big for Margate harbour—and carried
their goods to London. The Malt trade, despite the excellence
of Thanet barley, decayed because the malt was too coarse for
the distillers' liking, and competed unfavourably with malt

from Hertfordshire or the north. The taste for Northdown Ale was somehow lost, ' the Humour of the Gentry and People altering to the better liking of Pale North-Country Ale '. Little by little the fishery went to ruin; the big boats perforce were sold, and in little boats the fishermen dared not face the open sea in a gale. The catches of ' Whiting, Wraith, Wilks Red and White, Lobsters, Pungers, Oysters and Eeles ' grew scarce; perhaps because the rocks were stripped of ' Sea Woore ', so that the fish lacked both shelter and food. The loss of trade and of fishing led to the loss of substantial townsmen, who followed prosperity elsewhere.

At this crisis a new industry—the traffic in tourists—began slowly to fill the empty coffers. Margate air and sea-bathing came into fashion, and so have remained, until the last difficult years, when the revolution in road traffic again disturbs the town's well-being.

v

What a mistake it is when seaboard towns, grown out of old fishing-villages, are allowed to sprawl over the surrounding spaces without some coherent plan; allowed to set up squadrons of villas and bungalows along the cornfields, and to suck beauty out of the meadows, while they contribute nothing to delight the eyes. Perhaps health and happiness behind the curtains counter-balance the ugliness outside? Yet architects and builders might oftener consider how much is visible from the road where the country is flat and spacious; what crowds of good people are driven past ' Home Cot ' and ' Windermere ' between dawn and dusk. Good building furnishes this rather featureless landscape; bad building makes it dreary and distasteful.

You may not be tempted to settle in Birchington, despite a still charming coast-line. The bungalows are by no means all post-war: Mr. John P. Seddon, a friend of the Rossettis ' made ' the place in the early eighties. To one of his houses, ' West-

cliffe Bungalow ', ' a good-looking modern erection without
being a beautiful one ', Dante Rossetti came a broken man, in
vain search of health, and there he died. His mother and his
poet sister Christina came too, full of anxiety, to nurse and
care for him. He was creative almost to the end, working on
' Proserpine ' and ' Joan of Arc ', designing a statue of his
father, finishing his gruesome ballad, ' Jan van Hunks '. Sometimes Christina read aloud to calm his mind, weary of ' the
intolerable noise of wind, day and night '; she read Miss Brad-
don's *Dead Men's Shoes*, and Wilkie Collins's *Dead Secret*.
Dante Rossetti died on Easter Day, the ninth of April 1882,
and was buried in Birchington churchyard. One of the
mourners that day speaks of the old grey tower and grey
shingle spire going up into a pure blue sky; the churchyard
full of irises and wallflowers in bloom; the flowering laurus-
tinus and lilac bushes close to the open graveside. Closer still,
the old, old mother stood with her son and daughter's support,
calm, from self-command or the passivity of great age.

The Irish cross over the grave was designed by Ford Madox
Brown, and has three scenes sculptured on it : the Temptation
in Eden, the Marriage of Dante and Beatrice, and the death of
the painter-physician St. Luke. The stained-glass window in
the south aisle of the church, Mrs. Rossetti's memorial to her
son, was made by Shields, after a drawing of his own and one
of Dante Gabriel's.

Rossetti liked the turf stretches on the cliff, where he could
listen to the skylarks and look out to sea. One poem belongs
to the place and to a wayside plant which had caught his fancy :

> My eyes, wide open, had the run
> Of some ten weeds to fix upon;
> Among those few, out of the sun,
> The woodspurge flowered, three cups in one.
>
> From perfect grief there need not be
> Wisdom or even memory :
> One thing then learnt remains to me,
> The woodspurge has a cup of three. . . .

To Birchington belongs also Watts-Dunton's delightful tale of Christina's sunrise : ' She made up her mind that a sunrise she would see and one morning we went out just as the chilly but bewitching shiver of the dawn breeze began to move and the eastern sky to grow grey. . . . Christina was not much interested at first, but when the grey slowly changed into apple-green, crossed by bars of lilac, and then by bars of pink and gold; and finally when the sun rose behind a tall clump of slender elms . . . whose thin foliage allowed the sunbeams to pour through it as through a glittering lace-work of dewy leaves, she confessed that no sunset could surpass the scene. And when the sun grown brighter still, fell upon the silver mist-sheen in which the cows were lying, turned it into a sheet of gold and made each brown patch on each cow's coat gleam like burnished copper, she admitted that a sunrise surpassed a sunset and was worth getting up to see. She stood and looked at it, and her lips moved in a whisper I could not hear. Yet so powerful is the force of habit that I greatly doubt whether Christina ever took the trouble to see another sunrise.'

## VI

While I dally among the poets you must be longing to follow round to the North Foreland. You should pass through Kingsgate, and give a thought to that old roué Lord Holland, father of Charles James Fox. The sham ruins he erected inspired Gray's impromptu :

> Here reign the blust'ring North and blighting East;
> No tree is heard to whisper, bird to sing;
> Yet Nature could not furnish out the feast,
> Art he invokes, new horrors still to bring—
> Here mould'ring fanes and battlements arise;
> Turrets and arches nodding to their fall :
> Unpeopled monas'tries delude our eyes,
> And mimic desolation covers all.

The many ' gates ' around the Kent coast are ways into the sea made for convenience of the fishermen. Kingsgate was

formerly Bartholomew or Bartlem Gate, till, by command of
Charles II, who landed there on a voyage from London to
Dover, it was new christened :

> Late Barth'lmew the Right of Christnage claimed.
> But now, (so Charles commands) King's Gate I'm named.

Broadstairs was a small vill of St. Peter's, a mere knot of
houses, possessing a portcullised gateway, walled with flint,
built by George Culmer (1540). Not far from it was the chapel
of Our Lady, 'Star of the Sea', and to her image ships sailing
by used reverently to lower their topsails. Lewis called the
hamlet Bradstow, meaning in Old English Broad Place; the
name 'Broadstairs' as an alternative has been in use for centuries. Richard Culmer of St. Peter's-in-Thanet, who died in
1494, had six acres of land at 'Brodsteyr Lynch'. Certainly
the area has been inhabited far beyond the memory of man;
when a building estate was developed some twenty years ago at
Dumpton Gap, Bronze Age, Late Celtic, and Anglo-Saxon
finds were made. It may please you better to recall the memories
of Charles Dickens at Broadstairs. *Nicholas Nickleby* was
finished there, in a house 'two doors from the Albion Hotel';
in the intervals of stiff work, during a storm blowing great
guns, the writer 'staggered down to the pier, and creeping
under the lee of a large boat', watched the breaking waves
for nearly an hour.

Dickens lived also at 'Lawn House' and later at 'Fort
House', which stood, 'at the top of a breezy hill on the road
to Kingsgate, a cornfield between it and the sea'—a situation
after his own heart. In June and September 1840 he was working there at *The Old Curiosity Shop*, and the seascape sometimes wove itself into his narrative. When the proof stage was
reached he wrote to Forster : ' I really think the dead mankind
a million fathoms deep the best thing in the sentence. I have
a notion of the dreadful silence down there, and of the stars
shining down upon their drowned eyes, the fruit, let me tell
you, of a solitary walk by starlight on the cliffs.'

And here is a thumbnail sketch of a scene which must have burnt itself into many childish memories : ' It is the brightest day you ever saw. The sun is sparkling on the water so that I can hardly bear to look at it. The tide is in and the fishing-boats are dancing like mad. Upon the green-topped cliffs the corn is cut and piled in shocks, and thousands of butterflies are fluttering about, taking the bright little red flags at the mastheads for flowers. . . .'

So we are back again on the edge of Pegwell Bay, where the Stour, having travelled the impenetrable length of Stonar Beach, travels back again on the outer edge and reaches the sea at last.

Ramsgate as a watering-place, despite the fiction that at ' Romansgate ' Caesar landed, has a history no longer than its fellows : it too, in the early eighteenth century, was a fishing-town of a few mean houses. Successful trading with Russia and the East country brought it prosperity and many new residences, ' built after the Modern Way, in a very elegant and beautiful Manner '. One of these gave hospitality to the poet Gray, but the frequent visits of the royal child Victoria, ' who went thither by steamer, with Mama (very unwell on the voyage) and dear Uncle Leopold ' were an unparalleled adver-tisement. There, too, are Dickens memories, of the writing of *Dombey and Son*, of a visit one Saturday night in 1845 to the local circus, which may stand at the foot of a chapter :.

' Mazeppa was played ' (so the words run) ' in three long acts, without an H in it, as if for a wager. 'Edds and 'orrors and 'ands were as plentiful as blackberries : but the letter H was neither whispered in 'Evven nor muttered in 'Ell, nor per-mitted to dwell in any form on the confines of the sawdust.'

*Round about Deal and the Goodwin Sands—Dover and round about*

## ROUND ABOUT DEAL AND THE GOODWIN SANDS

### I

WHO has a better claim than Mrs. Carter, the famous blue-stocking, to be patroness, if not almost patron saint, of Deal? True, she arrived late in the town's history, long after Perkin Warbeck had landed there and Anne of Cleves and even Prince Charles. She was born in 1717 when the Chapel of St. George the Martyr, which her father, Dr. Nicholas Carter, served as perpetual curate, had stood in Lower Deal for just two years. St. George's is a pleasant example of a brick Queen Anne edifice, the east end surmounted by a bell-turret. Two centuries have filled its churchyard with grey headstones, and clothed its walls with a mantle of ivy. The interior is well-proportioned, fitted with galleries in dark-stained wood, dignified if not strictly ecclesiastical. A gaudy east window commemorates Dr. Nicholas, whose 'perpetuity' lasted for fifty years, and on the same wall is his daughter's oval tablet. It reminds Deal folk how she was 'a native and inhabitant of this town where her benevolence and virtues will long be remembered. In deep learning, genius and extensive knowledge she was equalled by few; in piety . . . excelled by none.' I hope she is remembered; although I vainly inquired for her abode of people who had 'lived in Deal all their days'; until a polite young policeman suggested that a rest home for invalid ladies was called the 'Carter

House', and the 'Carter Institute' might be connected with
the person I was looking for. I hope she is remembered, talked
of sometimes to the school-children, for never had Deal, or
East Kent either, a more loyal daughter. Her many letters
'full of bits and ends and snuffs of thought', have an under-
current of rejoicing in the surroundings, by day or night, of
her native place. 'The road from Canterbury to Dover was
quite new to me,' she wrote to Mrs. Montagu, after an outing
in a friend's carriage, 'and the prospects are extremely fine,
one half through a country highly cultivated and flourishing
and the other wildly and pleasingly romantic. However, as
highly delighted as I am with this new discovery, it has by no
means rivalled my favourite walks and prospects between Deal
and Canterbury,' that open wind-blown downland, rather
bleak for the most part. And when she visits Mill Hill her
imagination 'looks back with transport to East Kent'.

And she had probably a closer knowledge of the district than
most of her neighbours; this for two reasons. On to old age,
as I have said already, she was a great walker, and next she
had the poet's eye and mind, although she could seldom trans-
mute those long thoughts of hers into true poetry. When quite
a young woman she took to walking 'as if bewitched', pursuing health already impaired by over-study. 'I get up at four,
read for an hour, then set forth a-walking, and without vanity
I may pretend to be one of the best walkers of the age.' At first
she had companions on these rapid excursions, and would gaily
suggest a call a dozen miles off, just to enjoy their dismay and
their fairy-tales, when at last she led them home, of windmill-
sails torn off and cottages overturned in her impetuous path.

'Another of our troop sent me word last night she could
not possibly venture, as our last walk had absolutely dislocated
all her bones; so I have nobody to depend on now but my
youngest sister, who is as strong as a little Welch horse; she
. . . promises never to forsake me if I should walk to the
North Pole.'

These were youthful days; the habit of early rising, when the sexton pulled, from the garden, a pack-thread fastened to a bell at her bed-head, never left her, but in later years she had only a dog as walking companion. It was once attacked by a mad dog, which she drove off with sticks and stones. 'It seems,' she wrote calmly, 'there have been more mad dogs lately than ever I knew.' A conviction that any kind of weather was wholesomer than too much Greek no doubt helped to prolong her life to eighty-nine years, for she read and wrote habitually eight to twelve hours a day, rose at five and retired about eleven. This conviction, coupled with a passion for 'sublimity', made her indifferent to tempests which alarmed other people. She attributed her strength of mind to her father's example in early childhood. 'I perfectly remember that I was exceedingly frightened at a storm of thunder, but as it was not much my fashion to express what I felt I watched my father's looks; and the unconcern which I discovered there quieted my terrors.' Perhaps her fancy for describing storms, and Deal has its share, is the unconscious outlet of childish fears. Time after time she records the fire-balls and heaps of hail, the uproar of the winds, the east wind's 'ill-nature', or the earthquake (of 1776) when for a few seconds 'the wild tumult and hurry of the elements were as much beyond all description as the tumult of my thoughts'. Sometimes storm overtook her rambles, and she has 'the advantage of observing the whole progress of it through all the varieties of the sky'; and gaily risks cap and bonnet blown to the Goodwins although fastened with the largest pins procurable.

The house in which she lived from 1768 until her death lent itself to these idiosyncrasies. True, its little forecourt, where she watered the myrtles and geraniums, and set a jasmine and bits of tuberose brought from Lambeth Palace, gave her constant delight. She built a wall to shelter a cherry-tree with six blossoms and an apricot that never bore; but all the same the garden was apt to be torn up by the roots. Such accidents are inevitable if one chooses an abode, however 'riant and airy', which on occasions has cellars filled by the tide, and rocks with the wind 'like the Eddystone'. It stood somewhat isolated, last in the town, the elements playing round it 'with the most uninterrupted liberty', for it was open on three sides and had a wide unsheltered space before it. Into the window of her study lined with books the rain drove upon her writing-paper, but from it she could watch the sky-pageantry, a cloud spanned by a double rainbow, sunset colour on the sails of passing ships, the vanishing stars, the light of dawn. She loved to crowd her room with family and friends, though it was, as she says, 'in everything but motion an absolute cabin, and my prospects " Aer undique, undique pontus ".'

That house—which she bought with the profits of her *Epictetus*, surely the most lucrative translation ever penned, still stands on the east side of South Street. With its rounded end-gables, solid walls, and fine old roof, one can scarcely picture it rocking like the Eddystone. But nowadays it no longer meets the full gale, for a row of houses stands between it and the seashore. And it is no longer last in the town, as when the side windows took in a prospect of Deal Castle, where 'dear Lady Holdernesse' was living. Now the little garden borders the pavement; Deal and Walmer have touched hands; their houses have devoured the lanes where she gathered primroses and violets, and where the May bugs—'frightful animals'—reminded her of the northern army in Joel's prophecy.

II

Despite her devotion to Deal, Elizabeth Carter's biographer declares that she was 'not a woman of letters to her native town', but accounted a lover of whist and farthing quadrille. I fancy he does Deal an injustice; one has become not a prophet only but a proverb when Punch playing in a Deal puppet-show with less vivacity than usual,

'Why, Punch,' says the Showman, 'what makes you so stupid?'

'I can't talk my own talk,' answers Punch, 'the famous Miss Carter is here.'

The country-side was convinced such 'a cunning gentle-woman' possessed witch-like prescience of the seasons. In Canterbury Cathedral a verger's wife remarked : 'It will be a dreadful winter and a great scarcity of corn for the famous Miss Carter has foretold it.'

Deal in its lover's letters is just as Nature made it, the storm-blown place on the edge of Goodwin Sands, with much sun-shine and uncanny moonlight calms over the sea. In her day the soil was cultivated to the cliff-edge; she could walk to Ripple without seeing a house.

But there were startling echoes from the outer world. Some Polish prisoners captured by a man-of-war came to Deal in 1744; no one but Dr. Carter could converse with them, although they talked a Babel of tongues, 'One Latin, another French, a third Polish, a fourth high Dutch, and a fifth some-thing that sounds like no language at all.' Mrs. Elizabeth is too modest; she also could speak fluent French learned in her girlhood from a Huguenot pastor in Canterbury. The '45 brought a crop of rumours and (so frayed was the public nerve) a mortal fright when two idle lads got into Walmer Castle and scared the 'two old women on guard'; they ran into the village, declaring the French had the castle, and they had seen two hundred of them (supposed to be cows quietly grazing on a common). Upon this alarm the men took to their arms, the women ran away, and the messenger proclaimed himself through Deal streets, 'I am John Redman of Walmer, come to tell you the French are landed.' More genuine excitements were to follow. A Mr. Radcliffe and his 'pretended son', arrive mysteriously, prisoners on board the good ship *Admiral* in the Downs. There is much 'apparatus and affected reserve' which arouses suspicion that young Radcliffe is no other than the Young Pretender. He is 'not above twenty years old, has fair hair inclining to yellow, is ruddy, short-waisted, long-chinned, six foot high and appears dejected'. From Deal the prisoners are taken to Canterbury, where Mrs. Carter happens to be visiting and sees them pass.

These were moments of crisis, but smuggling went on continuously. 'There have been sad disorders here lately with the smugglers,' writes Elizabeth in 1779; 'they have killed one poor custom-house officer, and dangerously wounded another. The villains who did this mischief are fled to France, where they may be very useful to give our enemies all the intelligence of our coast in their power. Surely if people did but consider what a set of wicked wretches they encourage by the dirty practice of dealing in smuggled goods, they would make more conscience of it than they do.'

### III

Deal and Walmer were already something of popular seaside resorts, although the accommodation, even for royalty, was at times inadequate. The Princess Amelia took a house at Walmer in 1772, 'prettily situated for any plebeian gentle-woman', but in Mrs. Carter's view insufficient for the natural demands of a king's daughter. The kitchen being no bigger than a birdcage, her Royal Highness and suite must needs live upon shrimps or be starved off the premises. Our heroine's friends came not seldom to Deal for sea air and bathing and her pleasant society; she was invited out to meet friends' friends of reputation, not always to her enjoyment. Here is one more quarrying from the letters, where she digresses from books to their authors : 'I must tell you the celebrated Mr. Paul White-head has been at Deal with a family where I often visit; it was my fate to be once in his company, much against my will, for having naturally as strong an antipathy to a wit as some people have to a cat, I at first fairly ran away to avoid it; however,

I was dragged in at last . . . to hear part of a satyre ready for
the press. Considered as poetry and wit it had some extremely
fine strokes, but the vile practice of exalting some characters
and abusing others, with-out any color of truth or justice, has
something so shocking in it that . . . I had much ado . . . to
hear it out.' After this who could resist snatching from the
shelves that volume of *Chalmers' Poets* which enshrines the
largest number of forgotten songsters. Whitehead's muse
occupies only twenty pages, but there ' Honour a Satyre ' finds
place, dated two years after Mrs. Carter's audition.

> 'Load, load the pallet, boy,' it begins, rather promisingly,
> 'Hark! Hogarth cries,
> Fast as I paint, fresh swarms of fools arise! . . .
> On Satire, then! pursue thy generous plan,
> And wind the vice, regardless of the man.'

Which were the lines I wondered that shocked our Elizabeth?
I could guess at two; one refers with ignominy to Pulteney,
Earl of Bath, the other to Lord Lyttelton, both of whom
honoured her with a particular regard. Lord Lyttelton called
on her one late afternoon in 1756. She would not ring for
candles, and went on pretending to sew ' when it was impossible for one to see a stitch ', for fear the overwhelming guest
should notice her embarrassment.

## IV

' I have drawn Mr. Wright into the scheme of a romantic
voyage to the Goodwin Sands, where it is one to a hundred I
may be drowned,' wrote Elizabeth Carter, as one might write
in jest of whirlpools or avalanches. Born within sight of ' the
great shippe swallower ', she well knew the tales of tragedy
and heroism that have belonged to it ever since men went down
to sea. My first impression about a recent book on the Goodwins—E. C. Pain's *Last of our Luggers and the Men who
Sailed Them*—was the short time it embraced in comparison
with the long, long roll of disaster. It seems incredible that in

half a century (1858-1909) the wreckage in that one stretch of
sea can have been so tremendous, the indomitable courage of
the Deal lugger-men so constantly at strain. Every page tells
of struggles that to the landlubber seem superhuman, of lives
snatched from an ogre's maw. The author's object is to record
some achievements of the lugger-men—up to the point when
the courage that could wrestle with breakers had to own itself
mastered; by a force salutary, no doubt, and working for the
general good, but nevertheless in brave men's eyes an insidious
enemy. The tragedy can be put briefly enough; steam, the
steam-tug, by little and little superseded the boatman's calling.
The Deal lugger was a craft ' about 40 ft. long and 13 ft. beam,
more or less '. Shade of Richard Whittington—the smaller
sized lugger was called a ' cat '. The lugger had a forecastle
where a man could sleep in comfort; the cat was furnished
amidships with a movable ' caboose ' in which three or four
men could lie side by side. Here is an admirer's description :
' The luggers are splendid sea-boats and it is a fine sight to see
one of them crowded with men and close reefed, cruising in
the Downs, " hovelling " or on the look-out for a job in the
gale. While ships are parting from their anchors and flying
signals of distress the luggers . . . wheel and sweep round
them like sea-birds on the wing.' The passage usefully gathers
up just those duties of the lugger included in the good old
term ' hovelling '. It meant pilotage, the carriage of supplies,
life-saving, salvage operations, the provision of spare anchors
and cables and ' sweeping ' to recover those lost or parted—all
this rolled into one portmanteau word. . . .

The story of the luggers' last days is the more poignant,
because it passes from glorious effort to inglorious yet involuntary idleness : ' Where there used to be fifty galley-punts
there were now about half a dozen. A little bit of fishing in
the winter and pleasuring in the summer—that is all doing
nowadays. Men couldn't keep body and soul together upon
that, and so the youngsters had left the calling of their fathers,

or rather the calling had left them.' While it lasted how magnificent a calling, demanding the finest qualities of a man,
and a price to be paid. Between 1860 and 1887 fifty-three boat-
men were drowned from luggers and galley-punts within sight
of their own shore. Think of their antagonist, that shifting
sand, seventy-eight feet deep before solid chalk is reached.
Even rough statistics of losses upon Goodwin Sands make
one's brain reel. ' In the range of say 500 years,' one writer
calculates, ' at least one hundred millions sterling value of ships
and property and fifty thousand human lives have been lost '
just there. There have been, of course, projects for recovering
treasure from the dragon's cache; some day it may be ransacked
in reality, as it has been already in romance, in Herbert
Russell's *The Longshoreman*, by means of iron cylinders sunk
into the sand.

One of the uncanny horrors of the Sands is the way in which,
even on a fine calm day, they may engulf those who know their
' every spit and ridge, swatch and gulley '. Four Deal boat-
men went out, with many comrades, to get the cargo of coke
and coal from a vessel ' swaddled on the Goodwins '. These
four, with their boat, were lost; they never returned to shore.
They were seen running about the Sands, and this is almost
all that is known of their fate. ' Ships simply disappear,' said
the master of one of the Goodwin Lightships; ' my own theory
is they sidle off the Sands and sink in deep water.' This brings
one to the question of warning against the quicksands. Mr.
Pain says there was no lightship till 1795, when one was placed
upon the North Sand Head; and no lifeboat stationed at Deal
till 1865. The *Kentish Register* says this first lightship had ' a
very large bell to ring in hazy weather when the light cannot
be discerned '. One inventive mind had worked on the safety
problem more than a century earlier, although apparently without result. This was a Kent man, Colonel Culpeper; his
petition, interesting enough, shall stand here as a pioneer's
memorial :

' B.M. MS. 28094, f127)

' To the Queen's Most Excellent Majesty [Anne].

' The Humble Peticon of Colonell Culpeper.

' Sheweth that when your Petitioner had the Honour to be Engineere Generall of England, to be constantly attending upon the Royall person of King Charles the Second . . . to Councell and advise his Majesty in matters of warr and all maner of Fortifications, your Peticoner observed that the Booyes placed in the Sea to advertise Seamen of Rocks and Sands culd not be seene in the night, and therefore were of no benefit in dark and tempestious nights, when there was most need of them. And therefore your Peticioner invented a way to place a Light upon Goodwin sand, being the most Daingerous Place in England, lyeing in the middle of the Sea which separates England from France, so that all Ships and Vessels sayling through the sea from most parts of the world are in dainger thereof, as a safe direction for Ships hereafter to avoyd that daingerous Sand.' [Here he re-tells the story of the White Ship, and then comes on to more recent happenings.]

' Upon which . . . fower ships of war of the Royall Navey of England and other ships perished and one thousand eight hunderd men were drowned in the Late dreadfull storme, the 26 of November 1703 . . . . And for as much as the placing and maintayning a Light upon Goodwine Sands wilbe of great use and Benefitt to the Royall Navey of England and all other Ships . . . because it sheweth the very Place where the said Sands doth lye both day and night, which nothing else can doe; where some persons also shall constantly inhabit. . . .

' . . . Your Peticoner prayes that he may have a Patent for the sole Benefitt of his New Invention, and that all Ships and Vessels sayling through the said sea, shall pay the same Rates and prises to your Peticoner that ships and vessels agreed to pay to the Light House built on the Rock called the Eddystone nere Plymouth, blowne downe in the said storme; these payments to begin upon kindling the first Light upon Good-wine Sands . . .'

v

Mrs. Carter's excursions to villages neighbouring on Deal are recorded in letters to Mrs. Vesey. Sure of a ready sympathy from ' The Sylph ', she made ' ideal assignations ' with her friend who could range ' the chrystal wilds of air '; she led her to moonlit hill-tops, to the wild South Foreland cliff, ' where all is uninhabited waste around me and all blank ocean below ', to the little spring rising among the pebbles in St. Margaret's Bay. She often went to Woodnesborough, with its heathen mound, and writes somewhere of the venerable ruins of West Langdon Church between Deal and Dover, the mouldering arches and thick-strewn graves. Northbourne Court was another favourite of her rambles. She remembered the splendid old house, once belonging to St. Augustine's Abbey, where the Sandys' family lived for four generations, and marvelled at the lack of feeling which, in 1750, led to its demolition for what the materials would fetch. She used to sit among the ruins, recalling with true ' Gothic melancholy ' its former renown, the marble portico overlooking a shaded garden, three terraces like the hanging walls of Babylon. A babbling spring hard by the house still made music, but the rivulet flowing from it towards Sandwich Bay was choked with weeds and the moss-grown bordering trees ' looked like the abode of ill-omened birds '. Two great ' Gothic ' chimneys stood above the long gallery, and it and all the hundred rooms were lined with cedar, in every panel a golden arabesque. The glass in the gallery, painted with the Sandys arms, had been broken and thrown away. In Northbourne Church — a Norman church in the main—the fine monument to Sir Edward Sandys and his lady—but without inscription—was fast decaying. One memory of ' Norborne Court ', of which they were the first owners, belonged to the notorious Colonel

Edwin Sandys, the wrecker of Canterbury Cathedral, who came home mortally wounded from Worcester Field. . . .

While Mrs. Carter moralized, translated *Epictetus*, walked against the wind, another Kent lover grew up near by at Betteshanger. John Boys's mother came from Ripple, and he married the rector's daughter from Eastry-cum-Worth. As a farmer and grazier he was perhaps prouder of his Southdown sheep than of the book, *A General View of Agriculture of the County of Kent*, which he produced to please the Board of Agriculture in 1796. If one reads that work neither as farmer nor grazier, but to make the old Kent landscape live again, it can never seem out of date. Boys's Kent had a population from end to end of 200,000 persons, living in 45,000 houses. At the census of 1911 the people of Kent numbered 1,045,591; no wonder outward appearances have changed enormously. If you live in Birchington or Sittingbourne, Chatham or Sidcup, to-day it seems to matter little whether the soil beneath your bungalow is ' hassock ', which keeps fruit-trees from mildew; ' pinnock ', a sticky red clay good for filberts; ' coomb ', which ploughs heavy and crops flints; or ' hazel-mould ', which lines the hill-sides and ploughs light.

In the mid-eighteenth century Kent yeomen were fast increasing in number and prosperity. The estates, lessened in extent since the Civil Wars, were again being broken up and bought at good prices by farmer-occupiers. London merchants were once more building themselves good houses in Kent, like the Smythes, Weldons, Wottons of bygone days. They were coming out from the metropolis, as humbler people are doing in their thousands in our time.

Boys found much to condemn in the local farm-house, with its projecting upper floor. It was ' old, large, ill-contrived '; its age was proved by the heavy beams of chestnut, found in places where chestnut timber grew no longer for building purposes. Only Thanet farm-houses escape his criticism. There, too, the labourer is more comfortably lodged; his cottage is sometimes of brick and tile, and he has land enough to keep a cow; his modest rent is but two to three pounds a year, about as much as his successor now pays away in a month.

Not the philologist and antiquary only must delight in Boys's description of a farmer's implements, with their time-honoured names. The 'carriages', thirteen feet long, boarded at the ends and sides, which take the corn to market are, he says, called 'hutches', and are drawn by a team of four. In the Weald 'carriages called bavin-tugs are chiefly used for faggots, but many use them for corn and hay. . . . The hind and fore wheels are fourteen feet apart . . . so that the load lies very low and is less liable to be turned over; which otherwise would often be the case in the roads of the Weald.' The Kent 'turn-wrest' plough was famous. It was of great size and weight, built upon a ten-foot beam of oak, and wielding a share of hammered iron weighing fifty-two pounds. This stoutness was necessitated by the fact that four strong horses frequently dragged the plough 'against a rocky and stiffly flint patch' and ploughed to great depth. Boys gives a picture of this gigantic implement; once, when walking past an allotment ground near Hartlip, I am convinced that I saw one in use, resurrected perhaps from the obscurity of some old barn. Boys was a loyal admirer of this giant's peculiarities, and annoyed by the comparisons of the writer Marshall, who declared that its component parts nearly equalled those of a ship; a small north-country farmer would be glad of its beam for a gate-post; and the timber it contained would build a Highland cart. In one respect Kent was then like rural France of to-day; for, in the Weald at any rate, farmers still used oxen in their land-works.

'Here,' says Boys, 'it is common to see horses and oxen together, both in the plough and on the roads; eight or ten oxen, with a horse or two before' (not the white goat of the Auvergnat peasant), 'to lead them along. Frequently ten oxen, without any horse, are seen drawing a plough which would be more expeditiously done by four horses.' Boys indeed

thought the slowness of his oxen's pace made the ploughman
lazy.

Look again, when you are next in the north aisle of Canterbury choir, at the fresco of St. Eustace, where the fifteenth-
century artist has depicted ploughs drawn by ox, dog, and goat
harnessed abreast.

Certainly the soil tamed by the plough and many beasts
produced rich crops; the brown and yellow Lammas wheat,
the Kentish white straw, the egg-shell which Boys himself
preferred. The wheat was thrashed with a flail on an oaken
floor, or, in smaller farms, on an earthen floor. Boys himself
built the first thrashing-mill at Betteshanger, which employed
all hands on rainy days when they would otherwise have been
idle. Then, as now, fruit-growing was widespread and hops
a highly profitable crop, especially about Maidstone, whence
transport was easy to the London market. Has any one compared Boys's list of cider apples, Golden Rennet, Sharp Russet,
Golden Mundy, Risemary, Kernel-permain, and the rest, or his
cookers and eaters, Quince-apple, Loansmain, Golden Nob,
with those Tradescant grew a century earlier in the Cecils'
garden at Shorne or at Hatfield; or who has made comparison
of their cherries, black- and white-heart? Had the ' Arch-
duke's Cherye ' which Tradescant brought from Haarlem perhaps by now become the ' May-dukes ', which Boys's fruit-
grower sold, with Flemish Courones and Morellos, to the
higglers for peddling on Margate sands?

Filbert-trees, says Boys, are traditionally trained ' in the
shape of a punch-bowl and never suffered to grow above four
or five feet high, with short stems like a gooseberry bush and
exceeding thin of wood '. There is an orchard of filbert and
cob-nut trees close to Canterbury, where the long nut-avenues
are parted by turf-walks. Golden catkins of next year's crop
seem to film the bushes directly the nuts have been plucked.
In those green walks, as I often fancy, the spirit of many a
great gardener of old Kent must linger with delight.

## DOVER AND ROUND ABOUT

I

Across the bare upland plateau between Deal and Dover, scarcely out of view of the red-brick pavilions of the Duke of York's School, a ropeway stretches, along which the dangling iron cradles travel, carrying coal from Betteshanger Colliery to the sea. The existence of coalfields under certain rock-formations in south-east England is not a surmise of our own time. It was suggested in the mid-nineteenth century, and the discovery of coal under the chalk in northern France in 1846 increased the probability. Theory gave way to experiment, in 1890 ' coal-measures were struck at a depth of 386 yards in a bore-hole put down at Shakspere Cliff near Dover'. Since then pioneer work has showed that the area containing the most valuable type of coal covers some eighty miles, and ' within this area the borings and sinkings indicate that 1,500,000,000 tons of coal exist in seams of three to nine feet in thickness, lying at depths of 400 to 1,000 yards'. From the first a determined effort was made (alike by Kent authorities and the mine-owners) to keep the ' Garden of England ' as far as practicable unspoilt, while mining operations went on far beneath the fields and orchards. The depth of the coal-seams made this hope less chimerical. Up to now, although ash-heaps round the shafts are inevitable, the area of spoliation is limited. Great pains have been taken to create in the new mining villages, at Elvington and Eythorne, beautiful as well as healthful and desirable dwelling-places. How well I remember the ceremony of May 19th 1924 which started active operations in the Betteshanger Colliery. The company of Pearson and Dorman Long Ltd. had by now been formed and had acquired mineral rights under some sixty square miles of agricultural Kent. This, their first, colliery is on Lord Northbourne's estate, and takes in about 4,700 acres. ' The

top of the coal-measure ' (I quote from the official description)
' occurs at 975 feet. The water in these beds, viewed in the
light of experience in other parts of the field, will probably be
a very large quantity, possibly as much as 2,000 gallons per
minute.' I can hear now that great engineer, Lord Cowdray,
explaining to us what the presence of water in such a vast
amount had meant at the start, and how it had been overcome,
shut off by the sinking of great sealing-tubes. We were travelling along a little branch-line newly built to connect the colliery
with the Southern Railway. Sir Hugh Bell received us, and
the Archbishop of Canterbury (Lord Davidson of Lambeth)
spoke to the large assembly before he exploded a charge in the
shaft to begin the sinking of the downcast pit. Then Lady
Northbourne started the winding engine, which lowered the
master sinker and his men into the pit to send out the first
hoppit of earth. One could not but feel, foolishly perhaps, in
the presence of untried forces, a certain dread of what was
threatening our old-time Kent, its clear skies and quiet rural
places. The luncheon too, in the fitting shop new built on
the edge of the marshlands, seemed not only a joyful feast
inaugurating great enterprises, but also a farewell to humbler
things. The speeches were dullish, I remember, and so long
that the special train blew an insistent whistle, warning us
guests of a day to depart that labour in the new fields might
begin in earnest.

## II

Within the coal-area lie many pleasant old-world villages.
Tilmanstone, for instance, is near a pitshaft, but still ' by-
passed ' in rural seclusion. Ireland, the Kent historian, says
that the district is unfrequented and *contains nothing remarkable*; but the past reproaches such a misjudgement. True, the
history is chiefly manorial, of estate-owners and their servants
who tilled the soil. By Edward III the principal property had
split in two, and acquired the names of North Court and South

Court. The families who owned North Court in later times
were the Langleys (from Warwickshire), Peytons, Nar-
boroughs and D'Aeths. Sir John Narborough's two sons
were 'shipwreckt in the night upon the Rocks of Scilly'
with their stepfather Sir Cloudesley Shovel. Their grandiose
memorial in Knowlton Church has a bas-relief of the
doomed ship, and the inscription laments the two drowned
boys—'Happy in their Inclinations, Happy in their Fortunes, Unhappy only in their Fate'. Yet was it so unhappy? For in death the brothers were not divided: 'their
Mutual Impatiency of living long Asunder was the great
occasion of their dying both together'. South Court, from the
ownership of the Wardens, passed to John White, a Canterbury
merchant, knighted during the Wars of the Roses. A descendant of his sold it to a Cox, and after two generations Thomas
Cox, Customer of Sandwich, sold again, at the close of the sixteenth century, to one Richard Fogge. Then its history intermingled once more with that of North Court; for the two estates
were acquired by the Peytons, owners also of Knowlton Court.

Tilmanstone has had some famous vicars; the earliest—
well, poor Walter, under Edward II, was rather notorious than
of good fame. Yet his was a hard case. For as he and his
clerk Thomas and a neighbour Robert de Raundes were talking
together 'in the borough of Tylmanstone', a deadly quarrel
arose. Robert would have killed Walter the vicar in his sudden
passion had not Thomas drawn a knife and stabbed him fatally
in the back. Then Eleanor, Robert's wife, appealed from court
to court against the vicar and his clerk. Thomas was seized
and delivered over to the bishop, and died in prison. Walter
could not be found; he had 'withdrawn himself'. In his
absence the doom fell—he was outlawed, unheard but suspect.
Poor Walter. Two centuries after Tragedy came Contemplation, in the person of John Boys, of an Eythorne family; namesake, ancestor perhaps, of the grazier of Betteshanger. He was
educated probably at King's School, Canterbury, and Christ's

College, Cambridge. He held successively the Rectory of Betteshanger, the Mastership of Eastbridge Hospital, Canterbury, the Vicarage of Tilmanstone; in 1619, from all these country preferments, he went to Canterbury again as Dean. He was an eloquent man; preached in his youth at Paul's Cross, and in June 1625 before Charles I and his bride. Thousands of visitors know his monument in the Lady Chapel; there he sits in his study, among the book shelves so oddly furnished with volumes turned-on edge. His earnest face is uplifted to hear the Divine summons, which came to him, it is said, in this familiar place. He died on September 26th 1625.

Dr. Nicholas Carter was also Vicar of Tilmanstone for a while, leaving in 1734 after he had built a new vicarage-house.

Besides the two courts named for the poles, Tilmanstone had smaller manors. Dane Court belonged to the Fogges, who came into Kent under Edward I. The climax of their fortunes was reached by that Sir John Fogge, 'Lord of immense territory . . . of royal blood himself and by marriage the near connexion of his King', who re-built Ashford Church. After three generations his family suddenly retire to a small manor-house; after three more, and the Great Rebellion where they fought loyally for Charles, 'their estate is reduced to fifty pounds a year; the end is near; we soon hear of mariners and blacksmiths; till the last heiress of the race, descendant of kings and crusaders, is the wife of a poor shepherd living in a wretched hovel at Eastry'. 'Fogge's Feast', rival of the Barmecide's, provided Kent with a proverb. 'For it seems at a dinner made by one of the family the servant threw down the venison pasty in coming over a high threshold. He bade his guests not to be concerned, for there was a piece of boil'd beef and a dish of pease; but the dogs fell upon the beef, and the maid buttering the pease, flung them all down.' 'Fogge's Feast', the departing guests muttered to one another, and 'Fogge's Feast' for ever after said the disappointed man.

I like to remember that dear Dorothy Osborne stayed at

Knowlton in June 1654. Sir Thomas Peyton had married her
sister Anne as his first wife; she kept up with him and her two
nieces after Anne's death and his re-marriage to Cecilia Swan.
Knowlton did not fulfil her ideal of solitude, that ' melancholy
place and little company ' which best suited her humour. ' We
go abroad all day, and play all night, and say our prayers when
we have time ', she writes; and again, ' I am in Kent and in a
house so strangely crowded with company that I am weary as
a dog already, though I have been here but 3 or 4 days; all their
mirth has not mended my humour.' There were country-house
theatricals, when she acted in a tragi-comedy called the ' Lost
Lady ', by Sir William Berkely, the part of Hermione, deliver-
ing how fervently one may imagine, these lines :

> With what harsh fate does Heaven afflict me,
> That all the blessings which make others happy
> Must be my ruin.

But her time of weary waiting was nearly at an end. Her
brother Henry joined her at Knowlton to discuss her marriage,
and soon after she summoned her lover to meet her at Canterbury *en route*. There was one more sad trial, the smallpox,
which dimmed her beauty, and on December 25th 1654 she and
William Temple were at last made one.

Knowlton Court stands close to the manorial church; caught
in a network of twisting lanes; secluded, yet in open country
where fields are wide and unhedged and the sky is wide and
free. The house has been much changed by successive owners,
but in character is still a seventeenth-century mansion, with
rounded gable-ends, and solid walls faced with small rose-red
bricks—within, long galleries lead round the courtyards and
from end to end of each wing. The woodwork is chiefly
eighteenth century, but in the hall the panels are small and
dark; Dorothy's drama might have been played there. Some
armorial shields in painted glass brought in from church
windows to decorate court windows, must go behind the Peytons' to the Langleys' time.

III

Let us get on to our Cinque Port. There are many temptations to delay. The mighty contours of the Downs round Dover, the grim splendour of its headland, the depth of the chasm in which the town merges, seem to obliterate all petty detail. One ceases to notice the meanness of the huddled houses; they are touched into the panorama on the hill-side, or at its foot like a smudge of brownish shadow fading into smoke.

I met with an old writer the other day who described the starkness of Shakspere's Cliff—and indeed of chalk cliffs in general—as ' an unpleasant object '. He was an honest man, if it really made no appeal to his senses; perhaps the very awe its precipice aroused in him was the unpleasing feature. The passage occurs in some observations on the coast of Hampshire, Sussex and Kent, made by the Reverend William Gilpin, and published in 1804 by his trustees, with quaint sepia drawings, to benefit his parochial school at Boldre-near-Lymington. The bluntness of the book, its sedulous avoidance of gush—' enthusiasm ' he would have said—give one pleasure in reading it. Dover came in for a full share of his notice. He observed that the townspeople were ' a connecting thread between an Englishman and a Frenchman '; in Dover you might partake of English roast-beef or a French ragout, speak either tongue at pleasure and be well understood. The very street signs were in both languages—here at least 1933 shakes hands with 1804, for a large *Tenez la gauche* meets the eye at the top of Castle Hill.

Mr. Gilpin spent a disturbed night at Dover, clearly in the Lord Warden Hotel. A packet sailed at midnight, and a merry company of travellers arrived at the inn to wait for embarkation. They settled themselves in the apartment under his; they rang bells, clattered doors, shouted for porters to carry out their lumbering trunks; they chattered together, in what language it was impossible to distinguish. Mr. Gilpin could not sleep; so he dressed and sat at his window in the moonlight watching the busy harbour. And there, wafted on some little breeze, Inspiration laid her touch against his grim old cheek. For once in his life he was moved to describe with real feeling if sometimes stifling phrases a scene that human eyes will scarce see there again.

'The tide' (he says) 'was at its height; the sea perfectly calm; the moon full and perfectly clear. The vessels which we had seen in the evening heeling on their sides, each in its station near the quays, were now all in fluctuating motion; the harbour was brim-full. . . . Many of the ships, preparing to sail, were disentangling themselves from others. Their movements forward and backward . . . were entertaining : and the clamour nauticus, in different tones, from different parts of the harbour, and from ship to ship, had an agreeable effect . . . when nothing else was heard but a gentle rippling and suction of the water among the stones,

> as each slow-lifted wave,
> Creeping with silver curl, just kissed the shore,
> And slept in silence——

Some vessels had their bright sails expanded to the moon; while the sails of others, averted from it . . . were dingy and indistinct. At the mouth of the harbour a gentle breeze was felt and the sails appeared to swell. Ships, already at sea, were marked by lights which glimmered and disappeared by turns. . . .'

But poetry could make no long stay with the Reverend William Gilpin.

'Among other sights I had the pleasure to see, about two o'clock, my noisy friends issue out of the inn. I now saw plainly . . . they were French; and heard afterwards they were the suite of a French count. On this happy riddance I retired again to bed : and endeavoured to forget the busy picture I had seen.'

IV

The pathway, partly in steps, winding up from the old
dingy quarter of the town and crossing the broad motor road,
passes over a great rift in the promontory and ascends by the
Knights' Road to the topmost plateau. Three ancient buildings
keep guard aloft : the Pharos, the tallest Roman building still
standing in these islands; the church of St. Mary-in-the-Castle,
in part seventh or eighth century, with a wonderful south doorway arched in Romano-Saxon tiles; and lastly, the castle keep.
At one time the keep might have taken third place in interest;
but the Office of Works is changing all that. Already surprising discoveries have been made; presently it will prove the
most perfect example imaginable of a medieval castle. When
you have crossed the drawbridge, peering down at the slits in
the masonry where the mighty chains slid, the first marvel you
meet is ' Harold's Well '. As you peer over the edge an oily
rag drops burning from the guide's finger; it twists and turns,
a feather of flame,      . . . a little feather
                   Fluttering far down the gulf
—down, down, ever dwindling, till its spark extinguishes in
the tinder of millions of rags some 272 feet below. Even then
its ashes are far from the bottom of the well, which must have
a feeding-ground in springs at sea-level, a depth of 400 ft. This
may be the well that Saxon Harold swore to yield up with the
castle to William of Normandy. The builders of the Norman
keep in 1181·carried their steening ' of Caen stone beautifully
pointed ', 41 ft. above ground-level. Below this worked facing
the well-shaft narrows gradually and descends, unfaced, some
2 ft. 9 ins. in diameter, hewn through the solid chalk. · Only in
1930 was the well explored by a Dover citizen, Mr. S. A.
Payn, after precautionary testing of the air; fresh discoveries
followed his investigations. An elaborate water-system was
gradually revealed : it circulated by means of ancient leaden
pipes, containing three times as much silver as modern com-

mercial lead, from the well itself into chamber and hall. Some pipes had been cut, but enough remained in position to allow of experiment. Buckets of water were poured down each pipe, and by the sound of trickling, or by an outflow, the original courses were rediscovered. The engineer of the keep in 1181, Maurice by name, four years earlier had designed the castle at Newcastle-on-Tyne, with a similar water-supply. Earlier still, twelve years before, some one—was it Prior Wibert?—brought water into Christchurch Priory from the hills north of Canterbury, through just such a range of leaden pipes, and the drawing of that inventive genius still exists. Was there collaboration between the good brains of Dover and of Canterbury, as there is close similarity in style and ornament between the lovely Water Tower which housed Wibert's cistern, and the Chapels of St. Mary and St. Thomas Becket within Dover keep?

The water-system is not the only fresh point of interest for visitors to Dover Castle. The rifle-racks and partitions of the military occupation have now vanished; the fine proportions of the great hall can be appreciated; the hospitable fireplaces too, added by the Tudors, and the brick-work they fitted between massive Norman timbers. The passages though broad are tortuous, as begets approaches which must be defended in the last resort. The Norman windows are set in deep embrasures, but the sills are stepped, and the light entering each narrow aperture, caught on successive stone edges, is passed on intensified into the recesses of the room.

To relieve the tedium of imprisonment many a Frenchman and Dutchman has carved his device, or some prayer for God's mercy and the free air, upon these walls. Presently, it may be, some one will identify a Pieter Blondel or a Pierre Toussein of the sad company.

v

In November 1753 Wolfe, with six companies of the

Twentieth Regiment of Foot, spent a winter at Dover Castle. 'I lodge at the foot of a tower supposed to be built by Romans,' he wrote gloomily to his mother, 'and cannot help wishing sometimes that they had chosen a snugger situation . . . or that the moderns who demolished a good part of the works of antiquity, had been so kind as not to leave one stone upon another. The strength of our fortification is removed by discord and by time; but caissons are raised upon the ruins as prisons—and a proper mode of punishment for those wild imaginations that prefer the empty sound of drum and trumpet to sober knock of hammer in shop mechanic! Here's a ready deliverance down the perpendicular cliff to such as are tired of their existence. . . . One bold step frees them from thought.' This melancholy young man seldom stirred outside the castle gates; he was 'stupefied with smoke and sulphur', and growing 'little better than an oyster'.

Time hung heavy indeed on his hill-top; he could not even solace himself with 'good green tea', for none was to be bought in Dover. (Now had he but known it, a brisk walk to Deal, a knock at Mrs. Carter's door, and he had enjoyed, if not *chewed* as she did, that very green tea his soul desired!)

The castle had the reputation of being haunted, and by ghosts of both sexes. As Christmas drew near, and the sutlers made ready their mince-pies, people vowed they had encountered pale spirits 'in other words, there are minds unable to bear the darkness of the night without trembling'. In March 1754 Wolfe turned his back gleefully on the old castle. '. . . I am sure there is not in the King's dominions', he wrote, already in better spirits, 'a more melancholy dreadful winter-station than that we have just left; and the neglect of the Board of Ordnance adds to the natural horror that the situation raises in men's minds. . . . So much for the vile dungeon.' One trusts the Office of Works may be earning merit; may expiate the sins of the Board of Ordnance, its predecessor!

## Chapter IV: STILL EAST OF CANTERBURY

*Round about Richborough and Ash—Round about Wingham*

### ROUND ABOUT RICHBOROUGH AND ASH

#### I

THE new discovery of Richborough Castle, for the last ten years' work has meant little less, stirs the imagination in a hundred ways—never more than when you stand between the huge blocks of weathered stone, once the foundation of a mighty archway across the western entrance. For here your feet are upon the outgoings of Watling Street which, meeting the Dover portion at Canterbury, stretches out east to west, till it reaches the Roman walls of Chester. Everything about Richborough is stirring; every English boy should make his way there. The Claudian ditch riding north to south from point to point of the harbour of Rutupiæ, first confronted wild Britain with relentless strength. The triple ditches to which after some two centuries it gave place delve deep into the Thanet sand of which the island is an outcrop. Against incursions of the Saxon pirate in the late third century, the legions surrounded their encampment with impregnable walls, and ringed these again with stupendous earthworks. The wall-building was carried out in sections; the overseers' apportionments can still be discerned. For one faced his length with tufa, and one with rag-stone; one was unskilful and his courses of Roman tile fail to correspond with adjacent courses. Their joint labours produced at last something that is magnificent even when breached and ruinous; something to stir amazement at the towering designs of empire. The task of the

modern investigator has been arduous, but richly rewarded,
and is not yet complete.

Weeds and undergrowth have been cleared; corn-crops no
longer lean up against the outer masonry; the unspoilt ashlar
of the lowest courses can be seen, turret and bastion identified.
Near the tortuous north entrance the broken head of a couchant
lion protrudes from a buttress : it used to be known as ' Queen
Bertha's head '. Within the giant rampart is an emplacement
of soldiers' huts, where a conflagration, extinguished fifteen
centuries ago, left lines of calcined soil and charcoal fragments;
a cellar still guarded its wine-jars; there are tell-tale crops of
Juvenal's Rutupine oyster-shells. A nameless Roman legion
ary, put to rest in a walled grave, under a mound of earth, his
shroud fastened with a pin of bronze, lay hid while the west
wall was built above him, but came to light, poor skeleton, a
year or two ago. Some 50,000 coins, many of them overstruck
with barbaric designs, have been unearthed, the hoards of
sojourners here or the wages of the soldiery. In the midst of
all is a great cross-shaped foundation made in rough masonry.
It rests upon something older, mightier, and of finer workmanship : upon a block of concrete, solid as rock, going thirty
feet into the soil, which it grips with mighty flange. What
stood upon this base can be surmised only from numberless
shreds of white Italian marble, some graven with letters, that
lie around or have been built into the outer rampart; and from
fragments of wrought and gilded bronze, belonging to statues
of titan proportions. Was this the place where Rome proclaimed in bronze and marble her triumph over conquered
Britain? The idea of a hidden treasure chamber under the
concrete mass now abandoned—haunted the investigator even
in Leland's day : ' Not far fro the heremitage is a cave wher
men have sowt and digged for treasure. I saw yt by candel
withyn, and there were conys. Yt was so straite that I had no
mynd to crepe far yn.'

The mood of triumph which built that monument gave place

to sober utility. Down came marble and bronze, making way
—for a beacon was it, to survey the waters ship-ridden which
lapped the Rutupine shore?

After those silent, terrible years, when the legions had left
Britain at the mercy of barbarians, St. Augustine landed here,
among the debris of Rome's splendour. A stone bearing the
impress of his foot was visited by many devout pilgrims. Here,
too, on the east side of the fort, looking seaward, Ethelbert
(was it?) built for the newcomers a tiny apsidal church of
Kentish type. The foundations have now been marked out
close to the Roman bath-house.

II

Richborough lies within the Manor of Fleet, and a legal
agreement of Cœur de Lion's date enumerates twenty people
who cultivated fields around and within ' Ratteburg ' showing
that the area was then clear of buildings. Leland came here
during his six years' survey of England, about 1530-40, and
describes his visit with invaluable detail. ' The site of the old
town or castel ', he explains, ' ys wonderful fair apon an hille.
The walles, the wich remayn ther yet, be in cumpase almost
as much as the Tower of London. They have bene very hye,
thyke, stronge and wel embateled. The mater of them is flynt,
mervelus and long brykes, both white and redde, after the
Britons' fascion. The sement was made of se sand and smaul
pible. . . . Corne groweth on the hille yn mervelus plenty,
and yn going to plow ther hath owt of mynde [been] fownd,
and now is, mo antiquities of Romayne mony then in any
place els of England. . . .' Leland met a hermit on the spot,
clearly a born antiquary, who spent blissful days grubbing undisturbed among the ruins. ' I had antiquities of the heremite,
the which is an industrious man,' he wrote, but did not, alas!
describe the specimens he carried off. He saw within the
fort, still in use, ' the lytle paroche church of St. Augustine '.

Residents in Ash liked to benefit this 'Chapel of Rich-borough', rebuilt possibly in the twelfth century. Sir John Saunders, the vicar, bequeathed to it in 1509, 'one portuys [breviary] printed, with a mass book that was Sir Thomas's, the old priest . . . and 20*s*., to make them a new window in the body of the church'.

'The Friar that singeth at Richborough' inherited 8*d*. in 1519; ten years later a legacy for reparations is noteworthy; in that exposed position a few years' neglect would reduce the building to a ruinous condition. In the *Valor Ecclesiasticus* (1540-45) priests are mentioned as serving there.

Leland had antiquarian successors, more or less serious. Elizabeth Carter dined at an archdeacon's table where the salt-cellars were 'made of a piece of Roman brick' from Rich-borough. Can they have been Samian saucers? Then, too, Charles Stothard, who surveyed England, making drawings of marvellous accuracy for his *Monumental Effigies*, walked over more than once, in August 1811, from Margate to Rich-borough, '. . . a vast ruin; the walls now standing, in many places forty feet in height and nine in thickness'. Save for such pygmy interruptions the giant ramparts were abandoned to solitude. Once the receding waters had left the fields green around them, and the cavernous hollows in their southern range been torn perhaps by Norman castle-builders, they stood pretty much undisturbed from Roman times, until the ex-cavators of our day began to probe their secrets and unveil the fascinating story of their past.

### III

The 'Causeway', which leads up on a slope from Sandwich Marshes towards Ash, is very straight, as old at least as Henry VI, and travelled over with famous journeyings; but it does not embody the first lap of Watling Street.

The Roman track is lost for some distance; it might be re-

covered by excavation, unless the plough has uprooted every
trace. Possibly the hamlet of East Street marks its junction.
Ash itself, with the twelve manors of which Fleet is eastern-
most, is an ancient place enough. The eastern termination of
the parish is called 'Each or Eche end', that is, only Ash end
in Kent dialect. At the western entrance is Guilton; 'Gilton
Town', as Bryan Faussett called it—the 'Gilden Town' of
earlier inhabitants. A tradition persisted that 'on this spot
stood an idol of solid gold, three feet in height, which lay
buried beneath one of the tumuli'. Seventy years ago Planché,
who wrote *A Corner of Kent*, describing the Ash district, found
the belief still so strong that when he asked leave to dig on
land at Guilton, it was stipulated that if he unearthed the
golden idol it should belong to the land-owner. The ploughs
of centuries have laid low the tumuli, but from 1759 onwards
Bryan Faussett made discoveries here which brought wisdom
to the historian—and that is, after all, 'above rubies'. His
story is a Kent romance which should not belong only to the
dry-as-dust antiquary. He was born at Heppington near
Canterbury, and educated at some Kent grammar school, and
afterwards at University College, Oxford, where his fellows
named him 'the handsome commoner', and enrolled in the
volunteer corps which he organized during the '45 on behalf
of the Young Pretender. Jacobite proclivities were in his
blood. His ancestor Sir Thomas Godfrey had shared in the
Kent Rising; his father, despite strict surveillance, convened
secret meetings at Heppington, and planned to assist Charles
James on his southward march. The son, 'not to be behind
his family . . . nightly, with every glass, toasted King James
on bared and bended knee'. He once sent to an antiquarian
friend a ring with the Old Pretender's head, and a 1719 half-
penny found on Culloden Field. After leaving Oxford he
took orders, but with no great enthusiasm; from 1750 he was
living 'entirely rusticated' at Street-end House, Heppington;
later he became rector of Monks Horton and curate of Nack-

ington. His real ardour was for the past and its scattered relics. Dr. Godfrey Faussett has described delightfully how the passion was implanted in his childhood : ' Few persons of taste and education ', he wrote, ' can pass any length of time in Kent without becoming antiquaries at heart, if not in pursuit . . . the influence of the neighbourhood was strong upon my great-grandfather from an early age. . . . He could not walk a hundred yards in any direction from his father's house without crossing the ancient entrenchments with which it is surrounded; a Roman road, " Stone Street Causeway ", ran through the property. . . . The manor house of Heppington . . . a castellated mansion of the reign of Stephen, then lately reduced to Elizabethan comfort and shapeliness . . . was a fit home for an antiquarian mind. And he is said to have been immensely annoyed, though a boy of barely fifteen, when his father, being overburdened with ready money . . . pulled down the old mansion and built the present one,' in the Dutch style.

The existence of ancient cemeteries in the neighbourhood of Ash had long been known. Glass vessels had been taken in such numbers from graves at Woodnesborough that harvest home on an adjoining farm was toasted in good ale drunk out of Saxon beakers. A sand-pit north of the roadside, and close to two large windmills, a quarter of a mile short of Ash Street, had produced a crop of antiquities whenever the miller's servants dug deeply or there was a down-rush of sand due to frost or rain. Faussett's first experiment in excavation was at Tremworth Down, Crundale, in 1757. Two years later he was at Ash on some antiquarian errand and heard of the famous sand-pit. Needless to say he hurried off to the place where the miller's man showed him a spear sticking three or four inches from the pit surface and the discoloured sand which betokened a grave. He and a fellow-labourer fetched spades and ladders and began roughly to delve into the hard sand, Faussett having meanwhile clambered to the bottom. ' At the next stroke or two, part of a skull and a few vertebrae were

indiscriminately with the soil cast down into the pit, without
the least care or search after anything. That concern, they
said, they left to me and my servant, who were nearly blinded
with the sand falling on us, and in no small danger of being
knocked on the head, if not buried, by the impetuosity of my
honest labourers.' Such rough-and-ready methods were torture
to Faussett's scientific spirit. However, the season was too far
advanced to do more at the moment, and he returned home,
longing to hasten away the winter of inactivity. On the 10th
of April he went back to Ash, and next day set to his task.
This was the beginning of a feast of antiquarian discovery such
as is given to few men to enjoy. In all he opened 106 Saxon
graves at Guilton, 308 at Kingston, 108 at Sibertswold, more
still at Barfriston, Bekesbourne, and Chartham. Here at
Guilton he found shield-bosses, buckles, vessels of green glass,
broken at a touch, urns of black earth. In the women's graves
were coloured beads and exquisite ornaments, now a round
brooch of gold filigree upon copper, set with garnets in zigzag
patterns, now another in ivory and lapis, now a ring, a comb,
even a silken string.

Dr. Faussett pictures the old enthusiast at work, the stir he
made in the country-side, his heroic perseverance when dis-
abled by the gout. ' Tradition tells us of the boyish excitement
in which he superintended the opening of his barrows; of the
eagerness with which he sifted every crumb of earth . . . of
his good humour when his labourers worked well; his anger
when they flagged, and his rage and vexation when an unlucky
pickaxe shattered a vase or a patera.' Sometimes, despite the
gout, he would seize spade and axe himself; his ' good humour
and good pay ' made more impression than occasional out-
breaks of impatience. Neighbouring land-owners were not invariably sympathetic. When his son and fellow-worker, Henry
Faussett, discovered on Kingston Down that most famous find,
the large and radiant fibula which might have fastened a
queen's mantle, he carried it to Bryan Faussett, too lame to

leave his carriage, and he drove off with it. ' Next day a report was spread that the carriage had been so full of gold the wheels would scarcely turn; and the lord of the manor prohibited further excavations on these downs.'

In Faussett's younger days he is said to have visited every church in Kent, copying inscriptions and drawing armorial windows. Hasted found his notes of great value. He made a collection of some 5,000 coins, chiefly Roman and English, and under a whimsical impulse worthy of Sir Edward Dering melted down 150 duplicates into a bell, to hang over his house, and speak with brazen Roman tongue—so ran the inscription —of Rome's antiquity. The results of his excavations remained for more than seventy years unpublished and almost unknown, till their exhibition in 1894, at a meeting of the Archaeological Association in Canterbury, aroused a little tepid enthusiasm. Even then the British Museum refused to acquire them for the nation; and a collection which might have been the glory of Kent found a purchaser in Joseph Mayer of Liverpool, who gave it to his native town and printed, with fine illustrations, Faussett's notes under the title of *Inventorium Sepulchrale*.

#### IV

Although the twelve manors of Ash were owned by noble families in the days long past, their dwelling-houses of to-day have no great antiquity, or importance. The arms of Christopher Harfleet or Septvans in painted glass are still in the farm-house of Molland, which he set up at the end of an avenue of lime-trees about 1559. Philipot saw a Latin motto inscribed above the shield : ' I will scatter the enemies of my King like chaff,' an allusion to the winnowing fans or ' vans ' (at first seven, then reduced to three) which characterized the Septvans family coat. Chequer Court, along the same lane, possesses a moat, and once had a poplar avenue. Planché speaks of a forest of elms, from which the adjoining house of

Elmes, shortened to the friendly 'Nell', may have taken its name. He adds regretfully that 'immense numbers have been felled in this neighbourhood . . . and agricultural interests . . . are enforcing . . . the havoc, which, we fear, will only cease with the fall of the last of these beautiful old trees, still, for a few hundred yards, making a bower of this lane'. Let their memory at least be not wholly forgotten!

We are travelling now north and west from Ash. Between Bereling Street and Lower Goldstone or Goldstanton, which has lost its ancient mansion-house entirely, lies Paramore Street, named for an old Kent family we have met already at St. Nicholas-at-Wade. A John 'Pamore' was buried in Ash Churchyard in 1497, leaving his lands between his three sons, Nicholas, Thomas and William, 'each heir to the other'. Thomas must have succeeded brother Nicholas quite quickly, for he was living at Paramore Grange by the close of the fifteenth century. After him may have come Solomon Paramore, who wore a russet gown and white hose and left a quarter of malt to repair Ash Church. One of them probably built, at least in part, the existing Paramore Court. Little by little its ancient features are being rediscovered; the very day I called there last some plaster had been removed from the west wall, disclosing fine brick and flint patterning at the base of a massive chimney-stack. Inside the comfortable solid walls is a Tudor staircase black with age, adorned with oak pine-apples and planned with square turns which make a fine well into which one looks down, imagining ancestral Paramores descending the steps. Best of all is the painted room, so curiously decorated with a heavy black trellis in which many-coloured jewels are set. The Beatitudes in black-letter make a frieze round the top, and above the fireplace are the initials I.R., with a feather and an H. for Henry, Prince of Wales; the date 1603 suggests that the painting was completed just after King James succeeded Elizabeth. Thomas Paramore was Mayor of Canterbury in 1607 and 'obtained the Sword for the

City, not without great expense to the same'. He may have expressed his loyalty with the same lavish hand in decorating his own parlour. On the south wall two tiny blocked windows still keep their original panes and leading.

A return along Paramore Street and a westward bend by Warehorn and Ware bring one into Westmarsh. But first something must be said about these by-ways we traverse so lightly. Judging by many a fifteenth- or sixteenth-century testament, the 'foulness' of the roads lay heavy on the parochial conscience. The number of bequests for amending highways is remarkable; a road-rate could hardly have produced larger sums. There can have been few exceptions to the universal slough. Whether it be the way between Gilden town and Ash, between Ash Street and Holcombe, or Weddington and Bolney, east from Ash to Sandwich or west from Ash to Canterbury; all alike are fit objects for charity. Sometimes the testator orders how the road shall be made up at his expense : ' As much gravel or chalk to the value of 20s. to be layed between the Wallend and Sarre where most need is, this coming summer.' The vicar, Sir John Saunders, was occasionally put in charge of the road-mending; others made sure that their heirs or their friends would benefit directly, as well as the general public : 'The foulway afore my tenement, six loads of greivel.' I have led you far enough along the sticky lanes of long ago, only it is grievous that some vandal has modernized their ancient names. Fancy ' Knell ' for ' Nell ' upon a finger-post, and ' Cooper Street ' for ' Cop Street ' of centuries. Let us return by Warehorn, a slurring of the charming 'Wareshawthorne', an offshoot of Wingham Barton, where a plain-built manor-house, partly ruinous, still stands. Close to it, southwards, is Uphousen or Housden, another treasury of kingposts, beams, oaken floors, and peep-hole windows; it belongs to that country-side life of the past which seems, looking back on it, as sound at heart, as iron hard, as the oak which sheltered its sons and daughters. Uphousen has all too little history; the name occurs in one will only of my observation, when John Carpenter left to his wife Joan certain lands, ' whereof one acre and a half are at *Ophosen*, with the land of the Archbishop of Canterbury towards the north '. Carpenter lived in a house at Westmarsh called ' Peyndes ', with hempland adjoining, and two acres of pasture opposite. His will is dated 1484; part of the present Uphousen might well be as old.

Westmarsh, once a hamlet of Ash, now a separate ecclesiastical district, was earlier known as ' Coldmarsh ', so chilly a name that the inhabitants preferred to change it and bask in the rays of the setting sun.

v

After reading a number of those old wills one could walk along Ash Street and re-people the dwellings, ' needlework ' cottages of black and white. Refurnish them too; Margery Burton's, for example, with cupboard and best bed, standing-chest and little ' shippe cofer ', and an array of glittering brass and pewter pots. In the better houses, each away along its lane, one might admire the plate laid out with the linen napery, spoons with knobs of lions, ' nuts ' with silver covers, and gilded salts. The walls too are tastefully covered, like the room hung in white and grey, which Katherine Martyn gave to her granddaughter Margaret Wigmore. Or in the fields one might hail by name the beasts at pasture, ' Joan ' the pied red cow, ' Gryme ' the horse, the white-faced heifer of two years.

There is such a sense of life, rather of clinging to life, about these forgotten testators, a longing to ensure that the rhythm of every day, broken for themselves, shall pulse on for those left behind. Margaret Omer is still to burn ' the tops of ash trees ' in her grate; son Simon Penny to have the proud ' new garden '; wife Cecile ' half that Pome reall that shall be growing in that garden and half the next tree '.

Picking their way along the muddy tracks come the church-goers on a Sunday. Alice Christmasse wears the russet cloak which Thomas Mayhew left her; russet, that is cloth of reddish-brown, or neutral colour is useful country-side fashion. William Crofte is noticeable for his violet gown and tawny jacket, or he may have donned that 'gilded coat, or coat of white', which his neighbour Master Digge gave him. And now there is a stir; all eyes are turned respectfully to watch the gentry pass by; the Lady of Goldstanton first, Dame Matilda Clitherow in Murray kirtle and kerchief of fine Paris lawn. In winter she dons a cloak of crimson furred with marten, and in summer her mantle of red damask floats out behind her. She it was who left to John Norys, a neighbour's son, the sword and body-armour which her husband, Roger Clitherow, wore at Agincourt. And now the bells peal out from the massive tower, and the good folk pause a moment in the churchyard, where presently they will come to lie. Only for the wealthy and the great will room be found within the walls. William Lewies will presently order that stone for his grave, 'with the pykture of me and my wife', which is still under the tower towards the south-west pier. In the chancel Sir John de Goshall and his lady have rested long, and Richard Clitherow and his wife, daughter to Sir John Oldcastle, beneath their brass; Dame Matilda will join their company, and William Norys too, with a red cloth of baudekyn laid over his body. The Septvans (or Sevaunces, or even Sephams), John and Katherine, are to have alabaster effigies in Molland Chapel, and Christopher Septvans a large brass on the floor. . . .

One of these monuments, 'excessively interesting', brought Charles Stothard to Ash Church.

'At first sight it appeared an unintelligible mass, shewing nothing but that it was a human form; on a closer inspection I found it was buried in white-wash, in some places more than a quarter of an inch thick. . . . I set to work with my pen-knife and nail-brush to clear it from its coating. After a

four hours' job I was well recompensed . . . the figure from
its armour seemed to be of the time of Edward II (Edward
III) . . . on the shoulders are circular plates, having upon
them lions' heads. The surcoat is laced at the side, but left
sufficiently open to shew the body underneath covered with
small plates of iron riveted together. . . .'

The drawing made after this strenuous beginning represents
the effigy by the Molland Chapel entrance of Sir John Leverick,
Knight of Ash, who married Joan Septvans.

## ROUND ABOUT WINGHAM

### I

Ash Street nowadays has few picturesque features; its history
is more like a treasure-hoard, hidden and close kept, than that
of neighbouring Wingham. Between the two places the road
is straight and the country open, falling northwards to marshlands, with knots of green to mark an old farm-house. One
comes into Wingham down a little hill and past an apple-
orchard. At the entrance to Wingham Street a few magnificent trees are on guard, beech and chestnut, in a close once
perhaps a park; along it limes and chestnuts are planted in
ample belts of turf, and it is crossed by a little straight-bedded
watercourse. The place is situated, writes a great lover of
Wingham, 'on what was once a swampy marsh'. Some
Roman, attracted by the sheltered site and pure water, built
a villa 'of Roman tile covered with white and slate-coloured
mosaic' near the bridge on the Canterbury road; its laby-
rinthine pavement, bordered with black and white bands, was
recently uncovered. Some Saxon worthy left the place his
name, 'the homestead of Winga or Winc'.

'Probably the original Roman Road from Richborough to
Canterbury', we read again, 'was north of the village; but that
part across the marshes of the Lesser Stour being flooded in

winter a track was eventually made further south, along the
higher ground and crossing the marsh at Wingham where it
was much narrower; then the track turned westward, just
along the border of the marsh, and regained the old Roman
Road at the top of Littlebourne Hill.'

For convenience of passage to and from Sandwich Port the
Archbishop of Canterbury had a manor-house in the village.
He gave Wingham its market, which was so flourishing that
it was held to do Canterbury citizens an injury.  It must indeed
have been difficult to rival in abundance and cheapness the
wild-fowl of wood and marsh sold at Wingham fair; the geese
and swans, the woodcock and partridges netted or brought
down by hawks.

Guests came and went at the manor-house—Cœur de Lion
and King John, Baldwin and Boniface—and once an elephant
passed through the village on its way to the Tower, a royal
gift from France to England.  The college to which Wingham
still owes much old-world charm, was founded by the Fran-
ciscan archbishop Pecham, whose effigy, in bog oak, lies in
the Martyrdom.  'Friar John' had the soul of a reformer;
as he journeyed about his diocese on horseback, with a retinue
of a hundred men, he gave orders everywhere for greater
reverence at the sacred offices, and the revival of symbolic acts
that brought home to simple folk the beauty of worship.  He
was at 'Wyngeham' first in 1279, and often in later years, as
though he found peace in the quiet place.  At one visit he
arranged for the founding of the College for Secular Canons.
'We have turned our eyes,' reads the foundation deed signed
at the manor-house on August 2nd 1282; 'we have turned our
eyes to the church of Wingham as it were to a fruitful vineyard filled with branches and fruits, which cannot be easily
cultivated by the labours of one husbandman, nay further by
the labours of two . . . its revenues are sufficient to furnish
the payment of more labourers.'  So the manor is to be divided
into four parishes, and a college of six canonries instituted,

named from the places of their endowment—Bonnington, Chilton, Pedding, Ratling, Twitham and Wymlingswold. For three centuries or so the canons lived in their separate houses, carrying out their duties among a population of 900 souls. The college had few vicissitudes; adversity rather than calm prosperity fills pages of history. When Archbishop Warham visited in 1511 and questioned the canons, their complaints were of little moment: promotion was given to strangers; the rules were never read before the priest-vicars; how then could they know whether they were keeping them or not. Happy community which has no greater grievances. Change came with a vengeance at the Suppression; it meant the disappearance of provost and canons; it meant the dispersal of all their offerings of love; vestments innumerable and broidered banners; the silver Gospel book with the image of Christ and the four evangelists; the incense ' shipp of silver '. The Palmer family bought the provost's house—gone now from the walled enclosure east of the church. The canons' houses, gabled and heavily timbered, passed into lay hands; two of them still stand on the street which turns southward as one enters Wingham from Canterbury.

The Red Lion Inn, with a rampant beast on the sign, may have been one of the college buildings, or occupy the site of the old market-house. The Dog Inn with its hall or dormitory, may have housed the Vicars Choral, at first eight in number. The Palmer coat of arms bore a ' greyhound courrant sable '. Our Wingham historian, however, suggests that the sign over the inn is the portrait of a hunting dog, or talbot, introduced through the Oxindens. Sir Henry of Deane married Elizabeth Brooker of a family whose armorial bearings were ' three talbots passant—that is, three dogs walking with three feet on the ground, the fourth foot being raised and the tail curved over the back. Sign-painters of a later age, not understanding heraldry, altered the proper position of the dog.'

II

No one can mistake the Oxinden coat who goes into the south chapel of Wingham Church. A modern frieze illustrates their marriage-alliances by a long series of shields quartering various armorials with their own silver field and 'iii Oxen sabul, armed with gooldys, a cheveryn of the same'. In the centre of the chapel is a handsome pyramid, adorned with heavy swags of marble fruit and flowers, and four projecting oxen's heads, boldly modelled in black porphyry. Records of Oxinden burials from the sixteenth to the eighteenth century are set out on the pedestal. Sir George Oxinden, first Governor of Bombay, paid this stately tribute to his family's renown, and left a legacy of £300 to have the pyramid erected. The sturdy chestnut columns, which seem an odd substitute for stone in so large a church, have lately been explained to every one's satisfaction. A petition of 1555, unearthed in the Record Office by Mr. A. H. Taylor, revealed a forgotten scandal. It complains of the cruel advantage taken by one George Foggard, a Canterbury 'Bere brewer', of poor Wingham's delay in rebuilding its church, which fourteen or fifteen years since, 'being ruinouse and decayed, sodenly fell downe'. Foggard and his confederate had, it seemed, also presented a petition; in it they harped upon Wingham's poverty, and requested, as if duly authorized persons, licence under the Great Seal to gather alms for re-edifying St. Mary's. Safeguarded by these false pretences, Foggard and Co. had amassed, through sundry shires, the sum of £224. Any person who dared question their motives was subject to such insinuations of his not being 'a trewe Catholick man', that, just then—when Queen Mary's fires were lighting —he dared not refuse his contribution. The church's disrepair had extended over a quarter of a century; the north aisle had disappeared altogether (it has never been replaced), and there were bequests for the restoration which with Foggard's nest-egg would have fitted out St. Mary's nave with substantial stone arcades. But the £224 had vanished, and there the wooden posts still stand, after 400 years, a reproach to the dishonest man. A legacy in 1558 of '20s., to be delivered at such time as the sawers shall begin to work', must mark the abandonment of higher ambition. About 1776 the wooden stays were encased in stucco, and whitened, in a desperate attempt 'to simulate a masonry arcade of semi-circular-headed arches'. These shams were afterwards removed, but a lithograph of the church, *circa* 1840–50, proves their existence at that date, while Elizabeth Carter had already seen them on one of her visits to Wingham. 'In the Church which joins the house,' she wrote to Mrs. Vesey, 'the pillars are new cased with wood and joined by circular arches, to the infinite scandal of my gothic enthusiasm.' Now that Wingham House, the provost's house, has disappeared for ever, it is pleasant to read her description of the 'old mansion, which is spacious without looking uncomfortable and venerable without being dull. . . . Modern elegance, the great foe to ancient greatness and solemnity, has almost entirely banished all remains of its former appearance except a few gothic doors, which have hitherto resisted all reformation.'

Elizabeth's friend at Wingham was Mrs. Cosnan, who, as Bethia D'Aeth, had spent her girlhood at Knowlton. To her the verses beginning, 'Say, dear Bethia', were addressed; not great poetry certainly and yet perfectly sincere, for Mrs. Carter truly regretted Bethia's exchange of country quietude for the 'mad Circle of unsettled Joys'.

> Tir'd with unmeaning Sounds and painted Shows,
> Which this vain Theatre of Life compose;
> Let peaceful Thought to happier Scenes remove
> And seek the lov'd retreat of K——n Grove.

Sir Egerton Brydges, who knew Mrs. Carter personally, said that she had 'cold stiff formal manners', and ill-naturedly remembered how Hayley had dedicated his novel *The Old Maid* to her, and given her great offence. This was but one side of the picture; beneath a forbidding exterior was the warmest heart, profound loyalty to a coterie of good friends who could estimate her worth better, far better than cross-grained Sir Egerton. I should regret extremely that her nephew, Montagu Pennington, had dedicated her collected correspondence to Sir Egerton—had he not preserved her snuff-box in his library, with a volume of her letters to Miss Talbot.

### III

The Wingham neighbourhood is good ground for a walker, though a little spoilt nowadays by a tall chimney or two, a light railway crossing the high road. A few days ago my walking companion and I explored the hinterland bordering on the Lesser Stour marshes. There are some hilly spurs and dipping valleys, and then a windswept plateau on which little old Preston Church stands out. Ours was a voyage of discovery to find Old Wenderton, marked in Roman capitals on the ordnance map. Strawberry gathering was in full swing in the fields, and a steam-plough in the splendid hop-garden south of our lane prepared for the next harvest. Outside the barn at Wenderton Farm (an old house, disguised with stucco but betraying its age by the little red bricks of the side wall) a wagon was being loaded up with strawberry baskets. An old countryman came out of the yard and we bade him good day.

'Would you tell us if this is Little Wenderton?' I asked politely.

'No, mum,' he said, 'they calls this Great Wenderton Farm.'

This was disconcerting; it disagreed with our well-studied map.

'There used to be an old manor-house about here?' I went on tentatively.

'Well, yes; what they calls the Mansion, way up in the

woods; but there ain't nothing left of it but a bit of wall and an old cellar.'

'Is it long since it was pulled down, I wonder?'

'There you have me. I've been here meself a matter of forty year, but I've never known it other than them old ruins.'

'Forty years? Do you know, I read a letter the other day written in that house three hundred years ago?' (priggish of me, but true and irresistible). He roared with laughter.

'Three hun'erd years! That's a good bit; there you have me. In whose time might that be now? My word. Three hun'erd years!'

'It was when Mr. Vincent Denne lived there.'

'Denne, Denne. That ain't the name now. There's a couple o' cottages away in the woods, and if you turn left and cross the stile at the bottom and follow the path right up, the woman'll show you where the old mansion stood. You won't never find it yourselves.'

He laughed again good-naturedly, and came a few steps to be sure we took the right path.

What good fortune was ours. We felt as pleased as two children to be visiting at the manor-house. The field track followed a little stream bordered by green marsh-land where an army of yellow flags proclaimed June's triumph. And here we remembered the swans young Thomas Denne, when he inherited Wenderton, had kept in the river, and upped with his own swan-mark. We mounted now through a rising coppice planted upon a ledge in the hill-side which must, we thought, have been the old approach to the house; it was tangled and ill-kept, but bits of shrubs kept count of former cultivation. Then we emerged into a plantation of magnificent old Spanish chestnuts, and fancied we could trace the remains of avenues in their broken glades. A grove of gnarled walnuts came next, and then two ancient cottages, the brick zigzagged, the beams heavy and solid. Two little children ran out, and their young mother followed with two more, a red-haired

'Kathaleen', and Doris of the flaxen curls. They were
charmed—the whole party of them—to guide the ladies to the
old ruins, past the mole-traps set thickly along the grass-grown
track.

Well—the brick wall was the merest fragment, a couple of
feet high; the cellar past discovery; the relics of terraces we
found; and disentangled old yews and mulberries from a
thicket of dock-leaves. The jungle was too dense for much
exploration; as we emerged from it into an upper lane a finger-
board warned intruders in the next copse to 'beware of
poisonous snakes'.

Poor Wenderton; it was pulled down at some time after
1790. Would we had seen it when the chestnut avenues were
in their prime; and Tom Denne's orchards—six acres 'almost
come to the best'—clustered round the 'Cheife House' standing 'pleasantly for prospect' among groves of trees.

IV

Pensively we made our way along the Canterbury road; we
looked back once more at the dark cap of woodland which
hides Wenderton, and picked out Ickham Church spire and
Wickhambreux Church tower—near neighbours as they are—
across the cornfields.

As the road slants down towards a little bridge, the Park
on the left planted with fine timber, is Lee Priory; the house
just visible between the tree-stems was new-modelled 'at vast
expense' to the owner, Mr. Thomas Barrett, by James Wyatt,
'in the Gothic form'. Connoisseurs—Horace Walpole among
them—pronounced it 'one of the most beautiful specimens of
Wyatt's genius'. When Mr. Barrett died in 1810 he bequeathed the place to his nephew, Sir Egerton Brydges' eldest
son, then a boy of fourteen, who took the surname of Barrett.
Sir Egerton now left Denton Court and removed his queer,
moody self, his copious industry and thwarted genius, to his

son's property. At this time (1812) he became Member of Parliament for Maidstone, and, surprisingly enough, turned his thoughts from poetry and heraldry to the reform of the Poor Law.

In 1813, according to his *Autobiography*, 'a compositor and a pressman (Johnson and Warwick) persuaded me with much difficulty to allow them to set up a private press at Lee Priory. I consented, on the condition that I would have nothing to do with the expenses, but would gratuitously furnish them with copy, and they must run all hazards and rely on such profits as they could get'. The issues, strictly limited to 'a very small number of copies at high prices', sold readily to book collectors. The partners, however, quarrelled; Johnson departed in 1817, and by 1822 Warwick was some hundreds in debt, and the enterprise abandoned. Such rare tracts were printed at their press as the poems of Nicholas Breton, William Browne, and Raleigh; Greene's *Groatsworth of Wit*, the Duchess of Newcastle's *Autobiography*. Sir Egerton, as in honour bound, wrote 'to please the printers' the *Sylvan Wanderer* and *Bertram*, a poem; Warwick perhaps deserved the author's parting snarl, 'I value it least of all my poetical compositions.'

Litttlebourne, the old cottages set on the tiny green, the vista of its namesake Little Bourne or Stour, is full of charm, not wholly wasted, one hopes, on the cars careering along the village street towards Canterbury three miles off. The church has an unusual patron—St. Vincent—and stands, with pointed steeple, apart from the houses, just where the river escapes from a bower of trees into the marshland, and the heron sometimes comes for a little fishing. I have found two pleasing memories of old St. Vincent's and the candlelight twinkling through the panes on Sundays at eventide : one William Danyson in 1514 left his son Robert his stock of bees, to maintain 2 tapers of 1½ lbs. each in the Trinity window, under which, 'in the churchyard on the north side', he was buried; and this again—from a vicar's testament—Thomas Browne in 1544 gave the church its patron's legend, ' a book covered with white leather, containing the Story of St. Vincent ', and added this confession of an ancient grievance, and this bequest:

' If at my death the tapers standing on the high altar be burnt to the stumpes, or be half spent, then whole tapers to be set in their place; and bread and wine to sing with to be left in the box and botell belonging to the Church; so that the priest that shall come be not defrauded as I was.'

*Chapter V: IN THE STOUR VALLEY*

*From the Source by Postling to Ashford—Ashford and its neighbourhood—Round about Wye—Godmersham and Chilham*

### FROM THE SOURCE BY POSTLING TO ASHFORD

I

STONE STREET descends from its lofty ridge into the Stour valley steeply by way of Hampton Hill; 'Hempton Hill,' Gostling says in his little *Tour of East Kent,* ' so-called (as some fancy) for heaven-top hill, on account of its height.' He too had felt, as every passer-by will surely feel until the hills ' flee away ', the shock of surprise with which one reaches the extreme border of the Downs. From that vantage appears below, quite suddenly, a wide extent : first the tumbled foot-hills, then, in a farther distance, the sea-margin, a country-side scattered with villages, church towers, meadow and woodland. When the western sky holds the colour of sunset, the trees are gilded and the sheep have ruddy fleeces; this is one of the loveliest prospects Kent can show. If it could be made in reality a panorama of the centuries, nothing obliterated nor forgotten, vanished houses might be set in place again, and the figures of men and women of renown follow the ancient paths. Four people from four succeeding centuries are to be our particular heroes and heroine : four people as typical of their times as though they had lived, not among Kent hills, but in crowded and strenuous places. Much of this chapter relates to them; much more is left untold.

Probably the Stour itself first brought a population hereabouts, where the pitcher can be dipped at innumerable water-springs and the downside is interlaced with tributary brooks.

River-springs among the hills have always been the poet's freehold. We make less of our 'sources' than do the French; perhaps, on the whole, English rivers have less romantic origins. Has anything of ours quite the glamour of Druyes-les-Belles-Fontaines in the Morvan, or the Douix at Châtillon in the Côte d'Or, so quickly merged into the Seine? The principal source of the many-headed Stour is a romantic place. Following the road left from the foot of Hampton Hill you see, at one bend, shoulder beyond mighty shoulder of the Downs, each one jutting farther and steeper than its fellow, the highest culminating in wooded Beechborough. Behind Postling—north of the village, that is—a great bay opens out, and on its eastern slope, covered with beech-leaves, is a guardian tree. 'Here issue the Exterior Springs of the River,' writes old Dr. Packe, 'but particularly that which arises close to the Church, under the foot of the hill, that has a single Ewe-tree at the top of it: this is the Spring that comes out of the living Rock at five or six Spout-holes big enough to receive a Man's head; and this (tho' there are at least five or six Springs within half a mile of the place . . .) is what is commonly called the River-head, as it is a constant Spring that never fails in the dryest Seasons.' Nowadays the water gushes in a crystal ribbon literally from a spout of lead, and the yew has given way to the beech; from this cradle the young stream threads a bush covert towards the open fields. By the time it reaches Stanford, running behind the village gardens, it is wide enough to carry a little footbridge, close by the hillock on which the church stands. Next it curves past railway station and racecourse, through low meadows, around the ruins of Westenhanger House; under those grey walls it turns off west to Mersham and Ashford.

'Ostinghaungre', Leland writes succinctly, 'was Creal's lordship, of sum now corruptly called Westenhanger. Poyn-

ings a late hald it. The King hath it now.' History before the
Criols or Kiriels is a pale tradition. If the house was indeed
'a royal residence during the heptarchy' and Fair Rosamond
made there her lonely and perilous 'Bower', she could not
have drawn her last breath in one of the existing towers. The
earliest part now above ground dates not much before the mid-
fourteenth century; it is probably a near relation of Bodiam
Castle, perhaps designed by the same military architect.

An unfinished seventeenth-century plan in the British
Museum shows the vanished southern half of the house : by
fitting this sketch with the existing remains of the northern
side the ground-plan is recoverable. From a railway carriage
passing by two towers are visible—one round and roofed, the
other square, now a jagged ruin; an ivy-covered wall links
them together. Once there were four round towers at the
corners of a quadrangle, and half-way between four rectangular
towers. The entrance gate was defended with portcullis and
drawbridge.

## II

Here at Westenhanger we meet our first hero, that famous
Kentish worthy, Customer Thomas Smythe. His adventures
began at sixteen, like Whittington's, with a journey from his
home at Corsham to London, to build a fortune out of a tiny
patrimony. As a freeman's son he joined the Haberdashers'
Company, the Skinners' also, and he married Alice, daughter
of Lord Mayor Sir Andrew Judde, the founder of Tonbridge
School. Alice's portion was the Auchers' manor of Ashford,
on which Sir Andrew had foreclosed. Smythe was by now
' customer ', or collector of custom and subsidy on foreign
merchandise for the busy ports of London, Sandwich,
Chichester, Southampton and Ipswich. Queen Mary passed
him on to Queen Elizabeth; every time his ' farmer's lease '
was renewed he covenanted for a higher rent and deposited a
richer fine in the royal coffers. By the third renewal he found

BUST OF GENERAL WOLFE, QUEBEC HOUSE, WESTERHAM

no less a rental than £20,000 a year, with a fine of £5,000
worth his while.

The extent of his transactions aroused Elizabeth's cupidity
and suspicion of Smythe's good faith. The awful moment
came when he was charged with peculation, failure to keep
records, bribery of the Queen's Officers. However, on Burleigh's advice, she decided that to raise the rent immediately
by £6,000 a year, and exact the Customer's promise to dismiss
offending subordinates would meet the case. 'This being
nowe afresh gyven out from your Majestie,' Burleigh's
memorandum dryly observes, 'with some hard words to all
that move your majestie therein, will force him to forsake his
fryndes helps . . . to submytt hymself to your maiesties order,
and gladly to accepte what it shall please your majestie to
yelde to hym. For he hath confessed unto me in conference
that he hath clerely gayned by his ferme vj$^{mli}$ [£6,000] yerely :
and he confesseth his yerely charge not to be much lesse than
iiij$^{mli}$ [£4,000]. So as, though the plot I delivered to your
maiestie . . . be termed coniecturall; yet by this his owne confession it is proved true.' Now Smythe had other, not un-
productive, sources of income—sundry lead- and copper-mines
in Cornwall—and was well able to weather the royal tempest.
His life was crowded with interests, passed, as his epitaph
records (it was no empty boast), 'in relieving the poor, in pro-
moting literature, for the advantage of the State in fitting out
ships for long voyages, in discovering new countries. . . .' By
and by he purchased from Sir Thomas Sackville the manors
of 'Eastenhanger and Westenhanger', and he and Mistress
Alice moved into the magnificent house with its hall fifty feet
long and thirty feet wide, gallery for music, stone-vaulted
cloisters, and chapel, which Sir Edward Poynings, of Poynings'
Law, had built. They adorned the rooms (126 of them, lighted
by 365 windows) with magnificent furniture, a suite in
yellow velvet and one in green taffaty, Turkey carpets, chairs
broidered in silk and gold. On their guests' coverlids of Arras

famous romances were depicted—Paris and Helen, David and Abigail. The shining damask cloths which furnished the tables, five, six, and seven yards in length, had inwoven stories —of Holofernes or Samuel, or the Creation. Again Fortune's wheel turned back in restless hands; again the Customer fell under ' our high and heavie displeasure '. With a sick body, diseased mind, and trembling hand (these are his own words), the old man tried to propitiate his wrathful mistress by offering larger and yet larger rents. Nothing would satisfy her but such a sum as spelt ruin. Under the strain the end came in June 1591, when he was sixty-nine years old. Smythe's splendid alabaster tomb is in the south transept of Ashford Church. Could one have a better example than his of the Elizabethan merchant-prince?

### III

Leave the river valley now for the hills—northward. Monks Horton Priory is approached through steeply tilted lanes well braced with hedges. Once, in the narrowest, a traction engine nimbly descending collided with three bulky omnibuses, scaling as it were the heights of knowledge. 'Words' were overhead. Then a disgruntled procession shaped itself; the engine snorted backwards up the ascent; the empty omnibuses followed with grating brakes; the freight of learned archaeologists, more or less actively footing the hill, trailed after in a long-drawn line. The lane skewed into another, and yet another, before, with the fraction of an inch to spare, engine and omnibuses parted company, and knowledge wearily resumed its many thrones. After several such contretemps the K.C.C. forbade narrow lanes to East Kent Scarlets of the stoutest build. . . . What a sparkling description 'Fidget' would have scribbled off to her friend the Duchess of Portland; how she would have quizzed each detail with her sister 'Pea' and found, for one afternoon, the country-side less monstrous dull. Does it surprise you to meet her here, our eighteenth-century heroine, Elizabeth Robinson, presently Mrs. Montagu, queen of the blue-stockings? Mount Morris in Monks Horton was her mother Sarah Morris's estate; there Elizabeth lived until her marriage. Her father was a sociable being; compelled to ruralize, he promptly fell a victim to the spleen and required 'a double quantity of saffron in his tea'. 'Though I am tired of the country,' writes eleven-year-old Elizabeth to her Duchess, 'I am not so much so as my papa; he is a little vapoured, and last night after two hours' silence he broke out into a great exclamation against the country, and concluded in saying that living in the country was sleeping with one's eyes open; if he sleeps all day I am sure he dreams very much of London. . . .' After a year or two life in East Kent became more tolerable for the débutante at fourteen. Her early letters give us gay pictures of rustic society. The coaches rumble along country roads; winter, swelling hill-side springs, is apt to submerge them up to the seats, and force homeward the ball-goers in their finery. 'As I had never heard of any balls in the Elysian fields,' Fidget declares imperturbably, 'and so not so much as know whether the ghosts of departed beaux wear pumps, I thought it better to reserve ourselves for the ridotto than hazard drowning for this ball.' Arrived in the ball-room 'my papa' forgets twenty years and his nine children and foots it nimbly with the rest, only mortified by the ladies crying 'Old Mr. Robinson, Haysides and turn your daughter'. Lady Tufton of Hothfield, the moving spirit at these assemblies, is as democratic as you please. When the moon is full she calls in all and sundry to complete the tale of dancers. 'It is the oddest mixture you can imagine . . . every one has an eye to their trade . . . the mantua-maker treads upon your petticoat till she unrips the seams; the shoe-maker makes you foot it till you wear out your shoes.' And in the midst Elizabeth spins round to the squeaking fiddle, her bright eyes taking in every humour from Lady Tufton's frown

to Lord Winchilsea's flirtation with pretty Miss Palmer.
Presently 'Pea' falls ill with smallpox. Elizabeth is sent to
Hayton Farm, within sight of her home, to be safe from infection. 'I cannot', says Elizabeth, 'extract the least grain
of entertainment out of the good family I am with.' She finds
the chickens and a young calf but dull scholars in the school
of manners and apt to prefer the dairymaid to the fine lady.
She fancies herself a Pastorella, sits in Arcadia on a bed of
violets, gathers cowslips for an absent friend. But time hangs
very, very heavily on her little hands: 'Not a countenance I
delight in to joy me, nor any conversation I like to entertain
me; I am left wholly to myself and my books.' Poor Fidget,
her papa's own daughter!

IV

The Robinsons would certainly have preferred Monks
Horton Priory in its present guise of a modern country-house,
and indeed the owners have blended old stones and new
additions with great skill. Within doors every century has
left a token. The fourteenth divided out the Norman barn-
like simplicity with oaken floors and partitions. There are late
Gothic doorways, some oak-ledged doors with old strap-hinges,
an oaken kitchen-screen framed (*temp.* Henry VI) of thick
and thin planks.

Five mullioned windows light a great room on the upper
floor. Its stone chimney-piece, six feet high, has a carved
frieze, and an ample width of seven feet seven inches to hold
winter logs. Not sixty years ago one could look up from the
plaster wall-panels, in oaken frames, to the old ceiling, panelled
into squares. Within each square a crown of thorns was
painted surrounding the sacred I.H.S. in red, and the corners
were filled in with a flowering spray. Can you believe it?
The restorer of this room carried off its painted ceiling to
London. Where is it now? Would Fidget have sympathized
with the migration? In dry summer weather foundations of

the destroyed buildings on the eastern cloister range can be traced and some day may be excavated.

v

Sellinge, Smeeth, and Brabourne belong in memory to the Scots of Scots Hall. Brabourne Church, coeval with Monks Horton Priory, was built ' between the two choirs of Canterbury ' by Robert de Vere and his wife Adeliza. It is a perfect village church, with nave-columns of Kentish rag, strong as marble, a fine chancel arch, a precious fragment of Norman glass. The Scots have now no other home in the place but Brabourne Church. The heart of John de Baliol, Lord of Galloway, it is thought during the Scottish wars under Edward I, was brought here from Dulcecor Abbey, founded by his wife Devorgilla. She had the beloved's heart embalmed and cased in ivory and silver; she carried it everywhere with her and placed it at meal-times in Baliol's chair. At the end of all this restless grief the withered heart was enshrined by strangers among the North Downs. Two of Devorgilla's sons had Kentish connexions : Alexander, the fifth, was Lord of Chilham; the sixth, Sir William Baliol le Scot, was ancestor of the Scots of Brabourne. He was buried, like so many great people of the day, in the Grey Friars' Cemetery at Canterbury. His grandson and namesake, Sir William Scot, Lord Chief Justice of the King's Bench, Knight Marshal of England, was the first Scot of seventeen generations to be buried in Brabourne; his wife Sibella Lewknor brought him the manor as her dower. One canopied tomb belongs to William Scot, High Sheriff under Henry VI, who built Scot's Hall a little to the south of Smeeth. A brass in memory of his second spouse, Isabel, afterwards Lady Clifton, adorns the pavement. Her long hair flows to the knees from under a little circlet of jewels; here is her jingling epitaph :

> Hac necis in cella, iacet hic prudens Isabella,
> Qui nulli nocuit, sed Domino placuit.

A Scot marriage with Anne Pimpe brought into the family Thevegate Manor at Smeeth, and into the pedigree on the spindle side Lowys, the granddaughter of John Gower. This accounts for the burial of Robert Gower, the poet's uncle, in Brabourne Church.

A distinguished Scot was Sir Thomas, commander of the Kentish forces assembled against the Armada on Northbourne Downs. His cousin, Reynold Scot, wrote the swinging verses which begin :

> Here lyes Sir Thomas Scot by name,
> O happie Kempe that bore him,

and end with this proud eulogy :

> Let Romney Marsh and Dover saye;
> Ask Norborne camp at leyseur;
> If he were woont to make delaye
> To doe his countrie pleasure.

Reynold Scot himself was a champion of the oppressed, if ever there was one, a white name in an illustrious race. Being a younger son of Scot's Hall he made his home at Smeeth. Wood's *Athenae* tells of his early years, his studies at Hart Hall, at that time the Alma Mater of many Kentish men, his friendship with the Armada Sir Thomas. Reynold married Alice Cobbe of Cobbes Place in Aldington, and ' gave himself up solely to . . . the perusing of obscure authors that had by the generality of Scholars been neglected; and at times of leisure to husbandry and gardening '. The fruits of this idyllic existence were two famous books. The first, *A Perfect Platform of a Hoppe-garden*, interested the Elizabethan farmer so much that it is said the earliest hop-harvest in Kent coincided with its third issue. The other book was named *The Discovery of Witch-craft: wherein the lewd dealing of Witches and witch-mongers is notably detected, the knavery of Conjurers, the im-piety of Inchantors, the folly of Southsayers*, and so on, in leisurely preamble. Scot's work, inspired by curiosity which flamed out into indignation against human folly and super-

stition, shows ' profound research in many choice books '. For
a time the clergy and magistracy of England were deeply
impressed by his humane and reasonable arguments. Then
came along James, King of Scots; the preface to the royal
*Daemonology* denounced Reynold's nobler book : every copy
of the first edition that could be found was burnt by royal
command. No matter; his name is inscribed for ever among
those who have held high the lamp of mercy within ' cruel
habitations '. When, under Charles I, Henry Oxinden of
Maydekin interceded with his cousin Bargrave of Bifrons for
a Kent woman, Goodwife Gilnot, who was accused of witchcraft, he drew his argument from *The Discovery*, and requoted
Scot's plea for justice. Some of Scot's witches belonged to his
neighbourhood. The tale of Ada Davie of Sellinge is humane
after his own pattern. For Simon, Ada's husband, comforted
the sleepless, melancholy woman, who fancied she had bewitched him and her children and bargained her soul away.
He prayed with her in their cottage chamber and soothed her
disordered fancies. And at last their tragedy turned to comedy;
the rumblings of the Devil come to snatch his prey proved to be
but a dog gnawing at a mutton carcase ' hoong by the wals '. And
Ada, ' being now recovered remaineth a right honest woman,
far from such impietie and ashamed of her imaginations '.

This is the story of our seventeenth-century hero. For
twelve generations the Scots lived on at Scot's Hall. Sir
Edward Scot under Charles I enlarged the house; John Evelyn
visited there in August 1663. ' It was sold,' we read, ' with
the remaining possessions of the family, at the close of the
eighteenth century and destroyed in 1808. Some undulations
in a field on the north side of the road from Ashford to Hythe,
about half a mile east of Smeeth, alone mark its site.'

## VI

The Knatchbulls were of Mersham Hatch as the Scots, their

neighbours, were of Scot's Hall, time out of mind. Sir Wind-
ham Knatchbull and his family were turned back from the
same ball by the same flooded brook that covered Fidget's
coach-wheels. Indeed, they rescued the damsel and took her
home with them. Once she paid them a three weeks' visit; if
any one could, they should have taught her the inwardness of
country life; cricket—but not yet—and dogs and horses.
Edward Knatchbull-Hugessen, first Lord Brabourne, was the
chronicler of rural society in the eighteen-eighties, but yet had
ties with Fidget's century, as great nephew and biographer of
Jane Austen herself. Such distinction apart, he was the friend
of fur and feather; for all who remember his *Moonshine*
stories, he has peopled these woods and hills with enchanted
creatures. He loved the summer and the winter birds; the
great brown owls in Barrack Wood; the blackbird hopping
on green patches of the snow-sprinkled lawn; the oldest rook,
solitary on an elm top, punctuating with one loud caw its
thoughts of the hard winters it has known.

Lord Brabourne is this chapter's nineteenth-century hero.
Here, where time is not, he shall sally forth with its Elizabeth
and a bevy of dog-companions; Fitzy, his Skye terrier; Tippo,
the black and tan; Whisky and Dandy Dinmont; black and
white Bessy. He shall point to old Beechborough, towering
above the Channel and lay on us, once for all, the spell of
Bockhanger Wood. Here to conclude is his word-picture of the
place : 'Trees . . . oak, beech and hornbeam pollards, of immense
size and age untold, are cast about in most fantastic shapes;
some upright, some slanting one way, some another, some
split in every direction by the hand of time. . . . Beneath these
venerable trees, large patches of fern grow in woodland luxuri-
ance; where the fern grows not, rushes, moss or dried leaves
form the carpet beneath your feet. Go there in the spring, and
the noisy jackdaws start from their nests in holes of the old
pollards and ask you in pretty plain language what may be
your business in their wood. Go there later on in the summer

and a myriad birds awaken the echoes with their pleasant notes. The soft tender " coo " of the stock-dove; the sudden rush of the woodpigeon, scared by your footsteps from her leafy home; the friendly " tap-tap " of the green woodpecker; the quaint voice of the young jay, imitating the tunes of his neighbours; all these sounds greet your ears as you tread quietly over ground hallowed by the deep shade of old trees. You are in some enchanted place, where sin and sorrow cannot penetrate, where Nature and Nature's Master may without interruption be mused upon and loved.'

### ASHFORD AND ITS NEIGHBOURHOOD

The Stour valley, from Ashford down-water to Canterbury, is another stretch of Kentish soil trodden over with prints of history. Men and women unforgotten walk there together, in a primrose light that neither fades nor deepens; they talk of life lived once in time among these Downs and stream-fed pastures. Jane and Cassandra Austen are there, and Madam Dorothea Scott—oh, and what does our Jane make of the Puritan dame, the tub-thumper, the stern judge of princes, a creature out of drawing for her delicate page! Art first; for Chartham Rysbrack chisels his great Young monument; and behind Wye, at quiet Brook, a nameless painter makes the church walls glow. John Wallis, greatest of Newton's precursors, learns his tables in Ashford school and the ingenious John Ponet, Grecian and Reformer, leaves St. Mary's Vicarage for the Bishopric of Winchester. Kempe and Fogge and Knatchbull serve by their foundations the cause of education. These are few of many. . . .

But, of them all, our invaluable guide will be the celebrated medico, Dr. Christopher Packe of Canterbury. He it was who, on the 8th of April 1742 presented to the Royal Society a draft of his new chart of East Kent, a *Philosophico-Choro-graphical Chart*, whatever precisely that may mean. His offer-ing aroused great interest, for a contour map on so elaborate a scale was something new. This one set out 'the Country 15 or 16 miles round Canterbury . . . the Progress of the Vallies, the Directions and Elevations of the Hills, and whatever is curious in Art and Nature that diversifies . . . the Face of the Earth'. Dr. Christopher returned from London to Canter-bury glowing with satisfaction at the Fellows' compliments and bent on publishing his chart. But when he scrutinized it again, no longer as a hobby, but 'a matter of public right', so many errors emerged that his pride cooled to a profound dis-content. He determined 'for meer love of the work' to enlarge the scale without increasing the guinea subscription. Hitherto his notes had been made as he rode to and fro on his nag to physic the country-folk. Now he adopted exacter methods. He mounted Bell Harry Tower to take bearings, setting his compass by the Magnetic Pole. In this way four or five copies of the chart were begun, but not one completed. Here is his own account of the matter : 'As fast as I gained new Lights in my Journeys I saw they were not free enough of Mistakes to deserve the last Hand. And one grand Error I found run-ing thro' them all; as they in my apprehension, laid the whole country too Low upon the Line.' To rectify this miscalculation he ordered 'a large and very correct Azimuth Compass, in-scribed with everything suitable to my Design, and fitted with a Theodolite; in such a manner that the Focus of the Glass, at whatever Object it stood, gave the exact Bearing of it, even to the most minute part of a degree, by a Moveable Index which mark'd it upon the Circle of Degrees to which the Outline Circle of the Chart was exactly Correspondent. And having obtain'd leave to erect a Scaffold upon the Top of the great Tower of our Cathedral I plac'd the Instrument in its Centre. Here I had so Extensive a View of almost the whole Country that but very few places within my circle escaped my Sight.'

Sometimes on fine clear days, one imagines the doctor's sturdy figure, telescope in hand, on his scaffold up there against the sky; one overhears the drift of his bedside conversation towards that *Philosophico-Chorographical Chart*. After five years of patient industry it was published, beautifully drawn on four sheets of atlas paper. The *Gentleman's Magazine* greeted it warmly, and a contributor, the Reverend Mr. Sackett, penned a neatish epigram on Dr. Packe:

> Si quis lustrat agros; morbos abigatque feroces;
> Mercedem geminam Pan et Apollo dabunt.

To-day the unscientific may read with curious pleasure the introductory essay; the writer's eulogy of East Kent, his loving exposition of its every ' con valley ' and ' inosculation ', the place-names not invariably to be traced on an ordinary map. A copy is in the Royal Museum at Canterbury: here is a task for the hiker to pursue the good doctor's tracks and rediscover his landmarks. For where, O Kent lover, are, at random, Bumpit and Radewood, Hocketyhill, Wadnall, Uzzin and Querling? Dr. Christopher's second wife, on her monument ' Madam Maria ', but in her youth just ' Mary Randolph ', married to him in 1726, was the girlish confidante of Elizabeth Elstob. This is the moment to call upon the worthy man, because ' the Stour is the central part of [his] Work, and the Master Key to the natural knowledge of the whole Country ', and the Stour we are now to follow from Ashford to Canterbury.

II

Dr. Packe's exact mind does not merely note, like most geographers, two main sources of the Stour—one behind Postling Church, the other in the Lenham neighbourhood. He fills the hills with trickling springs that feed his well-loved stream. But with all his carefulness he does not give the Stour its older name in these parts, the name it lent to Ashford, so that in documents of equal date the old town is called both

Asheford and Esshetisford—the ford over the Eshe or Esshet or Stour. Dr. Packe bears out Hasted's remark, who, after noting the Estefort and Essetesford of *Domesday*, says that by his time (1790) the alternative name had long been forgotten. Lambarde knew it, yet perhaps thought it old-fashioned, although he explained that the river should not go by the name of Stour until on its way towards Wye. Seventeenth-century topographers begin to labour the obvious, to chatter of ash-trees near a ford (but one must remember that Ash was Esh in the Kentish dialect).

Sir John Fogge of Ripton Manor is the presiding genius of Ashford history. He lived in five reigns—from the sixth to the seventh Henry. Not once nor twice in those restless times his fortune faced about. He was Treasurer of the Household to Edward IV, but Richard III made him a landless outlaw. Henry VII brought him back to Ripton and prosperity, to his ample grounds and well-stocked fish-ponds. The inscription on his monument says that he ' renovated the Church at his own cost as well as the bell-tower, which he built from the foundation '. This is not strictly true, for the lower tower piers were only in part recased, the original caps and abutting arches remaining. But a little exaggeration is excusable, since the four skyward turrets—all, indeed, that makes a landmark across the Ashford plain—are of his building. His tomb, on the north side of the altar, once had brass effigies of Sir John and his two wives Alice Crioll and Alice Haute. On the tablet borne by an angel, which alone remains, a legend recounts Fogge's benefactions, the bell-tower he built, the books, jewels and ornaments he bequeathed. All these vanished long since, although placed by the testator ' in keeping of the best disposed man dwelling within the town of Asshetyford. . . .'

His benefactions did not end with the church. He gave Ashford a college which Edward IV endowed. It was a war memorial after the Wars of the Roses, and the two fit chaplains and two secular clerks on the foundation, were bound to pray for the souls of all faithful people of the county of Kent fallen in conflict at Northampton, St. Albans, and Sherburn field, as well as for a whole bevy of royalties. When the King died in 1483 before Sir John, the college plans were still incomplete; only three masters, vicars of Ashford, had held office when the Reformation put an end to it altogether.

Religious controversy was bitter in Ashford through Reformation times. Sir Michael, the priest, stood for past usages; the contemporary John Fogge with his Uncle Goldwell of Great Chart, 'favorers of God's word', and an interfering parson of Hothfield were hot upon the track of the Bishop of Rome. Ashford folk vainly tried compromise. After Becket was proclaimed traitor they 'transposed' his image in the church, and to conceal his identity took away his cross and put in place of it the wool-comb of St. Blaise. Some people were convinced that images thus transposed might safely stand, 'with new tokens in their hands'; but Fogge met prevarication with scorn. At Wye also the villagers clung to the familiar past. Being forbidden to burn tapers before likenesses of the saints, they took the saints to the tapers, setting them up in the rood-loft between certain candles which still flickered there unreproved. Hardest of all was it to stop the offerings made in love and sorrow before the image of Our Lady of Pity having her Son in her arms.

III

Ashford was a poorer place when Sir John's college was reduced to a fragment and robbed of most of its charm. The building was, as one old writer says, 'needlework', that is made in black and white like fashionable embroidery. It stood round three sides of a small quadrangle, the porter's lodge and a churchyard gateway completing the square. The abundant stained glass was the legacy of Richard Parkhurst, second master (1519–47). The hall (now a kitchen, with nine-teen white roses moulded on the ceiling) had windows full of tree-branches, birds and beasts. In the east window of the great parlour—the eighteenth century gutted that—were Queen Mary's badges, roses and pomegranates, and coats of arms in a glowing procession. In the south window the sun lit up figures of our Saviour and the Twelve Apostles. These were smashed during the Great Rebellion. Parkhurst placed his own rebus in an upper window looking to the garden, the acacias and ilex and lime-walk. The remaining college building now serves as the vicarage.

On the east side of the graveyard stood Sir Norton Knatchbull's grammar school, founded under Charles I ' for the Good of the Town of Ashford '. The governors were the successive owners of Mersham Hatch and the clergy of Ashford, Aldington, Mersham and Great Chart. Their guidance was upon master as well as scholars, for at their annual visit, ' If the Master shall be notoriously faulty they are gently to admonish him. If upon three several admonitions the Master does not amend, the Proprietors of Mersham Hatch are to displace the Master and choose another in his stead.' The original brick schoolroom, with a chimney for the scholars' fire, a study for the master, a little yard for playtime, was long, long since outgrown and the site abandoned to other uses.

IV

It is a pity that so much that was ' lovely and of good report ' has been allowed to perish, for the church tower now reigns over a large and growing railway centre. From the platform of Ashford Station, where most men of Kent spend hours of life each year waiting for trains, a veil of smoke broods upon serried ranks of engines. The suburbs present row upon row of uninspired cottages; the Stour here is a grubby ditch; all is flattish and drab. What an advantage to the town to possess a heart of beauty, where rest the memories of famous citizens and of their gifts to God and man. How every vestige of the old riches should be treasured, from the Smythe monuments to the secret chamber in the Tower with its spyhole cut through the arms of Charles II.

Central Ashford retained its medieval character till very late in the day. The old High Street lay between Marsh Street and Bank Street, which has nowadays a new outlet. 'The lord's copyhold boundary', says a writer in 1886, 'was clearly defined by an open channel running down the centre of the High Street, separating the roadway from the copyhold waste, portions of which remained until recently.' The untilled waste occupied roughly the space between the churchyard and Marsh Street, now a highway of locomotion which gives approach to the station and shelter to the motor-bus. The waste is hidden, covered up with shops and houses; some old-fashioned façades look out bewildered on the concourse of vehicles where once the channel ran. St. John's Lane near the top of Marsh Street was once called Copyhold Lane.

The fragment of a Middle Row, intersected with diminutive lanes and crowded with old black and white cottages, makes a bulwark for church and churchyard, and defies the traffic approaching from the Canterbury cross-road. This is the stronghold of old Ashford; its dignity well worthy of slackened speed, of a trifling respect for our origins. In far-back days the town markets were ranged along the waste : the corn, fish, butchery and butter markets, in that order, moving east. An old engraving of Virtue's shows the eighteenth-century cattle market in the middle of the town. The drovers stand about in smock frocks, the farmers in top-boots and low-crowned beavers, the wives, basket on arm, have broad-brimmed hats and white aprons to guard their gowns.

Yet to give new Ashford, busy, smoky, unalluring, modern Ashford, its due, it has done one God-like thing : it has planted in the midst a fair garden; a second war-memorial not so distant from the first. There too may the white rose flourish. Fine central schools have been built, not only ' for the good

of the town ', but to benefit the village children, who ' coach ',
in daily for the training of head, hand and heart; they are to
be founders of a new England in the country-side.

v

This is the moment, before following the river on to Wye, to
make an excursion along the adjoining spur of the North Downs.
. . . I reached Eastwell Church one winter's noon in pale sun-
shine, entering the soft dusk within through the little south door
and coming directly on two slumbering marbles, two figures
uncanopied. As real they seemed as though life had but for an
instant slipped away, and suddenly vigour must return into
those motionless limbs. Hasted says the monument had ' till
within these few years ', a fine dome or canopy, supported by
eight pillars of black marble, ' the fragments of which now
lie scattered about the chancel '. Who made this memorial to
two people of importance in their day I know not. The bust
high on the opposite wall which commemorates their son, Sir
Heneage Finch—a half-length effigy in gown and tippet,
appears in Nicholas Stone's diary :
' October 1632. Agreed with Mr. Frances Finch Esquyer
for 50£ agreed, for the tombe of Sir Hanegs Finch, Mr.
Recorder of London, and received 10£ in pres. Rest due to
me, the tombe being sett up and finished, 40£.'
The woman's figure on the greater monument represents
Elizabeth, only daughter and heir of Sir Thomas Heneage, a
high officer of state under Queen Elizabeth, and wife of Sir
Moyle Finch of Eastwell, who lies beside her. She long survived her husband, as indeed their effigies suggest, and received in her own right dignities due to him ' had not death
prevented it '. She was created Viscountess Maidstone in 1623
and in 1629 Countess of Winchilsea.
The elegant marble of a Victorian Lady Winchilsea, Emily
Georgiana, who died in 1849 aged thirty-nine, has a tiny chapel

to itself built out from the south aisle. The lighting sets off
its graceful charm, with slightly theatrical effect. It costs
something of a mental jerk to turn back to the dim-lit church,
to the old heraldic glass in the west window, the heads of
kings carved on the corbels. The dust of a king's son is perhaps contained in that nameless sarcophagus in the north
chapel. His is by far the most romantic memory about the
place. A Kent antiquary, Thomas Brett of Spring Grove,
embalmed it in a letter to a fellow-antiquary.

' Dear Will,' he wrote to the President of Trinity Hall in
1733, ' Now for the Story of Richard Plantagenet. In the year
1720 . . . about Michaelmas, I waited on the late Lord
Heneage, Earl of Winchilsea at Eastwell House, and found
him sitting with the Register Book of the Parish of Eastwell
lying open before him. He told me that he had been looking
there to see who of his own Family were mentioned in it. But,
says he, I have a Curiosity here to shew you. And then shewed
me (and I immediately transcribed it into my Almanack)
" Richard Plantagenet was buryed the 22 Daye of December,
Anno ut supra. Ex Registro de Eastwell sub Anno 1550 ".
This is all the Register mentions of him . . . nor is there now
any other Memorial of him, except the Tradition in the
Family and some little Marks of the Place where his House
stood.'

The tradition which Brett recorded was detailed and
picturesque. It began with the rebuilding of old Eastwell
House, and the bricklayer who read in odd moments, but hid
his book when any one came near. At last his employer, Sir
Thomas Moyle, surprised him, snatched the volume, and to
his amazement found it to be Latin. He questioned the work-
man closely and was entrusted with a secret hitherto un-
revealed. The man had been brought up at his nurse's house,
' whom I took for my mother ', until, at seven years old, he
was boarded with a Latin schoolmaster, somewhere in the

country. He had no kinsfolk, no visitors, but a gentleman who arrived once a quarter to pay his board and supply his wants. When he was sixteen this man took him away to a great house, and in one of the stately rooms a personage 'finely drest with a Star and Garter' came to him, spoke kind words, passed his hand over his boyish limbs and joints, looked narrowly at him, and gave him ten golden pieces. Then he was led back again to school. But a day dawned when the same guide appeared with a horse, and told the young fellow they must go a journey together.

'They went into Leicestershire,' so the narrative works up towards its climax, 'and came to Bosworth Field, and he was carried to King Richard's tent. The king embraced him and told him he was his Son. But Child, says he, to-morrow I must fight for my Crown. And assure yourself if I lose that, I will lose my Life too. . . . Do you stand in such a Place, where you may see the Battle out of Danger. And when I have gained the Victory, come to me : I will then own you to be mine and take Care of you. But if I should lose the day, shift as well as you can, and be sure to let no one know that I am your Father; for no Mercy will be shewn to any son of mine. Then the King gave him a Purse of Gold. . . . But when he saw the Battle was lost and the King killed, he hasted to London, sold his Horse and fine Cloaths, and the better to conceal himself from all Suspition of being Son to a King, and that he might have means to live by his honest Labour, he put himself Apprentice to a Bricklayer.'

Yet having learnt from his Latin schoolmaster to love books more than talk with his fellows, he spent all his leisure in their society.

Said Sir Thomas, the tale goes on, 'You are now old, and almost past your Labour. I will give you the Running of my kitchen as long as you live.' But the King's son begged to keep his solitude and to build himself a little one-roomed house in a field near by, and there to live and die.

After his death his plot was taken into the new enclosure of Eastwell Park, and the father of the Lord Winchilsea who told the tale pulled down Richard's dwelling. ' But ', said my Lord—all honour to him—' I would as soon have pulled down this house,' meaning Eastwell Place.

The story, remarkable enough, deeply impressed Dr. Brett; he speculated how and when the bricklayer had built his little home, and for how long he had enjoyed it; he concluded that Richard Plantagenet died when he was eighty-one years old and was ' 77 or 78 years of Age before he had his Writ of Ease ' and exchanged his hod for a Virgil.

What a strange company rest there in Eastwell Church— Richard the mysterious bricklayer and the ringleted Lady Emily, Lady Maidstone the stately heiress, and those men of affairs, her son and husband. Come out now into the church-yard; below it stretches a broad lake, lovely to-day with silver pools of winter light shining among a black-stroked army of reeds.

### VI

Westwell is on lower ground, as no one can forget who has wriggled along the twisty lane, so aptly named Tumble-down Hill. Outside Westwell Church, which once had Ingoldsby as curate, is a tiny village green, planted with an ancient chest-nut-tree and an ash. Inside, chancel and nave are separated by a remarkable stone screen; lancet windows are grouped in the east wall; and the original rough-hewn timber stairway leads to the belfry.

Eastwell Church is hidden by the park plantations; the cruci-form mass of All Saints, Boughton Aluph, of rugged stone with queer red-brick patching, breaks the line of hills looking eastward. Its lantern-tower, low set and powerful, gives an impression of long endurance against the winds of time. A very steep lane—' Tumble-down's ' fellow—leads to the church, a lane crowded in summer-time with lace-like hedge-parsley and waving grasses. Old stack-stones guard the church gate, and an old red-brick mansion close by is shut in with a flowering hedge of waxen pink montana. Once there was far more beauty within doors to chime with the beauty that surrounds the old church. The windows shone with bright colour, though only two figures, said to be Queen Philippa and Edward III, now remain; and old mural paintings have left a warm blur in places on the walls. One of the few fragments of Boughton's history (although it begins with the Saxon Leofwine the Red) tells that when Sir Hugh David was vicar —' the wyndowes of the churche of Boughton were broken by thevys ', not that they found much worth the stealing.

The vicar himself was bewildered by the destruction going on around him in the name of reformation. He got into sore disgrace for declaring that ' the best of England would not say that by the law altars should be pulled down ', but when asked whom he meant by ' the best ', replied lamely ' he meaneth nobody '. No doubt he had suddenly remembered the need of caution, for his squire, Sir Thomas Moyle of Eastwell, the royal bricklayer's patron, was one of Henry the Eighth's ' new men ' who shared liberally in the church's spoils. His estates came to his daughter, who married a Finch, and was the mother of our marble Sir Moyle Finch and ancestress of the Earls of Winchilsea. The Moyles were at Wilmington in South Boughton from Henry the Seventh's reign before Sir Thomas acquired Eastwell. A younger branch were living at Buckwell in the seventeenth century. The recumbent effigy, much mutilated, of Amy Moyle, wife of Josias Clerk of Essex, is in the north chancel at Boughton Aluph; she lies in frilled night-dress and veil, profoundly at rest, ' sub cruce, tuta quies ', three tiny broken images of her little daughters at her head and feet. Her rhymed epitaph is very charming, but the Moyles had a nice taste in elegies, and Sir Robert Moyle's competes with hers in interest : ' As soon as the Land had the happiness to receive again the King, he had the honour to receive Knighthood from the hand of the King,' but he enjoyed it only till June 1661. The elegiac palm must go to the lines which the mourning Priscilla Moyle (a daughter of Dean Fotherby and married in Canterbury Cathedral) dedicated to her husband, Captain Robert Moyle, who died February 23rd 1640 :

> Wisht ashes were it piety to pray
> Thy soul might once again inform thy clay,
> Each holy tongue a prayer-book would penne
> And force the heavens to send thee back again.
> I blame thy goodness; since 'tis understood
> Thou diedst so soon because thou wert so good.
> Say Heavens, when ye did want a saints' supply
> Did we not send a royal subsidy?
> This Moyle more treasure to their glory brings
> Than the proud camels of Arabian kings.

## ROUND ABOUT WYE

### I

> Naughty Ashford, surly Wye
> Poor Kennington hard by!

So, for some forgotten reason, the adage runs. If ever one could suppose pleasant Wye grown ' surly ', it befell when the new railway station obtruded so unmannerly on the entrance of the old town. The picture was already complete, with the Stour bridge (built in stone instead of wood under Charles I) and the vista of an ascending street. The Stour arrives here through green water-meadows; in Hasted's day it brought with it ' a great quantity of pike '. His description, written a century and a half ago, still strikes the proper key. Wye is still the same ' neat and well-built town, with two parallel and two cross streets ', although no longer ' unpaved '; church and college still stand north of a spacious green, built round with old-world houses. Beyond the old streets new ones now reach into the fields. The 213 houses and 1,400 inhabitants of Hasted's computation are long since outnumbered. To-day a township enlarges by stringing itself out along the roads of egress; once upon a time Wye picked itself up and sat down on a new site altogether. The ancestral Wye stood, as some think, ' in the valley which lies between Wye-down and Crundale, where the hamlet of Pett-street (Kentish for Pitt-street) now is '. There are, or were, deep disused wells pointing to former habitations, as well as the name of 'Town-borough '. Wye, as we know it, is ' new ' in the same degree as the New Forest or New Romney; the Conqueror gave its manor to Battle Abbey; it was there perhaps when St. Gregory, its patron on whose day Wye Fair was held, sent over his English mission. Antiquaries have always loved the place; they hum over its long past, and store the honey in voluminous collections. One was made by Thomas Brett of Betteshanger, who was schooled at Wye and went on to Queen's and Corpus Christi, Cambridge. His grandfather built a pleasant house at Spring Grove, from whence, as Dr. Packe says, ' the first spring of the Ashford Vale slides down thro' a large and fair Valley into the Meadows at Wye Bridge '. Our Thomas was at one time curate of Wye; then rector of Betteshanger and Ruckinge, till compelled to make a sacrifice for conscience' sake; for he was one of the most learned of the non-jurors. He gave up too, reluctantly, hopes of yet higher preferment to a canonry of Canterbury.

' I cannot plead any desert which may entitle me to such a favour,' he wrote to the Earl of Oxford in 1713, ' but a fair plea for it is that from the foundation of the Dean and Chapter to this day either the Dean or some of the prebendaries have always been natives of Kent. Dr. Belk, the last prebendary that died, was also the last Kentish man of the society . . . so that there is not at this day one man on that foundation who was born in this county, which never happened before since the Reformation. I acknowledge this cannot give me or any

other native of Kent a right to a prebend, but if it be allowed
that there has been such a custom, and that you are willing to
continue it, the gentlemen of the county in general must think
themselves obliged by the favour.'

The latest historians remind us of our town's importance in
former times; giving its name to a sixth part of the county,
the Hundred of Wye. 'Here Kings have sojourned, Saxon,
Plantagenet and Lancastrian; here banished in disgrace from
his father's court came the first Prince of Wales. Here Marian
martyrs suffered at the stake, and here men fought and died
in the . . . Great Civil War.' 'Wye Fight', as it is called,
when George Somner, the historian's brother, was slain, is
briefly recorded in the parish register : '1648. John Ingnor-
ham, a parliament souldier buried; he was slain, and three
more slaine weare not knowne; and weare buried in Wye the
sevent day of June; and thear wear slaine Thomas Laggat of
Crundale and Geo Grevel a wever; and John Godden of
Godmersham was bureyed the same day.'

II

Dr. Christopher is at pains to note that where Ashford Vale
and Stour Dale interlock at Wye there is 'a gentle hill'. On
this St. Gregory's Church stands up; from the churchyard is a
spacious and delightful outlook, over roomy fields to the high
downs; it is a place of wide horizons, a liberty of all the winds.
When the church comes into the landscape from the railway
it has a crouching, truncated air. Actually it is but the fragment of a magnificent building, first erected about 1200, on a
site consecrated perhaps centuries before. The aspect of the
church was changed by a disaster which happened during
Morning Prayer on Sunday, March 21st 1686. It was the last
link of a chain of mishaps covering over a century. In 1571
the wooden steeple was fired by lightning, and for ten long
years left unrepaired. Then Gregory Brett, an ancestor of

antiquary Thomas and churchwarden 1582–84, took the matter
in hand, bearing most of the heavy cost; not before prolonged
neglect had done its work. For even after Brett's intervention
' The Churchwardens present that our Church lacketh reparations; the rain beateth in and rotteth the principal timbers that
holdeth it up, so that it raineth into the Church ' (1586). At
last came the inevitable collapse, in the vicariate of George
Gipps. Three weeks after it happened Dr. George Oxinden,
Vicar-General to Archbishop Sancroft, sent in a hearsay report
as one suspects in the vicar's own vivid words : ' May it
please your Grace,' he wrote from Deane on April 8th, ' I
suppose your Grace may have heard the sad news that
the steeple of the Church of Wye fell down about ten daies
ago, and has beat great part of the Church downe, it standing
in the middle of the Church. The minister being at prayers
with the congregacion perceived the bell-ropes to shake, there
being no winde then, and immediately warned the congregacion of the imminent danger, and they all ran out and immediately the steeple fell down. I shall see it in my way to
Ashford and will give your Grace a more particular account.'

Once more Wye took its time. The ruinous east end was
boarded up, the pulpit and pews mended; then just before
George Gipps died, in 1706, the building of a new chancel, a
meagre thing by comparison, at last began. A visitor in the
interval, Harris, the Kent historian—describes the desolate
scene : ' I saw Fragments of several old Tombstones lying open
in the Churchyard, which formerly lay in the Isles and Chancel; and some Statues and Fragments of Monuments lay in
Heaps at the lower End of the Church.'

### III

No doubt the splendour of old St. Gregory's justified
Cardinal Kempe, John of Olantigh, statesman and diplomat,
in choosing his home town for the site of a college. 'The

chirch', he wrote, 'is feir, large, and convenable to a notable nombre of God's ministers, to be occupeyed therinne in divine service . . . the archebysshop was born . . . withinne the parisshe, wher also meny of the bodyys of his auncetre, alyys, and freends that be passid to God, the which he desirith especially to be prayyd for, restyn.'

In approaching Henry VI for a licence, the Cardinal made plain that he was building for heart's ease; the cares of Church and State had 'hindered him from minding as he ought his devotions'. He would recompense to God, and of his own wealth enable others untiringly to render the service in which he had come short. So he set up his College of St. Martin and St. Gregory, 'a felaship of God's ministers', on the church-yard's eastern boundary, to house a master and as many chaplains or Fellows as he could afford to salary. Their number is not specified in the statutes; probably Kempe had in mind a master, six priests, two clerks, two choristers; one of the Fellows to have the cure of souls in Wye, one to be grammar master and keep free and open school. To forestall bickerings between master and vicar, the old diplomat acquired the advowson from Battle Abbey and gave it to his foundation. Nor was he regardless of the town's prosperity, 'the which is like ellis, be process of tyme, greetly to decrees and fail, as it semyth'. For near a century the townsmen grew accustomed to the unceasing round of sacrament and prayer. Each holy day, when a bell chimed after compline, they knew that Fellow, clerk, and chorister were ranged beside the tomb of Sir Thomas Kempe and Beatrix his wife in the north transept ready to recite, as substitutes for their dutiful great son, a solemn De Profundis. The Fellows went about the streets always two together; always they wore long, straight cassocks to the heel of woollen stuff, 'neither too sombre nor too gay'; their sleeves were of moderate size, their shoes guiltless of the fashionable beak. They never sported with dice or ball, hunted, kept dogs, or joined in summer games; their sober recreations were writing, reading, singing, or some manual task. Then suddenly the familiar figures were seen no more. On January 19th 1545 the sixth master, Edward Bowdon, surrendered college, church and the Cardinal's broad lands into the King's rapacious grasp.

Queen Catherine Parr's secretary, Walter Bucher, now came into the place, on condition that he provided a schoolmaster, and two priests to serve the church. Generations of 'Free School boys succeeded the grave Fellows and made use of the College chapel, now called the Latin School '.

Anne, Lady Winchilsea, mistress of Eastwell, knew the young rascals' favourite haunts, and bantered them in Miltonic verse in her 'Fanscomb Barn'. Had she met them perchance, crowding round that valley spring under Wye Downs, where, as of ancient custom, they resorted in high spirits to drink the water sweetened with sugar? This spring it is:

> That flows near Pickersdane; renowned stream
> Which, for disport and play, the youths frequent,
> Who train'd in learned school of ancient Wye,
> First at this fount suck in the Muses' lore,
> When, mix'd with product of the Indian cane,
> They drink delicious draughts, and part inspir'd,
> Fit for the banks of Isis or of Cham.

Fanscomb Barn in the Lady Anne's day was a Beggars' Retreat.

Fanscomb Beech on the summit of the 'high pleasant downs' was a landmark to the country for miles around.

The college buildings changed hands time and again for a century and a half after the Fellows vacated them. Now the Damsell family live there, now the Twysdens, whose arms, quartered with the Monyns's are still over the door in the oak parlour. But the little flame of learning, lit piously by John Kempe, if it burned low had a strange persistence. Joanna, Lady Thornhill, a daughter of Sir Bevill Grenvile left part of her estate to educate the poorest boys and girls in the town. There is a reference to her own childhood, far off in Cornwall, in a letter of Mrs. Grace Grenvile's to her husband. His little

daughters, she says, complain that he has stayed away very
long already. 'Jone and Denis are allwaies prattling of you;
these are my poore companions which doe passe the tedious
houers away.' As a young woman, 'with a great deal of beauty
and modesty and wit enough', Dorothy Osborne grieved over
Joan's marriage to Colonel Richard Thornhill of Olantigh.
'This innocent creature', she wrote, 'is sacrificed to the veriest
beast that ever was.' But the Colonel, if drunken, spent his
substance for King Charles. Joan's brother, John, Earl of Bath,
was General Monk's friend, and she herself, till 1708, Lady of
the Bedchamber to Catherine of Braganza.

Until 1889 the Grammar School in the old chapel and the
Thornhill Charity School in the great vaulted hall, existed side
by side. The girls had a separate annexe for their spelling and
needle craft. In 1892 came the latest development: the South
Eastern Agricultural College was established, in a nucleus of
the old buildings, greatly extended by the County Councils of
Kent and Surrey. By the latest report (1932) 187 students are
at work there. They learn to be practical farmers, horticul-
turists; they study poultry-farming and forestry, harvest their
cereals, grow wild white clover on 'forty acres of the leys',
crop orchards and strawberry-beds. Their hens lay fabulous
store of eggs; they have a nursery of young trees from distant
lands. Where the schoolboy sipped his sugared spring-water
the modern student has carved a great crown in the chalk down
to commemorate Edward the Seventh's coronation. He
comes here from Kent or Surrey or from the world's end, and
brings into the old town a vigorous life.

IV

South of Wye, where the land is 'more inclosed and the soil
deeper', are the hamlet of Withersden and St. Eustace's Well.
Eustachius, a twelfth-century Abbot of Flai, came to England,
and first to this town, inspired by Sabbatarian fervour, the

kind of person to crusade against the Sunday opening of cinemas. Incidentally he blessed a little spring, and endowed its water with healing virtue. The results were sometimes horrific; the water expelled from one sufferer's mouth two black toads which turned to two black dogs and disappeared in asses' shape. Evidently Abbot Eustace had the diviner's instinct; at New Romney, which lacked a water-supply, he had but to strike a stone with his rod for abundant streams to flow. His well at Withersden has now no great attractiveness; although the virtue may be there as of old; a flight of steps leads to the water's brim where the buckets are dipped.

From Withersden, the roomy parish (seven miles long and five miles broad) puts out 'a narrow slip, between Brook and Brabourne, to Nacolt wood and the tile-kiln'. It is a flat, unattractive slip; the presence of brick-clay brings about a depressing atmosphere. But this only accentuates the charm when one draws near again to the hills, and hidden away between the greater wall of North Downs and a lesser spur comes upon the village of Brook. Good fortune took me there about St. Valentine's Day, in the month of snowdrops. They were everywhere—snowed thickly in cottage gardens, nodding beside the namesake brook, crowding—friendly sprites—by companies in the garden of the dead. The brook of Brook drops from the hills, flows above the village street, meanders through the fields, joins the Stour at Wye racecourse. Brook has a street of old cottages, and opposite the Norman church plough-lands, unfenced, border the road. One can imagine the medieval interior better at Brook than in any other village church I know. Once nave and chancel alike were overpainted; there is even a fine 'Majesty' in an oratory half-way up the tower. The colours still glow, a sunset glow of fading beauty; since Professor Tristram spent his skill on the place the trained observer can distinguish perhaps six out of nearly a hundred various subjects.

The hinterland of Wye, behind the eastern town barrier, is

a tangle of hills, intersected with steep valleys, wild, romantic, exquisitely beautiful. Villages are hidden there among tumbled woods—Hastingleigh and Crundale, Petham and Waltham; lonely still, almost as in the days when news some-how reached the villagers of the Peasants' Revolt and they descended from their solitudes to burn archives and achieve a new liberty. Along the face of the chalky steeps, fringed by beechwoods, rare and lovely flowers used to grow. I have seen butterfly orchids lifting poised blossoms in the hot sun-shine from a bed of crowsfoot, thyme, and wild strawberries; and peering between thin ash boughs helleborine, with the air of a foreign princess, beside the humbler tway-blade and tiny green men clinging to ladder-like stems. Long ago one could find toothwort in the thickets and spider orchids in the down-side turf. Alas! year by year they became more scarce. Were the flower-spikes so often gathered that no seed was left for wing or wind to disperse abroad? Yet the hill-tracks are ancient ways; for generations the villagers have passed along them, and the flowers grew on unmolested.

One May, not of late years, I saw in a beech covert the most exquisite sight imaginable. Some trees had been felled, and in the sunlit spaces numerous plants of the great brown-winged orchid were growing. The flowers quaintly resemble the human form in miniature; arms, legs and, beneath a shady sun-bonnet, an old woman's wizened face. Here the herbage was sparse : each plant had ample space to display in perfec-tion its glittering lilac spires and silver crown of leaves. Rare 'flowers of fantasy', they grew each one in stately isolation, yet sharing with its fellows the covert safely hidden, the quivering shadows of young leafage, the nightingale's singing. Two days later I visited the place again; beauty had died there. The flowers were roughly broken away, some heedlessly tossed on one side; leaves were torn, roots plucked up, trampled and already dying. A group of children passed me, chattering merrily together. Their hands were full of flowers, and in each nosegay I saw two or three bruised spikes of the fusca.

I stopped and spoke to them.

'What gay bunches you have picked,' I said.

'We are learning about the flowers of May,' they answered, 'and all we can find we take with us to school.' . . .

Ignorance and no eyes were, I fancy, less unkind to the rare wild flower than half knowledge and eager eyes. But more and more, I feel sure, botany is taught in the open beside the growing plant, less and less in the schoolroom over its mangled remains. And wantonness can only be combated by increase of knowledge, joy in beauty and reverence for all living things.

## GODMERSHAM AND CHILHAM

1

Godmersham at last, and Jane! She has beckoned all along from the copse on Canterbury Hill; but no! a lady of her agreeable gentility would never beckon, much less to a stranger, albeit an admirer. No, with a sweet dignity she awaits our arrival; the aura of Jane will surround us at Godmersham; but we may approach her bower along less enchanted avenues.

By Henry V the Brodnax family had arrived at Godmersham; they remained in the old house called Ford Place till the end of the eighteenth century. They were of yeoman stock, but after years, centuries, of comfortable farming began to aspire; and under Charles I social aspiration stank in the nostrils of the older gentry. John Philipot once thanked God *he* had no hand in providing a coat of arms for one such aspirant. Thomas Scott of Eggarton, Godmersham's neighbour, was at one with the Somerset Herald. Before Agincourt was fought his family bore their famous coat (argent, three catherine wheels sable with a bordure engrailed gules). Scott was author of a stately fragment, called *A Discourse of Polletique and Civill Honor*, addressed to his kinsman, the

Earl of Arundel, and ˜of *The Godmersham Goliah*, which
cannot be traced. The *Discourse* is at times an amusing piece;
it sums up the theory of social relationships then held by every
Kentish gentleman. They believed in a well-ordered society,
ranging from nobility, gentry, esquires and knights, through
the yeoman, to labourer, husbandman, trader, or franklin : a
place in its scheme for every one, and, until the crack of doom,
every one in his place. Yet, to Scott's rage and dismay,
ominous symptoms were abroad; only in the words of Solomon
could he express the 'hellish' confusion impending over
tranquil England : 'Folly is sett in great hightes and the ritch
sitt in lowe place. Servants ride upon horses and Princes walke
uppon the earth.'

He had actually seen a generation in which a clown could
'from the rise of his money bagg, leape over the heades of
antient and honorable Gentlemen'. It all sounds terribly
snobbish, yet was it so essentially? Scott's motto might have
been *noblesse oblige*; he was convinced that good breeding
counted for almost everything in efficient service of the State.
Dignity, pride of birth were for him synonymous with a call
to responsible office. He feels himself stumbling in a chaos
of mistaken values, when money usurps the place of nobility,
worship, and decorum. He is in a touchy mood even about
the degradation of the modest word ' esquire '; the pretensions
of his neighbour, Thomas Brodnax, catch him on the raw. ' I
can bringe you to a Tombestone,' he roars, ' where you shall
reade this Epitaph, able to make a horse breake his bridle :
" Here lyeth Willyeam Brodnax (the fourth sonne of Thomas
Brodnax, Yeoman) *Esquire*." . . . The Brodnaxes, all this
while have beene *mistaken* for yeomen. They are Gentlemen, or Esquires, even of royall blood, descended (as some
Plantaginetts in England whome yet theire neighbours have
called goodman Plantaginett) from Kinge Uter, the father of
that great Arthur. Their father wrot himself yeoman,' he
labours his indictment, ' theire elder Brother is Goodman

Brodnax. I have heard Sir Dudley Diggs call them clownes. If they be now gentlemen of bloud (which the Herauld did lately deny) they are but Parchment Gentlemen for their money, of some two or three yeares antiquitie.' Thomas Scott, choking over Brodnax presumption, perhaps remembered the old tale of Richard Plantagenet, the royal bricklayer. The Brodnax tombstone, with the inscription and misspellings Scott had mocked at, was removed from Godmersham Church at some time after 1793.

## II

At the date that Scott, an elderly man, wrote the *Discourse*, he was living in Canterbury, no doubt in his town house, as Member of Parliament for the city. When his daughter Dorothea was born, he was still at Eggarton, and she was baptized, on September 22nd 1611, in Godmersham Church. The little girl, destined to be a pioneer of Kentish settlement in the New World, was the youngest of six children. She was great-granddaughter of the witches' champion, Reynold Scot; her mother, Jane, was a Knatchbull of Mersham, and her maternal grandfather the traitor, Sir Thomas Wyatt. Somehow or other, the five elder brothers and sisters disappear, and on her father's death Dorothea inherits Eggarton Manor, together with rents of some £500 a year. She married in 1635, about the time she became an heiress, Daniel Gotherson, later of Cromwell's army, and bore him five daughters and a son, Daniel. With her husband she joined the Society of Friends in Canterbury—those ' few honest-hearted people turned to the Lord ' whom George Fox visited in 1655. Dorothea's restless spirit was attracted by their utter sincerity, ' a people could lay down their lives one for another . . . of one heart and one minde '. She became a notable minister among them, holding meetings, publishing religious exhortations. ' This Mrs. Gotherson ', Thomas Lovelace recorded at Pepys's request, ' had long been a great Quaker, and she had a particular congregation somewhere about the Hermitage, near the two great Brew-houses, which went under her maiden name of " Scott's congregation ", where he himself heard her preach.' The Hermitage was the old name for the house of Eremite Friars, entered from St. George's Street. Dorothea's meeting-house was perhaps in Canterbury Lane, where the Quakers congregated in quite recent times. She describes her conversion, in spite of which she found no spiritual satisfaction till she was twenty-eight years old. Her *Call to Repentance* may have been taken as an offering to King Charles II, when she went to court with other Royalists on a visit of congratulation. A disastrous visit was that, for at Whitehall she met her evil genius, the man John Scott, 'who tould me his name was Scott and that he was of the same family of the Scotts of Scot's hall, which I was ready to beleeve, because some of our ancestors' pictures were very like him '. On the strength of a family likeness, John, 'a nimble genius, though otherwise illiterate ', sold to Major Gotherson for £2,000 a quantity of land on Long Island, pretending he had bought it from the Indian chiefs. Gotherson sent over with Scott carpenters and materials to build two houses on the new estate, but it soon transpired that the property was none of his. The houses were dismantled and sold to support Scott's deserted wife; and the Gothersons were left practically penniless. Gotherson himself died in 1666 near £6,000 in debt. Pepys, who had championed their wrongs, was involved, and owed to Scott's transactions his committal to the Tower of London. Dorothea now remarried one Hogben. In 1680 she sold the Eggarton lands to Sir James Rushout, and with her children embarked for Oyster Bay, Long Island, where, even before the Scott meeting, Daniel Gotherson had bought a few acres in the New World. There they settled and there a younger Dorothea married John Davis of the Singing Quakers, and founded a numerous family; but Kent knew them no more. Dorothea's strange little book, half prose, half unpolished verse, has been reprinted. It is entitled *To all that are Unregenerated, A Call to Repentance from Dead Works to Newness of Life*, and is a trumpet-call to the England of her day; to the King, the bishops, the nobles of England, 'who are as Noble as the earth can make you' (a phrase her father would have applauded); the judges, the ladies, ' who walk with stretched-out necks and wanton eyes, mincing as you go, making a clattering with your feet, curling your hair, painting and spotting your faces '.

III

A century onwards and Jane is there, even strolling over the Quaker dame's estate : ' I am now just returned from Eggarton,' she writes to Cassandra; ' Louisa and I walked together and found Miss Maria at home.' It came about quite naturally, through those very Brodnaxes Scott denounced. By the eighteenth century their gentility had established itself beyond dispute. In 1727 one Thomas Brodnax, son of William, took his mother's name of May, and in 1738 that of Knight. He must have done much enclosure, for Dr. Packe's map in 1743 shows in Godmersham ' A New Park making '. His son, Thomas, dying without children in 1794, left his estate to a distant cousin on the maternal side, Edward, second son of George Austen and brother of Jane. Edward enlarged still further the Kentish connexion by marrying Elizabeth, daughter of the third Sir Brook Bridges of Goodnestone Park. He succeeded to Godmersham as early as 1797, thanks to the magnanimity of the widowed Mrs. Knight. She gave up the property to him, and went to live at the White Friars (the very ' Hermitage ' of our preaching Dorothea) in Canterbury, remaining on the best of terms with her supplanters. She was a beautiful and cultivated woman; Jane ' relished ' her society, and paid her visits, that were ' agreeable, with everything to make them so, kindness, conversation, variety, without care or cost '. Yet she placed, I fancy, no study of her among the immortals. So it befell that into East Kent circles Jane Austen, the dear famous little lady, stepped as among kinsfolk and friends, the company she most enjoyed. ' It is pleasant ', she wrote, ' to be among people who know one's connexions and care about them.' She was at Godmersham in 1805, and visiting at Eastwell Park, her hair elegantly dressed by an expert from Ospringe, at a fee of half a crown. With children she was a child; the young Knights found this out. ' Yesterday was a very quiet day with us,' she says in one letter, ' my noisiest efforts were writing to Frank and playing at battledore and shuttlecock with William; he and I have practised together two mornings and improve a little; we have frequently kept it up *three* times, and once or twice *six*.' She came again in 1808, driving of course, driving and driving, the long coach-road from Chawton. Her brothers met her at the gate; her sister-in-law and favourite niece, Fanny, greeted her in the Hall ' with a great deal of pleasant joy '. She was housed in the Yellow Room, and enjoyed the spacious apartment, a ' great place all to myself ', though it seemed odd to be there without Cassandra. ' Yesterday passed quite *à la* Godmersham,' she relates; ' the gentlemen rode about Edward's farm and returned in time to saunter along Bentigh with us; and after dinner we visited the Temple Plantation, which, to be sure, is a Chevalier Bayard of a plantation.' Bentigh had the charm of being Edward Knight's creation : he had made it from a ploughed field, planted the avenues, plotted the gravel walks. No wonder his guests sauntered there in leisurely fashion and took a short way through it to church. The high road at this time closely skirted the adjoining estates of Godmersham and Chilham; going towards Canterbury a traveller had the Stour on his right hand instead of on his left as now. The enterprising Mr. Knight crossed the Stour and planted round about ' the Temple ', a summer house one may still see from the highway.

How Jane enjoyed the space, the elegance, the ease; and

even a little unwonted luxury when there were neighbours to dine: 'I shall eat ice, and drink French wine, and be above vulgar economy,' she gaily tells Cassandra; and then returns to Chawton as lightheartedly; to orange wine new-brewed, and the joys of homely talk, and instinctive sympathy.

There were a concourse of children at Godmersham, eight of them and a cousin-ship innumerable. Not long after Jane returned home, Mrs. Knight died suddenly, leaving an infant of a few weeks. Cassandra then went to live at Godmersham and letters passed constantly to and fro. Jane's last recorded visit was in 1813, when she changed places for a while with her sister. By now her novels had brought her a modest fame —but she was still the same Jane. She may feel 'very rich'; but cares to know whether the new tea has been tasted or the new white wine. She dines upon goose and hopes 'it will secure a good sale of my second edition'. She loves as ever the sweet desultory ways, the neighbourly interchange of calls: 'How Bentigh is grown! and the Canterbury Hill plantation! and the improvements within are very great. I admire the chintz room very much. . . . I am now alone in the library, mistress of all I survey: at least I may say so and repeat the whole poem if I like it, without offence to anybody. . . .'

In 1927 there was a movement to set up a memorial of Jane Austen in Godmersham Church. A sketch was discovered, the large park pew as it was in her time, and a copy put 'near the place where she must have sat', in the south transept, where the village children may read her name.

## IV

Mr. Knight's ardour for improvement spread along the valley branching south, towards Eggarton on the Crundale border. He could brook no rival to Godmersham Park. Down came old Eggarton House, not the Scotts' house, but its successor. No one seems to know exactly where it stood, though

it is drawn on Dr. Packe's chart. I too walked out in search
of it. I enquired of a shepherd who struck me as an old inhabitant, but he had 'never 'eard tell' of such a place. I
climbed the high down and descended to the valley again past
an old cottage where love-in-the-mist grew in the garden and
the youngest baby had eyes to match. But there I had no better
fortune; the baby's grandmother 'never 'eard tell'.

The Downs, lined up behind Godmersham, are magnificent.
The headland named for Canterbury, standing in advance of
the rest, frowns down upon the sheltered church, a giant
leader of giant hills, on its brow a great helmet of woodland.
The Pilgrims' Way traverses the ridge, and passes through the
concourse of huge oaks and beech trees called 'The King's
Wood'. May bluebells people the glades in multitudes, throng
upon throng. You may drink in the heavenly colour as though
it were a draught of spring. Here is a song that once grew
in that wood :

> Who reigns a king in the King's Wood? O there the King am I
> Of beechen trees that brush the earth and oaken trees the sky;
> King of all that flitter and crawl, feathers and velvet pad
> (Saving Cuckoo the Vagabond—for he is no man's lad).
>
> .    .    .    .    .    .    .    .    .
>
> Follow me, Jacinth, speedwell-eyed, follow me through the green;
> Here are your maids; your minstrelsy hath music for a queen;
> And see, from stile to spinney-piece, from fern to cowslip-bed,
> Ruffled with shadows slender-foot, here is your mantle spread.
>
> At every stitch a sapphire bell, and every bell asway,
> 'Jacinth, Jacinth' upon its lip, hurries the passing May;
> Children all who go there by take hold of the broidered hem
> And pluck a patch of the Queen's gown, to bear it home with them.

### v

The former high road follows the forest margin to Chilham, and is now a country lane at its best. There you still
meet slow-moving wagons—yes, slow-moving—laden in
season with hay or corn or wood. The few cottages have
whitewashed walls, patterned with the curves of old ship's

timber. This May Day, looking across their gardens at the
distant Crundale Downs, through a maze of apple-blossom, I
could hear nightingales singing a duet from tree to tree, and
a blackbird determined to make the piece a trio. The thrilling
moment is when the left-hand hedge suddenly breaks and you
see Chilham Castle for the first time. The park is here confined by an open railing instead of thickset thorn, and peering
between the bars you gather your 'traveller's joy'. There is a
lake in the near foreground where armies of irises lift green
spears. Away up the hill are old terraces, banked with old
walls; based solidly upon these terraces is the gabled seventeenth-century mansion. The Norman keep stands a little
apart to the west, among velvet lawns. The panorama from
the terraces takes in the strategic point where the Downs part
asunder, and Stour, gently treading her green fields, flows
through that mighty gateway. Dr. Packe describes the scene :
' Jullaber's Hill ', he says, ' is the place where the high Down-
hills (whose roots descend to the banks of the River) begin to
Divaricate on each side, and retiring Wider from each other
the farther they go to the South form the great opening or
Chasm through which [the Stour] passes so Magnificently.'
The lime avenue at the castle entrance, planted in 1817, by
now shuts out the distant prospect of the cathedral. Bishop
Wilberforce's aspiration has been often quoted; he wished ' to
own all that the eye sees from the Keep as his estate, with
Canterbury Cathedral appearing just above the ridge as his
private chapel '.

Chilham Park has giant trees beside which the limes are
upstarts. The herons have nested here in lofty tree-tops during
almost seven hundred springs, for ' Le Heyroner ' is named
in a document of about 1280. ' Owners of Chilham ', writes
one owner in his history of the castle, ' have carefully preserved this wonderful colony. There is a tradition that the
birds return to nest every year on St. Valentine's day. . . . I
myself, on the afternoon of one fourteenth of February, went

up to the heronry and found it empty.  Turning homewards
I saw against the sky perhaps a dozen herons coming in towards the trees.'  Who can tell what strange rhythm of the
seasons bird-flights pursue?

VI

Sir Dudley Digges, who planned the present house in its
original shape, looms large in its history.  When he came
there its aspect was very different.  The Kempes, his wife's
family, or their tenants had by then spent a hundred years in
the remaining portion of 'a great house of the Badlesmeres,
not only commodious and beautiful for pleasure, but strong
also for defence and resistance'.  This house was, if not coeval
with the keep, at least of hoary antiquity.  Its destiny had been
never to remain for long in one ownership.  During the fourteenth and fifteenth centuries it see-sawed back and forth
between the families of Strabolgie, Earls of Atholl, de Badlesmere, and de Roos, as treason and forfeiture played their part
in succeeding generations.  The last treason of Lord de Roos
brought it, by royal gift, to the Scotts; from them it passed by
sale, more calmly, to Sir Thomas Cheyney.  He, with a trans-
atlantic gesture, removed the best of the stones, floating them
down the river to build himself a great new castle—Shurland
Castle in the Isle of Sheppey.  In his son's time enough stones
were left at Chilham, with the accompaniment of good farm-
lands, to tempt Sir Thomas Kempe to buy the estate; by way
of his granddaughter Mary's marriage we arrive at Sir Dudley
Digges.  The Kempe wheatsheaves and the Digges arms are
over the entrance.

Since Mr. Arthur Bolton carefully examined the tradition
that Inigo Jones designed the new house the discovery of a certain water-mark has put the matter beyond doubt.  Its lay-out is
unusual and remarkable; it is on 'a complicated hexagonal
plan : a court-effect at the back is visible by means of the open

sixth side of the hexagon'. Mr. Bolton compares it with the pentagonal fortress-palace of Cardinal Alexander Farnese, built in 1559 between Viterbo and Rome, like Chilham overhanging a lake, the Lago di Vico. This was still a nine-days' wonder when Inigo Jones went to Italy in 1604; it may have determined him to experiment on a 'geometrical set-out' of his own design, 'based on an equilateral triangle enclosing a circle, and consequently a hexagon', when a site among the English hills gave him opportunity. Chilham was inhabited, though not completed, by 1616; the last Digges died in 1718. Further changes were made by the Colebrookes, who followed after; they may have employed some architect of Wren's school. A ruthless 'remodelling' occupied David Brandon in 1862; even the outline of the towers was altered and their fir-cone finials swept away. Our generation has seen old beauties restored, some careful extensions to the plan, and much added loveliness.

## VII

Chilham Church has more and more artistic monuments than any other church hereabouts. Sir Dudley's pillar, set up in memory of his wife, Mary Kempe, is surrounded by seated figures of the severer virtues—Prudence, Fortitude, Chastity and Temperance. The monument by Nicholas Stone (perhaps an indirect argument for Inigo Jones's influence elsewhere, for the two men worked together) is not in his best manner: possibly the conception was Inigo's and somewhat outside his fellow-artist's range. Another seventeenth-century monument commemorates Margaret, Lady Palmer, Sir Dudley's sister, 'fairer than most women, wiser than most men'; one a certain Fogge, a 'harmlesse soule'. These are in Bethersden marble, finely incised with exquisite flowing designs of honeysuckle, vine and roses. The art of cutting back the surfaces and polishing the raised pattern to resemble an inlay of black upon white seems to be of local origin. It appears on monuments in

Upper Hardres and Hollingbourne Churches, and mantelpieces
at Chilham Castle and Godinton. That it is a Kentish, not
Italian, craft seems beyond question; or, if learned from a
foreign craftsman, it was practised in home-grown materials.
The mid-nineteenth century gave Chilham Chantrey's Wild-
man monument; the portrait-figures of the stricken wife, the
little kneeling daughter, the young man abandoned to his
sorrow, are most grave and dignified. The touching innocent
marbles of little Arthur and Edmund Hardy, modelled by the
Pre-Raphaelite sculptor Munro, were designed for the home
which knew its children no more; they find a fitting resting-
place in the Father's house.

VIII

Beautiful 'Robin's Croft' in Burgoyne Street was once called
'Cumberland House', from Vicar Robert Cumberland's having lived in it, perhaps also adorned it with panelling and
plaster-work. It is one amongst the many houses that make
Chilham so romantic a place. The village square at the top
of the street before the castle gate is surrounded by old cottages, for the most part of 'needlework' or dowered with
roses if they lack other charm. Of late the few blemishes on
the scene—an ugly inn here, an ugly cottage there—have been
skilfully transformed to the standard of beauty and fitness.
Long may this watchful sprite hover over Chilham Square,
and the traffic, which roars on to Margate round the base of
its hill, leave the village unperturbed! It was plotted out, as
some say, 'on a square plan, with four roads', in Roman times
—that is, after those woodland and hill-top skirmishes which
left Caesar triumphing.

There are ancient entrenchments in the woods to the north-
west; Shillingheld Manor once stood in their midst. Indeed,
the country on every side of Chilham cries out to be explored,
from the ancient corn mill—'French mill'—on Stour-bank,
away to Old Wives' (that is properly Oldwood's) Lees. The

Lees are bound up with a fantastic bequest of Sir Dudley's. He left forty acres of land in Preston and Faversham, still called the Running Lands, to provide rewards of ten pounds each in an annual foot-race. In Hasted's time, on May 19th, two young men and two young maids, between sixteen and twenty-four, still ran off a final 'tye' for these lordly prizes. The two couples, one from Faversham, one from Chilham, were nominally 'picked' by the Mayor of Faversham, advised by four jurats, and the lord (or the vicar) of Chilham, advised by four good freeholders. Actually there were preliminary tests : on May Day at Old Wives' Lees, the following Monday at Sheldwich Lees. For what jurat or freeholder could make choice of a runner like his or her own flying feet; Sir Dudley might have known better. And why did he fix on May 19th for his gala—and not for that only? By his bounty, on the same date, the young men of Chilham dined together and to his memory pealed the church bells.

*Chapter VI: IN ROMNEY MARSH*

WHICH for a stranger is the most striking approach to Romney Marsh? Should he come on to its western margin along the Wealden Ridge from Tenterden, slanting down by Reading Street to Appledore? Cobbett came by this route in 1823.

'In quitting Appledore,' he wrote, 'I crossed a canal, and entered on Romney Marsh. This was grass-land on both sides of me to a great distance. The flocks and herds immense. The sheep are of a breed that takes its name from the Marsh. They are called Romney Marsh sheep, very pretty and large. . . . The faces of these sheep are white; and indeed the whole sheep is as white as a piece of writing paper,' and so forth.

A flattering introduction to that Marsh hero, Sir Romney Sheep; but perhaps, in such company, our new-comer is a little deterred from the Appledore road; unfairly, however: he must come back there again. For the epic of Romney, if it all leads up to the fat sheep, white as writing paper, is a far more stirring history of endeavour than Cobbett's remarks might suggest. Let our traveller first confront the Marsh from some height—a cliff's edge like Lympne churchyard, for example. Let him gain a 'Pisgah-sight' of that immense green carpet, patterned with silver streaks which are fetters of river and ocean; stretching its levels away to the sea margin; roofed by the unfretted splendour of the sky. Through those wide spaces, above, beneath, the winds race towards him; cry to him of their liberty; his spirit companies with them, just touching the bending reed-tops, skimming the dikes, winging on, on, unhindered, unafraid.

382
148
383
379

The view from Lympne demands an eastern approach, crossing a spur of foot-hills, dropping to an ' inosculation ' of the Stour, mounting the last ridge, where Aldington Church stands high. Here one must stay a moment for Erasmus. Not that he was known there for long—only some fifteen months after his induction to the benefice. The whole episode is a contest of generosity between two great men. Archbishop Warham conferred the living, ' or rather ', says Erasmus, ' he did not give it but obtruded it upon me, in spite of my constant refusal, because the flock required that the pastor should be of the same nation; which condition I, being ignorant of the language, could not fulfil.' The Archbishop being at last convinced that his scholar, ' learned in the Latin and Greek Languages ', would accept no generosity at the expense of poor men's souls, allowed him instead twenty pounds yearly out of the parish and twenty pounds from his own pocket.

' When he converted it into a pension,' Erasmus continues, ' and found that I grudged to receive the money which was collected from a people to whom I could be nothing but unprofitable, the excellent man consoled me thus, saying, " What great services could you do, if you were to preach to one country congregation? At present, by your books, you instruct all pastors . . . does it seem to you unworthy if a small portion of the church's income returns to you? . . . I will provide that nothing shall be wanting to that church." And he did so; for . . . he appointed . . . a young man learned in Divinity and of good and sober life.'

Warham's young divine, Richard Master, shared the tragedy of Court-at-Street, that prelude to the Reformation, and suffered at Tyburn with Elizabeth Barton, the Nun of Kent. The Chapel of Our Lady, which Elizabeth visited in meek obedience to her visions, where she believed herself healed of fits and catalepsies, lies off the road to the south behind a ridge of farm-buildings. Where crowds once flocked to wonder at the maid's miracles there is now the merest shell of rough stones;

HARVEST FESTIVAL, LULLINGSTONE CHURCH

only the west window can be called an ' architectural feature '.

I remember the blacksmith from the forge on the high road directing me to the ruin and relating with all an antiquary's zest how he had found, beside the cliff track, a brass coin of the Emperor Nerva.

St. Martin's at Aldington, named in *Domesday*, has now a splendid perpendicular tower, with worked pinnacles. From the west door, between the sycamores, there is a Hollandish landscape of marsh and sea. Remember to lift the fifteenth-century choir seats and to look beneath at the misereres; all have rich foliage clusters, except the southmost; there you will find miniature vaulting and little castles fitted among the tendrils.

The modern east window illustrates the difficulty of blending harmoniously ancient and latter-day personages. In one light St. Martin kneels with Erasmus and the Venerable Bede —friends together, though divided by long centuries. In the opposite light Archbishop Warham is uncomfortably mated with a Victorian clergyman, and his wife arrayed in a black dress and ladylike cap. Will the time ever come when the incongruity is no longer perceptible?

The remains of the archbishop's manor, a chosen retreat of Cardinal Morton, is next the church, and from it the road drops to the village street, and passes by a black and white cottage standing apart in the fields.

II

But our faces are set due south, and to the Marsh. We will cross the Canal, leave Bonnington and Bilsington Priory unvisited to westward, scour out across green levels towards Dymchurch. Dymchurch—the name charmed me years ago in John Davidson's poem; round it shaped, like a rainbow, the colour, the sounds, which his lines induce :

> As I went down to Dymchurch Wall
>   I heard the South sing o'er the land;
> I saw the yellow sunlight fall
>   On knolls where Norman churches stand. . . .

A veil of purple vapour flowed
  And trailed its fringe along the Straits;
The upper air like sapphire glowed;
  And roses filled Heaven's central gates.
        .        .        .        .        .
Masts in the offing wagged their tops:
  The swinging waves pealed on the shore;
The saffron beach, all diamond drops
  And beads of surge, prolonged the roar. . . .

When I saw the real Dymchurch, summer had crowded those yellow beaches with trippers and the greens with campers-out. The vapours, the rosy light, draggled among sordid little bungalows; glamorous poetry had fled in dismay.

The opening paragraphs of *Joanna Godden* contain a useful summary of the Kent geography—which in a sense is also the history—of Romney Marsh. Actually it is not one but three marshes, 'spread across the triangle made by the Royal Military Canal and the coasts of Sussex and Kent. The Military Canal runs from Hythe to Rye beside the Military Road; between it and the flat white beaches of the Channel lie Romney Marsh, Denge Marsh, and Walland Marsh from east to west. Walland Marsh is sectored by the Kent Ditch. . . . Denge Marsh runs up into the apex of the triangle at Dunge Ness, and adds to itself twenty feet of shingle every year. Romney Marsh is the sixth continent and the eighth wonder of the world.' Indeed, it makes an early appearance in Nennius's eighth-century *Catalogue of British Wonders* :

'The first marvel is the Lomman (Limen) Marsh, for in it are 340 islands with men living on them. It is girt by 340 rocks, and in every rock is an eagle's nest, and 340 rivers flow into it, and there goes out of it into the sea but one river which is called the Lemn (Limen).'

What a wild tale it seems! Yet, after all, Nennius was merely creating symmetry out of the confused fact and rumour in some traveller's tale. For a stretch of shallow, brackish water, ebbing and flowing, locked already into shining watercourses, or merely turned this way and that by extruding 'islands' of rich ooze, his traveller, looking northward from the beaches, might well have seen. And, among the banks, fishermen navigating coracles or bending to their nets; and in the rocky margins, where the Weald sank abruptly to sea-level, nests of sea-eagles or gulls; and threading the whole region the Limen or Rother making their slow way by several mouths to the Channel. The rich Marsh soil is silt—river and sea compounded it; the Rother washing down the Wealden soil, the high tides sweeping it back again, intermixed with sand. There are huge shingle 'ramparts' at Holmstone and Denge Beach, embanked behind Dungeness; these barriers, flung together by 'the eastward drift of shingle from Beachy Head and beyond', first held up the silt the while it grew into the alluvial levels of to-day.

Our sixth continent offers problem upon problem to the geologist, the antiquarian. There is the question of its levels. Have they risen or fallen, and how long since? At least Lydd Church, embodying Saxon fragments, has stood unshaken for 1,000 years. Again, what was the old course of the Rother? The answer depends upon the origin and date of the Rhee channel and the Rhee walls. Once they were confidently attributed to Roman engineers—even to the Britons. A fine skill was certainly needed to excavate that immense channel, eighty to a hundred feet wide, with banks highest towards Appledore, lowest towards Romney; divert into it Rother waters, fortify it with more banks at the seaward end. By this means 24,000 acres of marshland were reclaimed and a new bay and safe anchorage formed at Romney. The latest scholarship leaves the Rhee wall unbuilt and gives the tides headway until medieval times—until the archbishops, from Becket onwards, had 'inned' Walland Marsh.

Certainly there was once waterway from Romney to Redhill in Appledore; in A.D. 893 the Danish Fleet sailed up it and harboured in the lake formed by the broadening river. In Drayton's version :

Those Danish routs, whom hunger-starv'd at home,
(Like wolves pursuing prey) about the world did roam,
And stemming the rude stream dividing us from France
In to the spacious mouth of Rother fell (by chance).

History then takes a leap of centuries till it can register, with Matthew Paris's pen, the terrific storms which from 1236 onwards to 1287 swept England, and not least the Kent coast. A shingle bank protecting Winchelsea and Broomhill was broken; the sea rushed in towards Appledore, and farther ebbing with every tide, presently drained off the reaches of the Rother till Romney Port had lost its waterway.

About 1258 Henry III tried to compel the fugitive waters back again, partly into their original course, partly into a new-made channel, so to save valuable trade. A new sluice at Appledore was planned ingeniously to hold back a volume of salt water at ebb-tide, so that the Rother, reinforced, might be able to ride out its journey as of old. Now came the first written Ordinances of the Marsh, made by Henry de Bathe, which, little altered, remained in use till 1930, 'the English parent of all embankment laws'. Scarce a quarter of a century passed; in 1286 fresh tempests, new devastation; the Rother at Ebony and Appledore again diverted. This time the invading sea provided the river with a new channel altogether, in length 1,000 feet, and shorter than the old by 400 feet. Not for thirty years was the broken trench filled in, although 'so obstructed by shingle and sand that ships can no longer pass by it to Romeneye as they used to do'. The battle was not yet over; for many a year the records of New Romney show how hardly it was fought to a finish. The years of struggle bred a determined race of men along those treacherous coasts. Throughout the fourteenth century England and France were at war, and organized piracy was waged impartially on all foreign vessels. Now the victim is a ship of Flanders; now a cog—the *Renelardi des Campes* of La Rochelle; the crew get safe ashore, but 'some evildoers of those parts' draw tackling and booty—

190 casks of good wine—by force out of the vessel, cut it into little pieces, and carry away wines, tackling and timber ' on horses and in carts and boats, whither they would '. The merchants' insistent outcry compels the powers of Westminster to order that goods in ships broken on the coast be restored immediately to their owners. In no time the King learns of fresh outrages. The men not alone of the Romneys or of Lydd, but from Rye and other towns of those incorrigible parts, had slipped the leash; they held, unransomed, tons of Spanish wine, pipes of oil, two chests containing two goblets of silver, a fine silver-edged girdle, being the freight of *la nawe Seinte Marie*, John Ortis, Master. 'Twere best, perhaps, to set a thief to catch a thief. The barges of Folkestone, Hythe, Romney, all the boisterous chorus, are now commanded to seize goods from enemy ships only and solely for the King's use. That is more after their mettle. A cargo of bulging woolsacks, grown on Marsh sheep and shipped to Flanders, is taken by French pirates and virtuously recaptured by the Romney barge. But virtue has limitations. Next time it is no question of woolsacks, but the glittering freight of three ' tarets ' of Catalonia, Genoa, and Naples; the King's bargemen hold themselves ' at defiance, in a place called le Chambre (Camber) ', by the sea-coast; even run the treasure ashore and sell it readily in the ports of La Rye. . . .

All this time Romney was herself exporting huge cargoes of Marsh produce, quantities of cheese, tons of butter, from those rich meadows of hers, which, in Drayton's words, appear to her attendant river :

> . . . most bravely; like a queen
> Clad all from head to foot in gaudy summer's green,
> Her mantle richly wrought with sundry flowers,
> Her moistful temples bound with wreaths of quivering reeds.

Despairing thought that the harbour mouth was steadily contracting as trade increased and wealth held out golden promise! What a drama lies behind dry entries in the town accounts. At several times Dutchmen were sent for to use their hereditary skill in making sluices and deepening water-courses. One Gerard Matthyessone came over for the huge fee of a hundred pounds, with sixpence Goddisselver, a gown and four hoods for himself and his three workmen. He constructed a great sluice, worked by a wheel and chain, and the citizens, and the chaplains too, put their pence together to pay for it. There was furious digging opposite the Quenehalle, a wall made around 'Jeffes Saltcote', but in a couple of years people were hunting out beyond the new sluice, 'in sprot-tyme'; and within twenty another watercourse had to be attempted, and eleven elms brought for 'bomying', that is, marking out the dwindling channel. Experts came—the bailiff of the Marsh very frequently—to 'make scrutiny'; some one rode to Maidstone to take the Lord Cardinal's advice. There was a proposal to bring more water from Gildford Marsh on the Sussex side. All to no purpose. By 1521 hope was dead: 'The sea hath now left and lost his course of flowing, half a mile and more from Romney, whereby four hundred acres and more were left dry and has become marsh-land and good pasture.' The mayor and jurats sadly told Lord Cobham there were now no ships, captains, or mariners belonging to their town, only masters of cock-boats.

About 1540 Leland summed up the whole matter: 'Rumeney hath bene a metely good haven, yn so much that withyn remembrance of men shyppes have cum hard up to the towne and cast ancres in one of the chvrchyardes. The se is now a ij myles fro the towne, so sore therby now decayed that where ther wher iii great paroches and chirches symtyme is now scant one wel maynteined.'

### III

There was another side to the picture. During the fifteenth century life at New Romney, even in the Marsh villages, was surprisingly varied, and a widespread artistic sense found expression in local drama.

The New Romney records give many glimpses of posturing figures, gaily bedecked, against the background of dune and sea, of buttercup pastures, white hemp-fields or patches of saffron. Some details may amusingly be fitted together. One finds entries like these in the Treasurer's books:

1422–4. To the men of Lyde (Lydd), when they came with their *May* and ours. . . .

1426–7. Given to the men of Wyghtersham (Wittersham) upon the shewing of their Interlude 6s. 8d.

1429–30. Given to certain persons coming from Hyerne (Herne) with a certain play 10s. 8d.

There were other Marsh players at Appledore, Brookland, Ham, Ruckinge, St. Marychurch, Stone-in-Oxney, and over the Sussex border, at Rye and Winchelsea; Wealden players at High Halden and Bethersden.

Hythe, Folkestone, and inland Chart and Wye, all had their companies, which played on holidays and at frequent intervals. The 'Hamme' players went to Lydd for the Translation of St. Thomas of Canterbury (July 7th); the Romney actors for the Church Dedication festival, and again on St. John Baptist Day and the Feast of SS. Peter and Paul. Many performances took place at Whitsuntide, or during long summer days: rehearsals, no doubt in some barn, or in the great barn-like Marsh churches during the winter. The theatres seem to have been under the open sky; one reads that the men of Wittersham showed their play, and drank their reward in good wine, 'upon the Crokhills', in the parish of St. Lawrence. 'Banners', or 'bann-criers', were sent ahead of the company. The banns were probably 'slips of parchment of a descriptive character', hand-bills as we should say, distributed to would-be spectators.

When the bann-criers arrived they were entertained at some inn: those from Brookland on one occasion were put up in the house of Edward Wodell at a cost of 5s. 4½d.; 6s. 8d. was the usual fee, whether for the benefit of banns or in recognition of the play. Occasionally 'in courtesy' the players received a few shillings more; but their refreshment was always inexpensive. Does that suggest the companies were not numerous, or the cheapness of bread and ale? Often there is mention of a watchman's fee : 'Paid to William Quikmanne for watching, at the time of the first play of Lyde, 4d.'

This 'watching' was a 'watching in the town', no doubt while the whole population save the sick and aged took a day's pleasure. The play was very much a municipal affair; but was it literally true one wonders that New Romney 'Paid the Bailiff and Jurats of Hithe, when they came to cry the banns of Hythe, 6s. 8d.'; or 'Paid as a reward to the Bailiff and Jurats of Lyd, when they came to cry their play, 6s. 8d.'?

Play 'wardens' were elected, often clergymen, chaplains who could lend vestments. Public money was sometimes lent to a warden of the town 'for the play in way of lone'; and when one John [the] Warden died, his widow received 3s. 4d. 'in full payment for the carriage of gere from London to Romene for the play '. From what London costumier were properties bought or hired? The famous silk-women carried on this branch of trade with much profit to themselves. Once a certain Mores hastened from New Romney to London to 'Master Gybson's' with 'the bill of arreyment for the play' and received 8s. for his trouble. His intention was no doubt to submit a programme and obtain a licence for the perform-ance. A few years earlier the Lord Warden's Serjeant had brought a mandate to 'the Barons', warning them not to play the play of the Passion of Christ without the King's leave.

Besides the Passion of Christ, which had been performed 'as from olden time', what other plays did the New Romney *Playboke* contain? Great store was set upon it, and between whiles the Common Clerk held it 'safely and securely . . . to the use and behoof of the town'. The Lydd play told the story of St. George. 'In expensis made the 4th day of July,' the Treasurer notes, 'beyng here Sir Thomas Keryell, the Luetenant of the Castill of Dovorre, and hi [their] wyvys, seing the play of Seint George, 18s. 6d.'; while the men of Lydd set up St. George's image at New Romney. Can actors sometimes have been engaged to play leading parts? Were women's parts—the Blessed Virgin, for instance—played always by men? And for what services did Agnes Forde receive in 1464 'For the play of the Interlude of our Lord's Passion, 6s. 8d.'?

Royal personages and great nobles or churchmen, like Cardinal Wolsey, lent their names to minstrel bands who, for a nominal fee, entertained the Marsh folk; there were humbler local minstrels like William Taberer, the Wayte, who was rewarded for his 'bourdyng' (thrumming on a little drum).

Sometimes the Lord Warden's beasts and the King's bear-ward came along; or the Lord Prince's Serjeant 'with the babyone' (baboon), or a man with a dromedary. The men of Romney held sports on St. Matthew's Day, when a crowd watched their wrestling matches. There were innumerable day-to-day incidents to relieve monotony. The town-crier went about proclaiming that hogs had strayed and must be driven in, or that shops were to be shut in service-time, or that towns-men must 'cease ball-playing and take to bows', or keep watch on shore or in the steeples. One news-letter announced 'the Frenshemen wolde come hedur'; there was a cry to make a muster, a provision of stone cannon-balls, and the jurats sat out on the Rype, refreshed by bread and ale, while the towns-men drilled.

The town officials were continually riding forth on some pretext. The belief in conference, or the personal interview, was profound—a modern touch! Lydd and Romney, faced with a dilemma, sought advice in Canterbury or London, seats of wisdom, 'to know how we should spede and be gydyd'. A mild form of bribery prevailed, if bribery it can be called which took toll of the bird-peoples of the Marsh. No filthy lucre was offered, but a curlew, or wild mallard, a crane, a 'cowpull of cygnets'. 'Two heronsewys' go to the Seneschal of Dover, and 'wildefowle, for having his friendship'. A conger reaches the Lady of Etchingham. 'The Captain', none other than Jack Cade, has a porpoise. The porpoise's escort on its last journey was expensive, but in the nature of insurance against a change of masters : 'Paid for the hire of one horse ledyng up the purpoys from Herietyssham [Harrietsham] to London, to the Capitayn 12*d*. For the hire of a horse that John Menewode [Manwood] rode uppon to Londone the same tyme, for to helpe to present the purpoys to the Capitayn 14*d*,' and so forth.

IV

I came upon a half-forgotten book called forbiddingly *Ermengarde*[1] which frames in those far-off times, evidently from a day-to-day knowledge of the Marsh. The heroine Etoile and Master Adam her escort are overtaken by a tempest, described after the manner of Holinshed : 'The roaring of the sea could now be heard approaching nearer in the gathering darkness.' Adam hampered by his age and Etoile's weariness hurries along, 'dragging his companion by the arm, entreating her to hasten her steps. Again their feet were on the shingle, and once more they had recourse to the backstays.[2] Strong gusts of wind hurled the sand, and even small stones into their faces, causing them sharp smarting pain. Flocks of seagulls and other birds flew wildly overhead . . . as if fleeing from some unseen foe. A high ridge of sand lay to their left. . . . Adam thought it advisable to climb the bank to take an outlook ere twilight should give place to night. Crawling on hands and knees, and holding on to the . . . long grasses, they

[1] *Ermengarde: A Story of Romney Marsh in the thirteenth century.* By Mrs. Hadden Parkes. 1893. (Elliot Stock.)
[2] Primitive wooden 'snow-shoes' for gliding over sand and shingle. They are still used by the villagers of Lade, a tiny hamlet on Dungeness Point, for crossing the beaches to the nearest road, two miles away.

peered over . . . and saw that Promhill, with its harbour, church and clustered houses was close to them . . . but that a wild raging sea was surging on the other side of the ridge, the level of which it had almost reached. A few moments and the hungry waves would pour over . . . and follow their flying steps like a pack of wolves. . . . The wave-crests shone in the surrounding darkness with . . . a lurid supernatural fire, as if the ocean itself were turned into . . . a basin of volcanic flame.'

In the course of the story the Marsh players are not forgotten, and among the audience on the Crockhills are 'the merchant and craft gilds in their distinctive dresses and badges, bearing images, pictures, banners and brazen horns '.

It is a true touch. The gilds fill an important role in Marsh history : possibly there was a gild of the Shepherds. None can estimate their share in the erection of those huge churches so out of proportion to the present-day population. Each fraternity must have room for its altar or chantry, and the number grew continually—until the doom fell. New Romney's Church of St. Nicholas was four times extended in the twelfth century; widened and enlarged, with a new chancel, in the thirteenth; and again in the fourteenth adorned by a chancel arcading of ' moulded arches on slender octagonal columns'. It had a glory of glass painting, fine tombs, numberless lights which the gilds kept burning. This is Leland's one remaining church of the original three—St. Nicholas, St. Lawrence and St. Martin; into its churchyard he saw the ships' anchors cast.

Once there were eleven more churches alive in Romney Marsh; of these seven have left no trace, and four—West Hythe, Hope All Saints, Eastbridge and Midley—are fragments of ruins.

The Marsh churches are full of interest : the ' cathedral ' at Ivychurch; the strange wooden belfry and leaden font at Brookland; lonely St. Mary in the Marsh; Appledore and

Brenzett; and Fairfield, isolated now almost as in the days
when it was unblessed because fashioned only of wood and
daub, and when the curate pastured lambs in the churchyard.
These churches are beloved of the antiquary, the architect; one
may read of them in countless monographs. I have rather let
the Marsh people crowd into my pages from the days of their
prosperity.

v

The best-known latter-day romance of Romney Marsh is
Sheila Kaye-Smith's *Joanna Godden*—a brilliant study of a
young 'farmeress'—in a Cinque Port one should say 'com-
baroness'—who is too ready to tilt against Marsh traditions of
corn-growing and sheep-rearing. Love is Joanna's undoing, a
tragedy first and last; in the death of her one true lover, in the
sordid sequel when her youth has gone by. Love holds the
foreground, but the Marsh interest lies in the skilful touches
which conjure the 'empty landscape and the flat miles'; the
'light mist over the watercourses, veiling the pollards and thorn
trees'; the fields with their 'tawny veil of withered seed-
grasses'; the 'little white sea-campions with their fat seed-
boxes', filling the furrows of unfrequented roads 'as with a
foam'. Or this of a May day, green, gold and white : 'The
new grass was up in the pastures releasing the farmer from
many anxious cares, and the buttercups were thick both on the
grazing land and on the innings where the young hay stood,
still green; the watercourses were marked with the thick clump-
ings of the may.'
There are background figures, too, more redolent of the
Marsh than the heroine and her ladylike sister Ellen : 'lookers'
inarticulate as their own sheep; the old farm-servant who drives
his mistress's gig, wearing a mulberry coat with brass buttons,
over his 'feet of clay and corduroy trousers tied with string';
the farmers and graziers who criticize, yet perforce admire, the
vigorous, gaudy Joanna. Yet I am not sure that the classic of

the Marsh has yet been written. Changes crowd upon it. In 1930 the Land Drainage Bill dissolved into a Catchment Area the Commission of the Level of Romney Marsh. Since the days of Henry de Bathe the Commissioners had controlled walling and ditching, gathered the ' scots ', faced the threatening seas unmoved; they had held their Lathes in the Court House at New Romney, feasted soberly in some ancient inn. Who could but regret their going?

The Marsh roads wind still along the dikes, but are less unfrequented by the measure of many cars and of omnibuses travelling from Ashford to Hastings. Late in the autumn I took this journey, rode out by daylight, rode back after dark. I was the only passenger on the return journey until we reached Ham Street. I could no longer see the landscape, but was conscious of it like an ample cloak of stillness. By the roadside we halted, and an old cottager brought out a bowl of steaming soup which, in good fellowship, driver and conductor drank by turns. Then we rolled on again; the dike edges were marked by coloured reflectors glowing and fading as our lights starred and then abandoned them to darkness. Those little glow-worms are a boon to unmotored travellers in the dark. Not long since an old priest from one of the villages, misled by a patch of shining tar, new-spread on the road, fell into a brimming ditch, which shone too, deceptively. There he lay, clinging to the steep sides, ready to be sucked down. By good fortune it occurred to him to lay his burning electric torch on the bank. A butcher-boy saw it, and rushing back into the village told the first person he met, ' There's a ghostie in the dik; I see'd his red eye ', and out came the rescuers only just in time.

I doubt if anything can rob the Marsh, except where it skirts the road, of that ultimate silence and oneness with the overarching sky. Nowadays the people suffer but little from agues and fevers, but they still have faith in their own herbal potions. Isolation sets its mark on them. They are little forthcoming, suspicious of the new arrival. ' It takes a thirty years' intimacy to win their confidence.' It is a lonely life too for the parson through the long winters, a life lacking most intellectual stimulus but that of the printed page. The monks were happier perhaps, who travelled from the central house to wait on their ministry. The problem is of long standing. Three hundred years ago John Streating wrote to Sir Edward Dering, begging for preferment, after nineteen years' labour at Ivy-church.

The living, his letter concludes, is ' worth allmost three hundred pounds a yeare, and I receivinge thereout only thirtie pounds a yeare, *though I live in the marshe, an unhealthfull place, and among rude and ill-nurtured people for the most part.*'

*Chapter VII: ON WATLING STREET*

*Canterbury to Boughton-under-Blean — From Boughton to Faversham*

### CANTERBURY TO BOUGHTON-UNDER-BLEAN

#### I

THERE are questions about the entrance of Watling Street into Roman Canterbury and its exit which may never be satisfactorily answered, now that the area is thickly built over. The iron bridge from Dane John to the Cattle Market certainly replaces the Roman Reding Gate, where Watling Street met the city walls. Farther along, in Beer-cart Lane, when the road was opened a few years ago, below the modern layers were seen foundations of the Roman way; no doubt just there it forded the Stour. Beyond all is uncertainty. Perhaps some vanished causeway carried the Street across the boggy islet of Binnewith, on to a second Stour Ford and more stable rising ground near Cock Mill. The site of this mill, as old maps show, was south-west of the Westgate, near some cottages on the bank opposite Tower House. The original Street may then have continued more or less parallel to the west side of St. Dunstan's Street, passing south-west of St. Dunstan's Church. Its line may have been that of St. Dunstan's Terrace, where a Roman cemetery was found not long ago in a bordering meadow. Then it went away to the left, much like the present London Road, soon reaching, by a miniature pass in the spur of hills, the thickets of Blean. For many centuries, isolated on the forest rim, stood, as it now stands by the busy high road, the Hospital of St. Nicholas. It was one of three

160

hospitals founded for the benefit of Canterbury citizens, who were lepers.

Eadmer the chronicler tells how Archbishop Lanfranc first ordered the wooden shelters to be built on a steep hill-side, a mile from the Westgate. He paid for the watchers the sufferers sorely needed, and saw to it that they were skilful, patient and kindly. A charter of Henry I calls the place ' The Hospital of the Wood of Blean ', and gives the hospitallers leave to grub up and ' riddaway ' ten perches of thicket on every side of their refuge. Time passes; spade and axe do their work. And now Henry II grants new favours to ' the leprous of *Herbaldown* '. Did ever name tell a plainer tale? In the interval from king to king the site has been cleared of woodland; now it is marked out from the uncleared hills around it as the Down of Herbage, or Tillage, the Pasture Down.

None of the archbishops but remembered his poor of St. Nicholas. Becket allowed them a one-horse cart to fetch timber daily from Shoerth Wood. Archbishop Winchelsey ordered a comfortable uniform, a warm outer garment of lambswool, black and not too costly; ' socks ' (in Milton's sense) of ox hide, laced half-way up the leg with thongs, or else boots of the same durable material. No brother might be seen out of doors unhooded; the sisters had russet mantles and double veils of cloth, not too fine, white within and black without. As leprosy gradually disappeared, the hospital was filled by ' sick, poor and impotent people ', of good repute, able to repeat aloud distinctly the Lord's Prayer, Creed and Ave Mary. A chantry priest ministered to them, by night and day : he lived in a house, ' honestly built ', on a site called Clavering, without the hospital gate, with pastures and garden and a dovecote. Such a long ancestry have the old brothers and sisters who nowadays live under the shadow of St. Nicholas, and from their neat almshouses, rebuilt and modernized, look out towards the hills. And what a prospect it is, across the lovely valley crowded with orchards and hop-gardens! In their

OAST HOUSES, BELTRING

common hall priceless ' mazers ', maplewood bowls, are preserved : one has a rock-crystal let into the bottom which perhaps adorned St. Thomas's shoe. ' In this house ', Somner says,
' was reserved the upper Leather of an old Shooe . . . worn
(as they gave it out) by Saint Thomas Becket; this Shooe, as
a sacred Relick, was offered to all Passengers to kiss, fair set
in Copper and Crystal.' Once, as we know, the shoe was
proffered to Colet and Erasmus; spurned by one, it moved the
other's kindly heart to drop into the almsman's rude old box
a little coin of charity. Pilgrims from London of necessity
came through the

> . . . litel town
> Which that ycleped is Bob-up-and-down
> Under the Blee, in Caunterbury weye.

Dean Stanley thought that the Black Prince, on a little pony,
and his noble prisoner, King John of France, on a cream-white
charger, might have halted there on their way to London, and
even gone a few steps down the hill, to the Prince's Well. Of
late years this part of the tradition has been a little ' blown
upon '. Yet the nearness of a medicinal spring might well
have suggested to Lanfranc the fitness of the place for his
hospital; and Edward, from some youthful memory, have
desired, in his feverish fits, a draught of the healing water.
Inside the church are ancient Norman carvings, shadowy wall-
paintings, scraps of old glass : a delicate sprig of Canterbury
bells is on one fragment.

II

Somewhere in Blean Wood was set up ' Le Hale ', the
famous pavilion of white woollen cloth, which, lacking a
palace in crowded Canterbury, gave shelter on summer nights
to the royal House of Lancaster. Queen Margaret, it seems,
first used it, on her pilgrimage in 1445. The baker's boy, of
a morning, bustled up the hill with ' choynes ', hot rolls, for
the royal breakfast; a wagon arrived from Graveney, containing an armchair for the royal nap, and another wagon from

Canterbury came laden with good wine. When the fun was over, the camp furniture was put away and the cloth-walls went to a fuller to be scoured. Where would a Scout or Girl Guide choose a site for Le Hale? There is a glade between the hills, just east of 'Hall-place', a glade sheltered from prevailing winds and planted with many-shaded rhododendron bushes. It is close to the high road, and but a mile from the city; in sum a perfect camping-ground for king and queen. The scenery all around is enchanting, and the enchantment lies over the whole country-side, from this point slanting upwards, and withdrawing, and slanting upwards again, to the crest of Dunkirk Hill. The spell partly lies in a gipsy wildness, the profusion of tumbled woodland, partly in the abundant cultivation; white mists of spring blossom, the glowing tints of cherry and oak, hazel and sweet chestnut when summer is done :

> Pleasantest corner the world can show
> Is a vale which slopes to the English sea,
> Where strawberries wild in the woodland grow
> And the cherry-tree branches are bending low,
> No such fruit in the south countree.

South of the Harbledown valley the 'pilgrims' road' tracks through the woods on the ridge-top. It passes by ancient Bigbury camp, where men of Kent in the iron age lived, high above the Stour valley.

North of Watling Street, Blean Forest mantles the hills towards the sea. If 'developed' as these forest-ridges must needs be, who is sufficient for the task? Here no man ever yet dug a foundation or laid brick to brick. How substitute the petty and commonplace for the freedom of forest ways? Yet, alas! already there are meagre hutments blotted on the skirts of the great wood. A stream of pilgrimage follows this historic road all the summer long. Is there no one to set a pattern here to all owners of English soil, those who can put England's beauty to ransom, sell her into thraldom, or release her, to delight generations yet to come?

Sibylla Holland has a charming fancy about the distances into which these hills look out. ' All beyond the immediate dark green of the garden ', she wrote, from her home at Upper Harbledown, ' is of a pearly grey. This is the prevailing tint of East Kent distances . . . a sort of reflection of the pale channel colours, clear but pale. The sea, the chalk, the wide cornfields, the great open sky above the northern waters, all combine to produce it.' A diary of the year round in East Kent could be made from Mrs. Holland's letters.

Here is the portrait of a good Man of Kent : ' Old Potts has cut down and bound together for burning the two apple-trees and pruned the third. When I went out to speak to him . . . he was recovering the wounded roots and said, I humbly beg your pardon, ma'am; I thought I was doing right in having of her down. I'll take and cover her up and comfort her a bit, and by the blessings let's hope she'll take no harm.'

### III

A century ago a jarring note was struck in this woodland harmony which yet vibrates as a tragic memory. The story of Sir William Honeywood Courtenay, Knight of Malta, otherwise John Nichols Thom, a Cornish publican's son, is a remarkable psychological study. So long as it unfolded in Canterbury it was pure melodrama, although with something shameful and pitiful intermingled, the shadow of ignorance and imposture. Courtenay arrived in the city in 1832; had the citizens but realized it, already the hero of a lurid past, eccentric to the verge of madness, swindler and impostor, a seducer of innocence, suspect of arson. Yet he still possessed irresistible personal attraction for simple people : his appearance hypnotized them and gave him a swaggering self-confidence. ' He looked a man of about thirty-five (he told the people he was two thousand years old), rather above the middle size, broad-shouldered, with a muscular . . . frame, an easy carriage and perfect self-possession. His hair was dark, parted in the middle, descending behind in long ringlets. He wore a fine coal-black beard, whiskers and long moustaches; his eyes were small and restless, but the features very regular, indeed . . . handsome.' In a mean and vague way he suggested a Raphael picture; the strangeness of his appearance was emphasized by the garb in which he burst forth as a parliamentary candidate at the first election under the Reform Bill. He wore a superb dress of crimson velvet, gold lacings, tassels and epaulettes, and menaced interrupters with a sword.

In three days' poll Sir William secured 374 votes, and at a bound stepped into the peerage as Lord Viscount William Courtenay of Powderham, unjustly excluded from his rightful inheritance. The tale so much took Harrison Ainsworth's fancy that he put back the clock by a century to introduce Courtenay into his novel *Rookwood*. The hero, Dick Turpin, visits the ' Vagrant Club ', a camp of thieves and gipsies, and meets Courtenay's prototype, the Knight of Malta in company with Jerry Juniper, Zoroaster, and other rufflers. ' Over his shoulders were thrown the folds of an ample cloak of Tyrian hue . . . upon his profuse hair rested a hat as broad as a Spanish sombrero.' The Knight swears by St. Thomas à Becket. At the feast he is croupier and toasts Canterbury with a song. It is a clever song in the right key of contemptuous braggadocio.

> Come list to me, and you shall have without a hem or haw, sirs,
> A Canterbury pilgrimage much better than old Chaucer's.
> 'Tis of a hoax I once played off upon that city clever,
> The memory of which I hope will stick to it for ever.
> With my coal-black beard and purple cloak,
> Jack-boots and broad-brimmed castor,
> Hey-ho for the Knight of Malta.

## IV

A trial for perjury closed this chapter of Courtenay's career, and the next four years he spent—one learns it without surprise

—in Barming Asylum. Then, on his father's petition, he was inexplicably released, and the scene shifted from melodrama in the city to tragedy in Blean Forest. Courtenay returned to the neighbourhood and lived first at Fairbrook near Boughton and next with some people called Culver at Bossenden Farm. There his restless brain shaped for itself fresh and far more mischievous delusions. Some have said that the soreness felt by the Kent peasantry at the Poor Law of 1835 was his sufficient opportunity. Apparently this was not the case. The peasants of Hernhill, Boughton and Selling were by no means destitute. Work, especially woodman's work, was plentiful : not a few were small land-owners. No, Courtenay's attraction lay elsewhere : the evidence of his followers cannot be gainsaid. ' Sir William he sat upon the ground,' said one, a charcoal burner, ' with his back against a tree—like, and there was all the women a-crying and praying to him; and they says to him, " Now do tell us if you be our blessed Saviour, the Lord Jesus Christ," and says he, " I am he "; and then he shows 'em the mark of the nails in his hands, which was made when he was put on the cross. Now that's no lie, and I knows him well as see it.' Thus with the vision of their Lord returned, riding His white horse forth to conquer, these poor people left their homes at a madman's bidding—a madman unmasked already a few miles away.

Early in May 1838 Sir William prepared for a ' demonstration ', its object characteristically ill-defined. He possessed himself of pistols and shot, a huge cavalry sword, a white and blue standard with a lion rampant painted by his women supporters. On Sunday May 27th he anointed some of his followers at Waterham Well to make them invulnerable, and next day left Bossenden Farm with a train of devotees. They made their way through Fairbrook to Goodnestone-next-Faversham, carrying a pole stuck through a loaf of bread. The leader's white horse was saddled with a skin, and he wore the famous sombrero, a velvet coat, and plaid trousers. The marsh road

was traversed back to Dargate; in the evening the party returned to a night in Bossenden barn. Weariness perhaps
induced the symptoms of failing courage; at any rate, next
morning began with a threat to shoot deserters, and off the
procession set once more, to Sittingbourne, and thence to
Newnham, Throwley, Selling, and to Bossenden again when
darkness fell. This aimless wandering could not continue in-
definitely. A crisis was brought about by a Hernhill farmer,
who applied to the authorities for the arrest of his truant
labourers. Accordingly Constable Mears and his brother went
in the early morning of May 31st with their warrants to head-
quarters at Bossenden. They were under no illusion; here was
no saviour for them. Mears's brother made his calm decision.
'It is certain,' he said, 'one of us must die in this attempt;
which shall it be? It shall be I. I shall not leave any children.'
Without a tremor he took his brother's office on himself, faced
the fanatic leader, explained his errand, received the fatal
pistol-shot and wounds from the great sword, and was flung
aside into a ditch. At 8 a.m. after this foul murder, Courtenay
administered to his band a sacrament in bread and water. An
old woodcutter, hiding terror-stricken in the undergrowth,
listened to the madman's wild words. Sometimes he said he was
the Christ, sometimes under divine direction. From the great
oppression in the land he would lead his followers to glory and
share among them the gentry's estates, forty or fifty acres
apiece. He had come to earth on a cloud and on a cloud would
be taken away; neither bullet nor weapon could harm him or
his friends; and if 10,000 soldiers came against him they would
fall dead at his feet. These lunatic sayings strangely affected
the unlearned and emotional peasants. They believed he could
hear a mile off what they were saying and repeat every word.
Some worshipped him, kneeling at his feet, and cried aloud
joyfully that he, the saviour, had accepted them as his followers.
None dared leave him in face of the terrible doom he called
down on defaulters. Thom was clever enough to realize that

the simplest stratagem sufficed to deceive these people in their
excited state.  If he fired off his pistol loaded with tow and iron
filings, one of his victims, as she watched the bright sparks float
to the ground, heard ' divine harmony ', and believed a miracle.
But it was only Wills, the village flautist, piping somewhere in
the wood.   About noon on the fatal day a major and a hundred
men of the 45th Foot, summoned from Canterbury by local
magistrates, appeared on the scene.   The Courtenayites were
parading defiantly up and down the fields, with fire-arms and
heavy clubs.   The danger was acute, because he had promised
them glory that very day, and announced a march upon the
city, when he would seize the Hales estates.   Three thousand
men it was credibly believed would have flocked to the lion
rampant had it appeared at the West Gate.   There was no time
to lose.   At sight of the troops the peasant rabble drew back
into Bossenden Wood.   Yet they took no shelter, believing
themselves and their leader to be invulnerable.   The first to fall
was a young officer, Lieutenant Bennett.   He was shot by
Courtenay, who knew no fear and shouted to his men, ' Boys,
come forward and do not behave like dastardly cowards.'
Eight persons were killed in the short, sharp fray which
followed, Courtenay among them, and some five-and-twenty
of the rioters were made prisoners.   The bodies were taken
to the Red Lion Inn by the roadside on Dunkirk Hill.
Courtenay, his beard and hair shaved away, lay among the
rest ' like a giant ', his white, blood-stained blouse torn by relic
hunters.

v

In the inn parlour that May afternoon were the jury of
inquest; in an upper room the prisoners; in the yard frantic
wives and mothers struggled to get a sight, through the narrow
window, of the faces of the dead.  Most of the fallen were old
men, and the prisoners were young, all but the one woman
among them.  This was Sarah Culver, the farmer's sister at

Bossenden where Courtenay had lodged. The end was now at hand. Some women assembled at the 'Lion' with bits of oak bark stripped from the tree against which their hero had fallen; thousands of sightseers flocked to see him in his coffin, paying a last foolish homage to his inglorious career. Then a van carried off the mortal remains to Hernhill. No bell tolled. There were a few watchers on the ridge; a little crowd gathered in the churchyard. A grave but four feet deep had been dug, four paces northward from the north chancel door. As the clods fell on the coffin one of the spectators cried out, 'Cover him up quickly. Let us have no more of him.' For a time watch was kept by the graveside, because many of his followers expected that their messiah would rise again, and it was feared the body might be exhumed. For this reason no mound has ever marked the place.

With the passing of a terrible illusion the storm of sorrow fell on Hernhill.

'The voice of wailing was heard in almost every house, for the villagers intermarry so much that all are more or less related. One poor young woman whose brother had been committed to Maidstone Gaol for wilful murder was sitting at her door, pale, exhausted, stupefied by grief. Another was singing most dolefully to the young child in her arms and ever and anon breaking off to bewail her dear, dear husband.' . . . The funerals began at four o'clock on the Monday after the riot. The clergyman met each of the six coffins, one by one, and all the while the bell tolled. There was no sign among the mourners of extreme poverty; all the dead were buried at their own charges. The service took two hours amid such abandonment of grief as the spectators prayed they might never see again. Yet perhaps the most poignant moment came at evensong on the Sunday following. 'There was no psalmody attempted. Not even a hymn was given out. The great body of the rustic choir was either among the dead or among the captives in Maidstone Gaol. Wills the flute-player, whose flute

was with the spoils found in Bossenden Wood, was absent—
and along with him who played, nearly all those who usually
sang to his music—in prison.' Those who were left behind
could not raise a song and melody in their heaviness. For
some minutes only the silence spoke for them.

VI

Events in the Blean did not fail of their effect. Thoughtful
people asked themselves when Parliament discussed the re-
grettable liberation of a lunatic whether this was not really
beside the point. Whether heart-searchings were not rather
due about the condition of a population upon which such madness could take hold.

The Central Society for Education sent their emissary, a Mr.
Liardet, to look into the ' State of the Peasantry in the County
of Kent '. Grief and dismay speak from every page of his report, which is still well worth reading. In the Ville of Dunkirk, numbering about 700 inhabitants, he found smuggling
rife. ' There was nothing in the neighbourhood ', he says,
' calculated . . . to inspire any regard for order and law.
Living within view of the spires of Canterbury there was not
a church where they could attend the ordinances of religion,
nor clergyman to guide them. . . . The place did not even
possess a day-school, in which the lowest degree of learning
could be imparted. Not to speak of a gentry, there was not a
medical man, a farmer, or even a shopkeeper in the place.
. . . It is not to be wondered that the people fell into pernicious courses, and acquired the character . . . of a desperate
and lawless community.' The stir of conscience led quickly
to the building of a little church on the crest of Dunkirk Hill.
Education Acts, time and improved communications helped
to wipe away the old reproach. But memories were long and
pitifully sensitive; there are those yet living who have seen a
weeping woman kneel at Courtenay's grave.

To-day Hernhill is one of the most charming villages in Kent, the grey flint church tower, so quiet and so reverent, the village green with the old 'Red Lion Inn' on the north and timbered cottages on the east side. Wooded hills and valleys hem in the place and safeguard its quietude.

Close at hand is a stretch of country offering the most surprising contrast. From Hernhill tower, ' northwards may be seen the German Ocean; ships passing to and from London, the northern ports and the English Channel; the fleet of fishing-smacks off Whitstable; colliers and other craft making for the Swale between the Island of Sheppey, tapering into the sea, and the coast.' And the link between forest and ocean is the spreading marsh—Graveney Marsh. The light catches dikes and pools amongst the string-coloured grasses; the softest of winds suffices to flutter the purple reeds on the road margin.

## FROM BOUGHTON TO FAVERSHAM

### I

As I took my way along the Street to Faversham, at the foot of Dunkirk Hill, that steep descent towards lowlands laced with cherry-blossom, a cavalcade moved slowly in my direction. Then I remembered : Chaucer's pilgrims are on the road. Straight from his joyous imagining they amble into my world ' at spring '; to-day is an April morning.

Not long ago, only some five miles back, the Nun, Prioress Eglentyne's chaplain, finished her tale of ' bright Cecilie '; now, ' at Boghton under Blee ', the party is overtaken by a man on horseback, dressed in black over a white surplice. His dapple-grey hackney is steaming hot, so hard has he ridden it. His companion, the Yeoman, has also pressed his horse almost beyond endurance; its dark coat is flecked with foam like any magpie. The man-in-black travels light in this warmish weather. All his belongings are stowed away in two pockets

hung upon his crupper. For a moment or two Master Geoffrey
is puzzled to place the new-comer. Then he notices:

> How that his cloke was sowëd to his hood,

and by this token of clerical attire

> I demëd him some chanon for to be.

The Canon is a jolly soul. If his horse is hot he is hotter; he
has stuck a dock-leaf under his hood; all the same, his forehead
is beaded like a still that squeezes the sap from plantain or
pellitory.

'God save you all,' he shouts, as at last he reaches the party.
'I rode as hard as I could to overtake your merry selves, and
go along with you.'

'Nay,' interrupts the Yeoman, 'it was I who saw you starting from your inn, and pointed you out to my lord and sovereign, such a lover as he is of good company!'

'Very wise of him, too,' said mine host; 'but tell me; can
this master of yours tell a merry tale?'

> Who, sire? My lord? ye, ye, withouten lye
> He can of murthe and eek of jolitee
> Nat but ynough . . .

And little by little the truth comes out. The Canon is no
better than a swindler; he borrows a pound here and a pound
there on the plea that by 'elvish crafte' and alchemy he can
turn one pound into two. After serving such a master for
seven years the 'Chanon's Yeman' is none the wiser and much
the poorer and sadder man. Dolefully he confesses it, among
all those jovial and well-clad folk:

> Ther I was wont to be right fresh and gay
> Of clothing and of other good array,
> Now may I were an hose upon myn head;
> And wher my colour was bothe fresh and reed
> Now is it wan and of a leden hewe.

And, lo! and behold, the Canon, his shameful secret betrayed,
turns his horse and flees the company he so lately joined. It is

the Yeoman's turn to beguile the way—the way to Herbaldown over the wooded hills.

Those riders of Chaucer's company saw the veil of forest drawn right over the western hill-brow and down the slope as far as Boughton Street. Now it is withdrawn almost to the rim of the hills; but that westward face has still the air of a squatters' settlement. Cottages scatter in the bushes as though each of them had alighted in a little clearing of dense Blean Wood; they face all ways, unrelated to any cottage-community, linked by no particular path. Towards the foot of the long slope they pull themselves together into a well-ordered village street. Houses of every date hobnob sociably over the days when thatch and timbering went out of fashion, or the days when Queen Anne brought along a pretty porch and small-paned casement, or, to-day, when King George's men set out those gaudy hoardings.

The tower among the trees just north of Selling Station belongs not to Selling Church, but to SS. Peter and Paul, Boughton-under-Blean, and the approach from the village-side (turning by a fine timbered cottage) displays to even more advantage the wonderful beauty of its situation. There is a long path open in the fields, not a roadway, yet wide enough when need is to carry the dead along it to their resting-place. Gradually this path brings you nearer the grey tower bowered in trees and, as you walk, the spaciousness, richness and dignity of the country-side fill your heart afresh with praise of ' England's Garden '.

Inside Boughton Church Sir Thomas Hawkins's alabaster tomb (1616) is a link between Boughton and Lynsted Church, farther along the street, and a little enlarges our knowledge of an English sculptor who has lately taken a new lease of fame. Mrs. Arundell Esdaile has inspired visitors to parish churches to search for the infrequent work of ' the most exquisite artist Mr. Epiphanius Evesham '. Epiphan was no man of Kent, but the youngest twin son of William Evesham of Wellington in Herefordshire. He was born in 1570 and had his sculptor's training, unusual for a lad of gentle birth, under the Dutchman Richard Stievens, in the Southwark School of Alabaster Workers. His monument-making covers a series of years. Kent possesses some early though minor examples: three tablets to the Collyns family, two in Hythe Church, and one, to Margaret Collyns, at Mersham, which are dated respectively in 1586, 1595, and 1597. Epiphan was already a master of his craft when he adorned the Hawkins's tomb at Boughton with those little panels so characteristic of his graceful fancy and delicate craftsmanship. The Lynsted memorial, to Christopher Roper, second Baron Teynham is a yet more ambitious and mature work of middle life. It is inscribed in capital letters along the base ' E. Evesham me fecit '; and of late a cursive signature an ' Evesham fecit ', has been found also, rather clumsily scratched, on the Boughton tomb. Evesham's genius lies rather in the execution of small, realistic scenes in bas-relief than of large figures in the round. On the base of the Roper tomb kneel the Baron's sons and daughters; the elder lad is in armour, his helmet and gauntlets laid beside him; his brother, in cloak and doublet, ' like another Inglesant, is lost in devotion; his face is the face of a mystic '. In place of the graduated family group nursing their tiny skulls, with which pious convention supplanted the medieval ' weepers ', Evesham's fancy led him to attempt the portrayal of real grief: here each daughter gives natural expression to her sorrow; Bridget at her faldstool is wrapt in prayer; Mary, with face bowed down, has her hand upon her heart; Elizabeth lifts her head with radiant hopefulness to join the cherubic songs which reach her from an overhanging cloud.

II

' Faversham, Faversham, a dull old town; all beer and gunpowder, isn't it? No, I have never gone to see it; why should

I? Isn't there something about "Arden of Faversham";
Feversham, do you tell me? What should take me there, I
wonder?'

Have you not heard comments like this where strangers
were discussing places worth seeing in our county? I have;
not seldom; a little while back I should have expressed myself
much on the same lines. Yet the story of Faversham is varied
as any topographer, antiquary, or historian could desire. The
threads in it are so many it is hard to disentangle a few and
weave a pattern for this book. The outskirts are featureless.
Do not stay there; drive on between the gabled houses; listen
a while to forgotten voices. And at first the children, the
schoolboy at least; the girls are not so easily enticed out of the
shadows.

Old Faversham Grammar School lies along a quiet alley
edging the Town Meadow, 'a very fine gravel walk for the
inhabitants to divert themselves on', which takes you north
of the church. The schoolhouse, now used as the Masonic
Hall, has the appearance of a two-storeyed building; but as
originally built the upper storey was a schoolroom supported
on stout oaken posts over a paved play-yard, which it roofed in
and made available for the boys' recreation in all weathers.
The old paving, worn and broken, remains, but the yard has
been walled and made into an office; the north side of it was
always closed in, so that the boys could not run right across
their play-ground. A fine oak doorway, with carving on the
door-posts, leads into what was originally the School Library.
The whole lay-out probably represents a common type of
Elizabethan school building; it was much the same at old
Ashford Grammar School. The large schoolroom, which has
kept its original barrel-roof, was built in 1587, on the town's
petitioning Queen Elizabeth that the school, after the suppression of Faversham Abbey, might be restored 'for the sake
of good Literature in her Kingdom and for the promotion of
learning and good manners'.

The walls are panelled with black oak, iron-hard, yet scored over with initials, names, dates, little ships even, copied from those the scholars saw daily coming up the Creek. The window has good modern glass, Masonic devices, fitted into the original oak mullions. The usher's desk remains, and the poppy-heads, which were bench-ends in the scholars' time, are now made into stalls for the Masons. They use too for their ballots the boys' old marbles, hardly any of them true spheres, found in odd crannies about the place. By the entrance are two delightful carved panels, 'portraits', so 'tis said, of King Stephen and Queen Matilda (who wears her hair in a bun); they came from a room over the Town Gate. The 'Free Grammar-School of Elizabeth, Queen of England, in Faversham, in the County of Kent', still its proud title, has had a career longer by centuries than its monkish predecessor. The Abbey School apparently came into existence December 10th 1527 under a tripartite deed between Abbot John, Mayster John Cole, Clerk, and the Warden and Fellows of All Souls. John Cole, confident that the abbey would continue for all time, intended Brethren and Novices as well as 'all othre Children that be disposed to lerne the science of Gramer', to get instruction through his endowment. Abbot and convent appointed the schoolmaster at ten pounds a year and a gown-cloth. His pupils, before admission, must repeat the Latin services, and afterwards were to take religious learning, grammar and writing at convenient hours, 'with reasounable correccion and puneyshment'. Novices and monks were taught 'in a certayn House adjacent unto the Scolehouse', at the same time as the rest; the master being expected to go to and fro between his lay and religious pupils. Holidays were strictly regulated. Nobody, save at Christmas, might, on any pretext, stay away longer than six days, unless he were ill, or pestilence was in the town; three absences meant expulsion. The scholar's friends saw to his books, and 'in Wynter Season . . . that the Scoler have Candyll, for hym and hys Felowes of the Forme that he ys of, every Evenyng and Mornyng, when his course shall come about; so that they may se to rede on theyr Bokes and not lose theyr time '. Lighting thus cost the school nothing and was no great expense to any one else; provided all the friends were equally generous with their tallow dips. Opening prayers were offered for the King, Founder and Abbot, the boys' families, and their own health of mind and body; at closing time there were Latin collects, Salve Regina and De Profundis. The connexion with the abbey was close; the head master lodged there, and tabled in the Frater, or at the abbot's board.

### III

John Cole's abbey—St. Saviour's Abbey for Benedictine monks of the Cluniac order—had already stood in Faversham since 1147 : little wonder he thought it established ' for ever '. King Stephen and Queen Matilda were the founders of this ' Mynstre of French Monkes . . . in the worship of the Croys ', for their own souls' sake, their son Eustace and other children, and their predecessors on the English throne. There were to be an abbot and twelve monks to symbolize Christ and His Twelve Apostles. King Stephen was buried there in 1154; in the rhyme of John, Abbot of Peterborough :

> At Feversham he lis, at a heven in Kent,
> In an abbey of pris he founded with lond and rent.

His corpse was probably plundered at the Suppression for the lead, and thrown into the Nailbourne, the little stream which comes to Faversham from Ospringe.

The abbey meadows lay near the Creek and were damp and foggy; the water supply was brackish; but, all the same, the brethren lived and flourished to a great age. The abbey church stood on the east side of the Abbey Green. The parish church close by is mainly of the thirteenth and fourteenth century. The dedication to St. Mary of Charity is an echo from the mother house at La Charité-sur-Loire, that most

beautiful church which the Huguenots broke and ruined. The
loyalties of the men of Faversham, 'the King's Little Town
and Royal Vill', were unusually complicated. They were for
ever in danger of infringing somebody's liberties; whether
king, abbot, or the Court of Shepway, representing Cinque
Ports jurisdiction; for Faversham was a limb of Dover, and
had to furnish one ship, with twenty-one men and a boy to
serve forty days on summons.

The town, first known as Favresfeld, then Favresham, was
plainly built for the sake of its Creek. Leland describes it
succinctly : 'Ther cummeth a Creke to the Towne that bereth
Vessels of XX Tunnes, and a myle fro' thens, North est, is
a great Key called Thorn, to discharge bigg Vessells. The
Creke is fedde with a bakke water that cummeth fro Ospringe,
a thorough-fare a myle and more of.'

One must annotate his words, imagine much of the surrounding marshland still under water; the head of the Creek
near Swalesmouth deeper and broader than it now is. Till
Edward IV the Swale was the usual passage way for all vessels
London-bound; hence the favourable position of Faversham
port. From the time of Henry VIII large vessels could, as
Leland says, 'lade and unlade at the Thorn'; 'This', comments Mr. Giraud, who made close study of the records, 'was
at the entrance of the Liberty, where the tidal creek branched
off in two directions; one branch ran to the town, forming a
channel for the smaller craft; the other ran towards Clap Gate,
forming . . . Thorn Creek.' The ordnance map nowadays
shows indeed the two-branched Creek; and the word 'Wharf'
appears on it a little northward of Oare; but the old names
have disappeared with the old facilities, under the slow process
of silting which the town is not now prosperous enough to
arrest. Trade is not brisk in the Creek to-day, but it is still
a picturesque, if rather melancholy quarter, lying under the
steep ascent of The Brents. Barges come up with the flowing
tide and lie there at the ebb, stranded in the mud; an ancient

heavily timbered warehouse stands on the bank, cheek by jowl with the corrugated iron roofs of modern commerce.

IV

I have gathered at random several old 'tales of Faversham folk worthy of remembrance. There was once in the church an altar, dedicated to St. Crispin and St. Crispian. Would you believe it, these saints, to avoid the persecution of the Emperor Maximinius, fled to Faversham, ' where they learnt to make shoes for a livelihood, and followed that trade at a house in Preston Street near the Cross Well, now the sign of the Swan '. Our information is wonderfully exact. Their dwelling became a goal of pilgrimage for brethren of the last, who journeyed ' from all parts of the Nation, to pay their love . . . to the saints of their profession '.

A benefactress of the church was Dame Joane Norton, formerly Joane Hornby, a Lincolnshire woman. She was buried with her first husband at West Horndon in Essex (he was her number one, but she was his number four), but had evidently once meant to lie elsewhere; for she bade her executors 'fynyshe upp my tombe in feversham churche, according to the bargeyn that I have made with oon Alen, a mason of Bersted in Kent; and it to be used for a sepulchre-place in the same churche '. This, then, is the origin of the beautiful Easter sepulchre in St. Mary's. The indent of a lost brass at the back of the recess shows Dame Joane kneeling, in her hood, ' with a scroll extending from her to a representation of our Lord rising from the tomb '; that glorious mystery to which she desired to do great honour. Outside the church two recluses took up their abode. The anchorite was William Thornbury, for twenty-two years vicar of Faversham, and for eight more (1473–81) an inmate of the ' chapel and parvise ' in the north-east corner of the churchyard. The anchoress, to whom he left a legacy of fourpence, and twopence to her servant, had her cell also on the north side of the graveyard. She was, it would seem, one of a long line of saintly women—reckoned in the category of the church officials with vicar, choristers and bell-ringer—which extended back perhaps a couple of centuries to that Celestrina, nun and anchoress, named in the obituary of Davington Priory.

To the seventeenth century belonged Zutphania Ower, wife of Robert Ower of Syndal. She inherited her Christian name from her mother, Zutphania Wood, a daughter of Sir Christopher Clyve, who was born at Zutphen in Guelderland, and named after her birthplace, no doubt, for the sake of Sir Philip Sidney. The first Zutphania died at nineteen when the second was born. Who brought the little motherless child up I know not; or who taught her to pen those letters of a deceptive politeness which remain among the Oxinden Correspondence. But her connexion under the rose with Thomas Oxinden brought misery on him and his young wife.

Last among the gleanings I shall set this charming story of a great soldier. In 1838 the Town Council of Faversham, since the passing of the Municipal Corporations Act had abolished the mayoralty, proposed to sell by auction the town's ancient maces. The last mayor of his long line wrote in desperation to the Duke of Wellington, Lord Warden of the Cinque Ports, begging him to intervene. The reply came punctually, a model of diplomacy. The Duke had no right in law to interfere, as the Corporation had undoubted right to part with their maces. He had no right to give an opinion, much less power to prevent the sale. But : ' The Duke laments exceedingly this state of things. He was always sensible of the consequences of the Measures of the last seven years. He is not responsible for them; he can only lament them with others.' The maces were not auctioned; they still lend lustre to Faversham's civic treasury.

v

The mention of Arden of Feversham (the name was in fact Ardern) led me to re-read that lurid drama. I read it with Faversham in mind, and found I had not taken account enough of the local features. Sir Lionel Cust (in *Archaeologia Cantiana*, 1919) based some argument for Marlowe's part-authorship on the local colour to be found in the play : Marlowe would, he thought, as a Canterbury man, have been better able than Shakespeare to supply this element. It may be so; although after Marlowe left the King's School his Kent connexions are problematical. There seems no real reason why in boyhood he should have known Faversham intimately, thirteen miles away from his home, though he may have ridden through it towards London; but true it is that Alice Arden suffered at the stake for her crime in Canterbury, only thirteen years before Marlowe's birth. The author of the play makes dramatic use of the fact that Arden had acquired by patent royal ' all the lands of the abbey of Faversham ', so as to oust former grantees, and in particular his neighbour Richard Greene, who cherished a bitter grudge against him :

> Your husband doth me wrong
> To wring me from the little land I have. . . .
> Desyre of welth is endles in his minde
> And he is gredy gaping still for gaine . . .
> And tell him this from me,—I'le be revenged,
> And so as he shall wishe the Abby lands
> Had rested still within their former state.

Thomas Arden, as a young man, served in the office of Sir Edward North, Clerk of the Parliament, and married, in an ill-omened day, Alice Mirfyn, North's stepdaughter. Arden's usefulness to his master was rewarded by the lucrative post of Commissioner of Customs of the Port of Faversham. It is true enough that he obtained a grant of abbey lands, but the recent discovery of documents has proved that they came to him through Sir Thomas Cheyney of Shurland. Arden prospered exceedingly : his house by the abbey gate, dismantled now and stripped of the old panelling and old stone fire-places, stands there to-day. It was once a handsome house, suited to Arden as the foremost citizen in the town, and in 1548 its mayor.

In the tragedy Sir Thomas Cheyney plays an important part. Just when Greene, Black Will, and Shakebag are about to do Arden to death as he rides along Watling Street, close to ' Raynum Downe ', ' Lord ' Cheyney and his men arrive opportunely on the scene. Cheyney says :

> 'What, Mr. Arden? You are well met.
> I have longed this fortnight's day to speak with you;
> You are a stranger, man, in the isle of Sheppey.'

Then he recognizes one of the hangers-on :

> 'What! black Will? For whose purse wait you?
> Thou wilt be hanged in Kent when all is done.'
> *Will:* 'Not hanged, God save your honour.
> I am your bedesman, bound to pray for you.'
> *Lord C.:* 'I think thou nere saidest prayer in all thy lyfe.
> One of you give him a crowne;
> And, sirra, leave this kinde of lyfe.'

And then, little imagining he affords his friend brief respite from the fatal knife, he carries Arden off to feast in Shurland Castle.

The play is full of trivial incidents such as must daily have occurred among the riders of Watling Street; the horse that ' halts down-right ' and is led back to Rochester to be shod; the ' annoyance of the dust '; the encounters of old acquaintants :

> Your way and mine lyes four myle togeather.

At the close the ruffian Will seeks sanctuary at Flushing aboard some oyster-boat or hoy sailing from Faversham Creek. Then, too, Arden is almost stifled by a Sheppey fog in his throat and Will cannot see his road—for that same island ' smoake '.

' I pray thee,' Shakebag answers his companion, ' speake still, that we may mete by the sound, for I shall fall into some ditche or other unles my feete see better then my eies.' And into the ditch he falls sure enough, till the Sheppey ferryman comes up at his cries and grumbles out : ' You are well enough served to go without a guyde in such weather as this.'

When the awful deed is done the Mayor and Watch of Faversham come to the house ' with glaves and billes ' to search for the murderers, and at the ' Flowre de luce Inn ', whither Alice Arden had once sent those silver dice, pledges of stolen love, Mosbie the arch-villain is arrested. For two years after the crime, that *cause célèbre* which set all London talking, ' in the place where [Arden] was layd being dead all the proportion of his body might be seene . . . as playne as could be; for the grasse did not growe where his body hadde touched but betweene hys legges, between hys armes and about the holownesse of his necke and round about his body '. That place was the Town Meadow, and through the stone arch between the abbey precincts and the Gravel Walk the dead man had been dragged in the snow. Last of all, there is the thrilling possibility that Shakespeare himself played in Arden of Feversham—can it have been in Shakebag's part?—when he visited the town with Lord Strange's company in 1590.

VI

Up a steep hill from the Creek, on the outskirts of Faversham, Davington Church and Priory look towards the marshes, and (twice for their misfortune) towards the Powder-Mills. In 1932 the Central Board of Finance of the Church Assembly acquired and most carefully restored those historic buildings; extinguished private ownership, and secured a spiritual ministry for the adjacent area. The Church of St. Mary Magdalene on its hill-top may occupy the site of a Roman cemetery. Almost certainly some earlier building stood there; when Fulk de Newenham established his priory in 1153 he found a ruinous Saxon church partly constructed with Roman bricks and mortar.

The priory added one more to the little group of Kentish

nunneries, though it never had the great possessions of the two Minsters or Dartford Abbey. The number of its Black Benedictine sisters at first reached twenty-six, but soon dropped to fourteen. By 1527 only the prioress, one professed nun, and a lay sister remained; before 1536 two of these were dead, and the third, Sibylla Monyngs—who can wonder at it?—had left the forlorn place. So that Davington suffered no ' suppression ' except by the hand of Time. After the nuns' disappearance the domestic buildings were granted by Henry VIII to the omnivorous Sir Thomas Cheyney, who demolished much and re-partitioned what remained.

When the antiquary Willement bought the property in 1845 he found the house divided into weekly tenements, and the buttery licensed for the sale of ale, beer, and cider. (Strange Kent of that age, which could discover no better use than beer and skittles for its historic sites!) The plight of the nuns' church was almost as deplorable. If you enter it to-day you will notice two pointed doorways in the east wall; these originally led through an ancient nine-foot partition screen into an adjacent building, probably the Saxon parish church of St. Lawrence, taken down between 1534 and 1580. The foundation-stones were dug out and sold, so that the ground-plan cannot be recovered. After this, the lay owners of Davington Priory allowed the parishioners to worship in the nuns' deserted sanctuary. The Norman fabric suffered terribly in two explosions of the gunpowder mills in 1767 and 1781, and within the ruinous walls services became more and more irregular. Willement found the windows mostly stopped with brick and the tower capped by a red-brick parapet. Ewes at lambing time were sheltered within the walls, and it was a hiding-place for contraband goods. Who will not rejoice at the beauty and order given back to this ancient House of God, at the restoration alike to church and nunnery of their forgotten dignity, their quietude, and contemplation.

*Chapter VIII: THE ISLE OF SHEPPEY*

I

UNTIL of late years Sheppey has had but two approaches, by ferry-boat from the mainland. The lesser ferry still crosses from Oare to Harty, west of the Horse-Sands, which lie in mid-stream. Harty was once itself an islet, but its tiny strait was drained out long ago. A little way inland, as you look from the trees of Oare and Uplees towards the trees on the high island ridge, the silver streak of the intervening Swale is scarcely perceptible. To reach the ferry you turn right from Oare, past the little church and skirting the spacious unhedged fields. Oare is supposed to owe its name to the sea-wrack which was gathered all along these north Kent shores. The word goes back to the Old English for sea-weed (*wár*), and takes many shapes, 'waur' and 'ore' among the rest. The growing plant was cut away from the rocks, carefully dried, and burnt to make cinder-ash or kelp for the potter's use. It was a poor man's summer trade. The gatherers roasted their harvest in holes dug on the beach, and the stench was so horrible that Queen Elizabeth forbade the practice, because the inhabitants 'are thereby much annoyed in their health and greatly hindered in their fishinge'. There is a foreign look about Oare village from the Faversham Road, with the pyramid of its red roofs piled on rising ground above the tiny creek.

The second approach to Sheppey from Watling Street once proceeded by the King's Ferry. Only the signposts remember it. Even the inn close beside the new Queen's Bridge, which for a time kept the old name, is now called the 'Lord Nelson'. The ferry's story is full of picturesque detail. A special court was held on Whit-Monday at Kingsborough to assess the islanders for its maintenance—those ' sons of Sheppey ' who ' go into England ' whenever they cross the Swale. The cess might be no more than a yearly penny an acre upon fresh marsh or a penny for ten acres on salt marsh. The actual passage was free except on Palm Monday, Whit-Monday, St. James's Day, and Michaelmas Day; horsemen then paid two-pence and footmen a penny each. There were two large ferry-boats and a skiff on the route, moving on a long cable of 140 fathoms fastened from bank to bank. A little stone ferry-house stood on the island, built by George Fox, who had waited shelterless in the cold and wished to spare others the experience. Sometimes outlaws and tramps wandered into this out-of-the-way corner for security. Was it at the Ferry Inn under William and Mary that a man was seized, ' neare the Isle of Shipay ', who had ' for some tyme gon about a begging '? ' One night ', runs his tale, ' at the house where he lodged, hee bespoke a joynt of mutton for supper, and talking somewhat more pertly than beggars use to doe, the people of the house . . . the next day, after he went out, persued him and tooke him, and upon search found he had quilted about him 500 guynees. So hee is now in Maydston Gaole, upon suspition to bee the Lord Montgomery in the proclamation.'

I crossed the Queen's Bridge into Sheppey for the first time in a sweeping rain-storm which was dashing the cherry-blossom on the mainland. Close to the bridge a stately barge was coming up, its brown sails full set. The river-water bore along green reflections from the bright spring colour of the surrounding marshes, and the ditches were full of white water-buttercups. They hinted at the treasury of marsh-flowers which await a botanist hereabout. Many and many a time the name of Sheppey occurs in Gerarde's *Herbal*. He found ' Sea Rag-weed ' and abundance of sea-lavender close to this very King's Ferry; ' Cat tails ', with shaggy leaves, in the ditches; yellow horn-poppy on the sands. He speaks of the sea-starwort, an excellent herb against poison, which 'women that dwell by the sea-side call in English blew Daisies, or blew Camomill '.

It is tempting to botanize in such good company; but Sheppey has other harvests than the marsh-flowers. Hasted writes of the rich grasslands, and about Minster and East-church of the great corn crops, grown in small enclosures with elm hedgerows to break the sea-winds. 'The whole face of the country ', he truly says, ' is exceeding pleasant in fine weather, being interspersed with much small hill and dale and frequent houses and cottages.' Then he adds warily that fresh water is scarce and brackish; that at times the air, in this morsel of an island, but thirteen miles long and six broad, dominated by the North Sea, is ' very thick and much subject to noxious vapours '.

In the Swale marshes there are but two small villages, Elmley and Harty, and scattered cottages of the ' lookers ' who oversee the flocks. The population occupies chiefly the ridge of low hills, rising at Kingsborough to 200 feet, which traverse Sheppey from behind Queenborough to Warden on the eastern extremity. The clayey cliffs backing Minster are a hundred feet high, and the tides, urged by easterly gales, waste and fret them for ever away. Hasted says that ' so great is the loss of land at the highest parts that sometimes near an acre has sunk down in one mass . . . upon the beach below, with the corn remaining entire on the surface of it, which has afterwards grown and increased to maturity and been reaped in that state '.

There is a narrow winding road to the left after Minster Church, going steeply down like a Devon lane. At the bottom is an inn, and beyond it the cliff path, well worth pursuing to see the acres of tumbled earth-masses, padded with brown bushes and starred by the golden pussy-willow. Between the huge broken clods water lies in leaden-grey pools. The pros-pect is a thing by itself. All this foreground of wreckage : the yellow gravelly cliff-face, hiding the treacherous clay; beyond it a sea of delicate grey; then the Essex coast dimly seen; westward the shore falling back to Sheerness; opposite, nearer than Essex but still mist-hidden, the Isle of Grain. There is a noisy kennel of beagles somewhere about here clamouring for a run over the marshes after the flying hare.

II

Here in this narrow slip of land, swept by sea-winds, cloaked by sea-mist, where one may gather milkwort and wild flax in salty places, or soldanella, the 'sea-bindweed, like a bell of bright red incarnate colour'; where the sheldrake—'bargander' as Sheppey calls it—nests in the marsh: in this romantic setting the Lady Muse of History has staked many parts. She draws up her toes out of the marsh and plays chiefly among the higher villages. But no! that is untrue: she points first to Queenborough on the flat westerly shore. Its castle was built 'in the time of bows and arrows' to defend the western arm of the Swale, which, making an S turn at the end of Long Reach, passes into the Medway by Queenborough Spit. Why was the building-stone brought from Yorkshire quarries, from Stapleton and La Roche, to distant Sheppey by land and water transport? Did the stone-hewers also come from the North, and was homesickness the cause of the unceasing labour troubles? For the labourers were repeatedly ordered to stay on the works, at the King's wages, so long as required, on pain of imprisonment. Their Comptroller was a clergyman, John Barler, vicar of Wormshill, away on the North Downs, who was paid sixpence a day and twenty shillings a year for his robe. Can he too have been a North Countryman, who knew their speech and could alone keep discontent within bounds? Kent and Sussex folk also complained loudly of oppression by the royal purveyors for the King's castle in Sheppey. At last the plans William of Wykeham had prepared were completed. Edward III was at his

castle in September 1363 and in May the year following. He
made the tiny place a free borough, changing its name from
Bynnee to Queenborough in honour of Queen Philippa, and
gave it many privileges, including a mayor. These were the
days of its glory; sunset came after two centuries or so. By
Henry VIII the castle had become ' little more than a mansion
for the Constable ', though many of those officers were distinguished personages.

A description of the time of Charles I tells of twelve rooms
below stairs and forty from the first storey upwards, 'being
circular and built of stone, with six towers '. In a little round
courtyard paved with stone was the famous well; a great court
surrounded the whole with a heavy outer wall and moat. One
visitor, the botanist Thomas Johnson, admired the ' noble large
castle hall '; around the cornice were shields of the nobility and
gentry of Kent; Queen Elizabeth's arms had verses inscribed
beneath :

> Lillies the lion's virgin breast explain,
> Then live a virgin and a lion reign. . . .

Soon after Johnson's visit, in 1629, the castle was pulled
down to the last stone. Even the well gradually silted up.
The town had always been the smallest of royal boroughs;
under Queen Elizabeth there were only twenty-three inhabited
houses, at the end of the eighteenth century about 120, in one
long, unlovely street : a little fishing-town inhabited by fishermen, oyster-dredgers, and alehouse keepers.

One Monday morning in 1620, a fair-day, too, when the
place was crowded with visitors from the marsh villages, there
was a stampede to the quay, started nobody knows how. Close
to the water's edge lay the oddest craft man or woman ever set
eyes on : a skeleton-boat, kept afloat by eight large bladders—
four on each side—and propelled by two stock-fish tied to two
canes. In it sat two men, weary and bedraggled, for they had
been at the ' oars '—save the mark!—since Saturday ' at even-
ing-tide '. They had, in fact, for a wager, started out to journey

from London to Queenborough in a boat of brown paper. Before they had gone three miles the paper bottom fell out; there they sat, ' within six inches of the brim ', paddling along, hour after hour. One of them, Thomas Taylor, was waterman enough to keep the vessel stirring, and poet enough to turn their Odyssey into rhyme when they safely rounded the Spit. The other, Roger Bird, a vintner by trade, unused to any sort of craft, meanwhile put up to heaven the prayer of the fool-hardy. Taylor's *Praise of Hempseed* is the story of this crazy voyage :

> Thousands of people all the shores did hide,
> And thousands more did meet us in the tide,
> With scullers, oars, with ship-boats and with barges,
> To gaze on us they put themselves to charges.
> Thus did we drive and drive the time away,
> Till pitchy night had driven away the day. . . .
> The tossing billows made our boat to caper,
> Our paper form scarce being form of paper;
> The water four miles broad, no oars to row;
> Night dark, and where we were we did not know;
> And thus 'twixt doubt and fear, hope and despair,
> I fell to work and Roger Bird to prayer;
> And as the surges up and down did heave us,
> He cried most fervently, good Lord, receive us !

When at last they landed, they had the grace,

> Ere they two steps did go,

to offer their thanksgivings :

> His mercy us protected
> When as we least deserved and less expected.

Now the fun began. The mayor, with the rest, came hurrying up to the quay. Not every day such adventurers rounded Queenborough Spit. A collation awaited them; with mock ceremony the bones of their lunatic craft were solemnly presented :

> . . . to glorify that town of Kent
> He meant to hang it up for monument.

But human nature never changes; while hungry Tom and Roger sat down to their beer and oysters, the populace fell upon the boat, tore the eight bladders, the two stock-fish, and the two canes to fragments and carried them back as mementoes to their villages.

The castle well was rediscovered just a century after the round towers had been demolished. A shortage of water for His Majesty's ships at Sheerness led to the brilliant idea that the old castle supply might be brought back into use. A party of officers, with Peter Collinson, an eminent botanist, as their scientific observer, went to the round courtyard. Finding but very little water at the bottom of the well they began to bore. For three and a half days they bored into the close, bluish clay, till at last one evening, when they were near giving up in despair, ' the auger slipped down at once and the water rushed up violently '. In eight days' time there was 176 feet of water in the once-empty well. They calculated that the spring lay 166 feet below the deepest place in the adjacent seas. ' The water proves excellent,' Mr. Collinson joyfully reported to the Navy Commissioners, ' soft, sweet and fine . . . it lathered well with soap, and boiled old pease . . . and they had great reason to believe . . . will sufficiently supply his Majesty's ships. . . .'

Outside Queenborough Station is a large grass-grown mound, with traces of a moat about it. It is fenced to protect from annoyance the iron cisterns which crest its summit. Into those gloomy cisterns the famous spring still bubbles up. The inn, hard by, of yellow Sittingbourne brick, bears Queen Philippa's name on the signboard. *Sic transit gloria.*

From Queenborough one may work round, skirting the Medway marshes, to Sheerness. The famous dockyard is closed in these days, and the seagirt place is becoming a health-resort. It grew out of a morass into martial fame about 300 years ago. Under Charles II a small fort of twelve guns was made there to defend the passage of the Medway, and the King went twice in the early part of 1667 to see its erection.

III

Minster has the most ancient of the island churches, a land-mark from the Kent coast.

St. Sexburga, Queen of Kent, niece of St. Hilda of Whitby, founded a college here thirteen centuries ago for seventy-seven novices. The church began with the nuns; it is dedicated to St. Mary and St. Sexburga, their ideal and their foundress. (For centuries children in neighbouring towns were named after Sexburga.) The north chancel was the nuns' choir; fragments of early masonry can be seen among later stonework. The conventual buildings were on the north side of the church, and part of the entrance gate, with much Tudor chequer-work in the walls, still remains.

Edward III's new-built castle must, I think, have encroached on the convent water-supply. When he provided Queen-borough with ample well-water, he granted the prioress and nuns, ' those two wells or stanks in a place called Bynnee in the isle of Sheppey, by the water of Swale, in which the rain-water falls ', and the land around the wells. Their servants were allowed to plough channels for the rain-water round the stanks, to draw off a supply at any time, convey it to the priory by boat, cart, or horse, and to use the castle causey or any path from Queenborough to Minster.

The nuns had powerful patrons; Archbishop Corboil re-stored their church in 1130, when already it was 400 years old; in 1286 Sir Roger de Northwode, a Sheppey landowner, ' with no sparing bounty ', relieved it from great poverty, and earned the name of the nuns' ' restorer '. Records of the ' Plunder ', when there was a prioress and ten nuns, allow us to scrutinize their belongings, in company with Henry's ruthless Commis-sioners. At that time they farmed extensively, and had outbuildings for every practical purpose—cheese-house, bake-house (with a horse-mill and grindstones), brew-house, boult-ing-house, milk-house, and garners stocked with grain. They had cattle, too, sheep, and horses, a dun, a white and an 'ambelyng grey', perhaps the prioress's mount. Every department was well staffed: Jhon Gyles, the Shepherd, Ellyn at my ladye's finding, a horse-keeper, carter, thatcher, cowherd, and two or three chaplains. One of these, Sir Jhon Lorymer, turned traitor and told the Commissioners the nuns had carried away valuables which he had last seen on Relic Sunday. Four chalices were missing, a blue velvet cope bordered with gold stars, the head of St. Mary Magdalen silver-gilt. It was a mean charge, even if true, when one considers what remained to satisfy Henry's rapacity. Clearly confusion had reigned when the rumour of the visit got about: treasured objects had been hastily thrown together. Tumbled into the 'Shrine of Timbergilt' in the church was the oddest assemblage: 'olde relyks in purses of sylke'—such as the nuns made in stray half-hours; an ivory box with more relics; 'an olde sleve of St. Syxborow with xviij peces of sylver therein'; a hanging for the prioress's seat, of 'verders, with whyte rosys'.

In the Great Chamber more precious things still were heaped up: the 'crosse clothe of Sarcenet of vi colors, with the image of S. Syxborowe broderyed thereon'; a pyx of beryl set in silver; the bone of St. Blaise, glittering with gems; the lector-table of ivory finely wrought. These, and countless others, the piety of the ages had deposited in St. Sexburga's lap. . . .

Once upon a time the ferryman plied busily for the messengers bringing gifts on their way to the convent; on one sad day also, when the plunderers returned, bringing loot for the robber king.

### IV

Since the early fourteenth century, when Margaret de Shurland married Sir William Cheyney of Patrixbourne, his family had lived in the old Shurland manor-house, standing due east of Eastchurch on rising ground. They had a distinguished record, in Margaret's sons and sons' sons. Fuller describes Sir

Thomas Cheyney, one of St. Sexburga's 'visitors', rather
pleasantly as a 'spriteful gentleman . . . a Favourite and Privy
Counsellor to four successive Kings and Queens in the greatest
turn of times England ever beheld'. Sir Thomas's motto was
'Le meus que je puis', and his was a good best. He mopped
up quantities of Church land about Kent, priories and manors
unending. We have watched him already, transporting the
hewn stone from Chilham keep to build his new mansion in
Sheppey. He needed an abundance, for the plans included
nine quadrangles, enclosed in stone walls, covering several
acres. To crown the efforts of this 'Strenuus Miles', Henry
VIII and Anne Boleyn visited Shurland—Shurland *Castle* by
now—in 1532, and surveyed the banqueting-hall, chapel, and
gorgeous chambers. Forty years later it stood dilapidated,
empty of inhabitants: the next heir, Sir Henry, preferred his
mother's estate in Bedfordshire. Twice he entertained Elizabeth; then, having lived a spendthrift, he died a beggar, his
huge inheritance all melted away. By and by the Queen leased
Shurland and turned it into a barracks. When Gerarde gathered flowers in Sheppey, the castle belonged to 'the Worship-
ful Sir Edward Hoby'. Nothing of the nine quadrangles now
remains; the great wall encloses empty space, and the façade
with two red-brick turrets stands up like a proscenium. . . .

Eastchurch Street looked very attractive that spring day, with
clouds of pink almond and armies of nodding daffodils. The
church is a less melancholy monument to Cheyney generosity
than Shurland is to their lavishness. It was built in 1431 on
three roods of land given by William Cheyney. Its predecessor
had gone to ruin 'by reason of the sudden weakness of the
foundations', a perennial difficulty in Sheppey because of the
London clay. For the new church the Abbot of Boxley saw to
it that lasting foundations were laid—a deep trench filled with
solid blocks of chalk from the mainland. Diagonal buttresses
support the building at every angle, and it stands up hand-
somely on the ridge. A dated church of one period is of special

interest, and this is a fine example, with its beautiful rood-screen traversing three eastern chapels. In the chancel is the tomb of Gabriel Livesey, the father of Michael Livesey the regicide. The design of it reminded me of the Thornhurst monument at Canterbury, only the position of the figures is reversed. Here it is the wife, Anne Sondes, who leans up in the background, her elbow on a cushion. In front is Gabriel's recumbent figure, holding a book in his left hand. A little baby in a long frock occupies a lonely niche beneath its parents. The memorial window to two young airmen makes a splash of strong colour on the south wall. In it the female figure has an armful of almond-blossom, and her seraph-companion a broken sword and wings of flame; their message to the mourners is 'Turn ye to the stronghold, ye prisoners of hope'. A large aerodrome is perched castle-like on a hill above the Swale marshes, just south of the village.

This chapter began with the view northward from Oare towards Harty; it may end by looking southwards from Harty back to Oare and Faversham Church tower. Clouds of gulls share the brown fields of Harty with a few barrows—'coterels' was the old name—a few stacks, a silver-shining ditch. There are more gates than houses on the winding leisurely road, and in the churchyard few dead even; three solitary altar-tombs and a leaning wooden cross. The church, lonely still, has been here for centuries. The bellcote has an oak frame of rude carpentry and an arch opening into the south chancel goes back to the twelfth century. Some seafaring man may have brought to Harty Church its chief ornament, the 'Flanders Kist', carved with a jousting scene between two mounted men.

## Chapter IX: ON THE MEDWAY

*Rochester—Chatham and neighbouring places—Old Maidstone —Tonbridge and Tunbridge Wells—On Visiting Penshurst*

### ROCHESTER

#### I

ON first visiting Rochester Cathedral I had a guide of the best kind—one of those who progressed long ago beyond mere acquaintance with their building, skipped the stage of a dull over-familiarity, and have arrived where all do not reach, at a third stage, which is vision. There a guide becomes a true lover who finds continually fresh charm in a worn countenance. My guide had one grievance. Travellers who visited his Rochester, he said, had always Canterbury in prospect. They gave scanty time where careful attention was due. I consoled him, admired everything he had to show; and secretly postponed my departure by an hour or so.

I have since thought, when travelling through Rochester, seeing that ancient panorama of church and castle across the broad Medway, and when the bridge is past, the 'close-up' of St. Andrew's above the brown huddled houses, at how many points the stories of the two Kent cathedral cities interlock. Both, as it were, sprang from a river and a Roman road. In both the main interest is shared between a great church and a highway from London to the sea. Lanfranc, the Norman builder of Canterbury, links his name with Bishop Gundulf's in the Norman building of Rochester. Not so long ago the foundations of a Saxon church like St. Pancras and St. Martin were found to the north-west of St. Andrew's Cathedral. Gun-

dulf began his task with a great detached campanile built eastward of the Saxon church; the ruin of it, about forty feet high,
remains on the north side.   Once it towered up some sixty feet,
and in it hung two great bells; one was called 'Thalebot',
from the sacrist who made it; the other 'Bretun', because it
was paid for with the money a drowned man had left in his
brother, Ralph Bretun's, keeping, when he went his last
voyage.   There is a fascination about these named bells of the
Middle Ages, these in Gundulf's tower, and others at Rochester
which Bishop Hamo de Hethe placed in his new steeple, calling them Dunstan, Paulinus, Ithamar and Lanfranc; and
Canterbury's Bell Harry and Bell Dunstan.   Their voices intermingled with the lives of countless generations; they rang on
up to the stars while their makers and their hearers fell away
to dust.

Ernulf's task, both as Prior of Christchurch and afterwards
Bishop of Rochester, was to complete and adorn what others
had begun.   He finished Gundulf's nave, and in 1130 there
came, within four days of each other, two dedication festivals:
at Christchurch on May 4th, and at Rochester on Ascension
Day, May 8th, when Archbishop William Corboil, the castle
builder, hallowed St. Andrew's Cathedral, in the presence of
Henry I, eleven English and two Norman bishops.

And the great churches shared their sorrows as well as their
joys.   Both suffered terrible conflagrations, and what medieval
cathedral escaped them?   Rochester had two, in 1137 and again
in 1179, five years later than Canterbury's greatest disaster.
The stonework of the chapter-house still bears the mark of
that scorching.   After the fires there sprang up in both churches
a new cult to be the magnet of pilgrimage, and in both a rebuilding of the choir on a new and splendid scale was made
possible by the offerings of the faithful.

Now in the year 1201 a certain William of Perth, a baker, so
charitable that he gave (surprising Scot!) every tenth loaf to
the poor, vowed to visit the Holy Land.   He called on the way

at Rochester and next turned his face towards Canterbury. He had not gone far when his servant beguiled him from the high road, robbed and murdered him, and took to flight. The monks retrieved the body and buried so generous a man in their choir. The story spread like wildfire and grew into legend; the saintly baker's bones became the object of popular veneration. Miracle followed miracle, and for three centuries Becket's pilgrims halted first at William's side. When the jubilee of his murder had gone by, some further recognition of his virtue seemed due. Bishop Laurence of St. Martin went to Rome and obtained official canonization: ' St. William ' on pilgrims' lips he had long since become. Some say that at this time his body underwent, like Becket's, a ceremony of translation to the Chapel of Our Lady in the north transept.

The records of the thirteenth century are a mosaic of construction and destruction. King John pillaged the choir in 1215; 'not even the pix with the Body of Christ was left over the high altar '. On Good Friday 1264 Simon de Montfort's men ' entered the cathedral on horseback with drawn swords, while priests and people were celebrating the Passion of Christ'. Poor 'people' on whom the scourge of war eternally falls!

There seems little doubt that, offerings permitting, the monks intended to construct in greater magnificence the whole of their church. Happily 'their plan . . . came to an end when they reached the nave '. So that in it Gundulf's work may still be studied and from it Lanfranc's vanished nave at Canterbury be reconstructed in imagination. While at the west door there stand those strange elongated figures in thin-folded draperies, the statues, some say, of Gundulf's patrons, Henry I and Queen Matilda, which recall the mystic kings and queens beside the west entrance of Chartres Cathedral.

The tomb of Bishop Walter, founder of Merton College, Oxford, says Sir William St. John Hope, ' was originally of Limoges enamel, probably of wood, with an effigy of the bishop covered with metal plates . . . the whole being placed under a stone canopy, with a double window pierced in the wall behind, to throw light on the effigy'. The costs are detailed in the executors' accounts preserved at Merton. The artist was Master John of Limoges; the executors went to France to consult him, and he finally escorted his masterpiece to Rochester and superintended its erection. This was in 1282; the college went to the expense of a new tomb in 1598, when two Latin epitaphs were added. At the foot is this couplet:

> Quam breve spatium hec mundi gloria
> Ut Umbra hominis sunt eius gaudia.

The words proved sadly apposite to the tomb itself; for by 1662 it had again to be renewed, being half-destroyed by the fanatical mob; while in 1852 the effigy and the ancient grill were displaced and modern work substituted.

The Parliament troops came to Rochester Cathedral in September 1641.

'They brought', says Mercurius Rusticus, 'the same affections which they express'd at Canterbury, but in wisdom thought it not safe to give them scope here as there.'

Whether or not Rochester folk were less destructive than Canterburians, the frescoed Fortune, safe hidden behind the old pulpit, continued to turn her wheel on the north choir wall, and on the south a few of the fleurs-de-lis and leopards, painted in the fourteenth century, to adorn the plaster. The choir stalls, in part the oldest wooden choir-fittings left in this country, also escaped destruction; and 'wild zeal' spent itself on so-called 'popish innovations', the Laudian rails and velvet altar-cloth, and the removal of the holy table. Part of the building was used as an ale-house, and saw-pits were dug in it, where the city joiners framed great beams for timbered houses like some of those in the High Street.

Nothing of St. William's Shrine remains, except a slab of Purbeck marble, which for many years lay upside-down in the transept floor, and is now set up on posts in St. John Baptist's

Chapel. Rochester, like Canterbury, had its box of bones found just under the pavement in the crypt.

II

The monastic buildings here are difficult to reconstruct, and with good reason. Bishop Gundulf made the earliest, about 1082, after replacing the secular priests of St. Andrew's by sixty Benedictine monks. He erected his church walls parallel to the wall of Roman Rochester, which left him little room on the usual site, south of the nave for the cloister, and obliged him to place it south of the presbytery, where the space was less confined. Bishop Ernulf built a dorter, chapter-house and frater, forming two sides of a new cloister, still farther east than Gundulf's, and used the Roman wall as a party wall between cloister and frater. The cloister occupied this same site until the suppression in 1558, when it was adapted for a royal residence, while the new cathedral body housed themselves elsewhere. The King's Lodgings occupied the old dorter : in one of the windows the arms of Katherine Howard were set, and then as quickly removed. The monks' refectory became a great banqueting-hall. No trace now remains of the adapted building; long before the alterations were complete it was granted to Lord Cobham, who left it at his death back to the Dean and Chapter.

Before the end of the sixteenth century ' a clean sweep had been made of almost everything in and about the cloister and the area of it had been subdivided . . . into gardens '.

South of the city wall lay the Monks' vineyard. St. Augustine's of Canterbury also had its vines, in a place cleared of the thickets which had harboured robbers. The wines of Rochester were perhaps the more renowned. They were thought worthy to fill a king's goblet; Bishop Hamo de Hethe offered a draught to King Edward II. And the bishops' tenants are known to have placed at their disposal large quantities of blackberries, the gipsy's grape, to colour the episcopal vintage.

When the sixteenth century began the monks were still occupying their cloister and dining in St. Andrew's Hall. A surgeon of the town, Richard Qwyke, buried in 1501 in the cathedral, before St. Ursula's image under a 'marbyl stone', provided for the greater comfort and decency of their meals. He left 'to the gentylmen's table in the hall, to wash daily therein, a bason of laton, and an ewer with a rose in the middle'; as also 'three sylver spones, an ownce of broken sylver and iiis in money *to make the spones in the fratrie an honest dosyn*'. What odd little tale, what perennial joke it may be, lay behind this quaint provision?

III

Medieval travellers to Canterbury might ford the little Stour by a timber foot-bridge. Travellers to Rochester had the broad Medway to negotiate before they could pass along the High Street to St. William's Gate. The ferry of Roman times was early supplanted by a wooden bridge 'over against Strood hospital'. The force of the tidal waters being so great and the passage of such vital import, elaborate provision was made to ensure repair of the bridge. Pier by pier, plank by plank, it was apportioned out between the King himself and his villages of the Medway valley and the overshadowing hills.

'These shall repair the bridge at Rochester whenever it is broken; and let it be observed that all the beams which are placed in this bridge ought to be of large dimensions that they may well support the planks and the great weight of all those things that pass over them.'

This bridge was about ten feet wide; it had a wooden tower of defence, 'built with marvellous skill', probably near the east end. The view of it from Frindsbury height, when the basin was crowded with sailing-craft, the air clear of smoke, the hills green behind Chatham, is delightful to think upon.

In 1281, after a great frost, the bridge was ruined by ice-floes sweeping against the piers; and it continued ruinous till Edward III (1344) wished to march his troops across it on their way to the French wars.  The laden wagons and the tramping feet during his campaigns overstrained the old wooden erection. About 1387 the first stone bridge was begun, finished under Richard II, and in use till 1850.  The bridge builder was Sir Robert Knolles, who rose from 'a common souldiour to a most commendable Capitaine'.  Lambarde says that he built his bridge with the spoils of towns, castles and churches, which he burnt and destroyed ' in such wise . . . that long after in memorie of his acte the sharpe points and Gable-ends of over-thrown Houses and Minsters were called Knolles Miters '.  At least what he spoiled in one place he spent in another; but it brought little comfort to ravished France that out of her sorrows arose this fair bridge across the English Medway.

The new stone bridge, with eleven arches and solid piers, was more than a hundred feet longer than the old; the expense of maintenance was heavier : a plank here, and there a stout beam, no longer sufficed.  It crossed the river forty yards higher up stream, and so was out of line with the High Streets of Rochester and Strood at either end.  This defect was remedied when the next bridge, a cast-iron successor of wood and stone, was erected in 1856.  The last to bridle the Medway with a bridle of steel is still a very young bridge, dating only from May 1914.  Dr. Plot of Borden, who collected 'rarities ' like all good eighteenth-century antiquaries, sent a very ' rare ' tale to Dr. Charlett of University College, Oxford, about the Medway reach at this place.  He declared that, as medicine for a mad dog's bite, Dr. Maximilian de l'Angle, Prebendary of Canterbury, his wife and daughter were all 'dipt in salt water, a little below the bridge . . . last Friday morning, by two fellows of this town, the spectators . . . being very numerous '. It was August weather, but Dr. Plot was incredulous.  ' That the Rev. Dr. was really mad,' he slyly adds, ' I hope you will not doubt; but whether the medecine had its due effect I guess I shall hear by the time I reach Canterbury. . . .'

### IV

John Fisher was the last Bishop of Rochester to make a home in the palace which Bishop Lowe had built opposite the cloister gateway. About 1524, when Fisher's ill-health was causing his friend Erasmus the utmost concern, 'I shrewdly suspect', he wrote, 'that the state of your health principally depends upon your situation. . . . The near approach of the tide, as well as the mud . . . exposed at every reflux of the water, renders the climate severe and unwholesome. Your library too is composed of thin walls, which let in through the crevices a subtile, and . . . strained air . . . highly prejudicial to . . . tender constitutions. . . . I could not live in such a place three hours without being sick. I would rather choose a chamber · . . . well floored with wood and wainscoted, for the exhalations . . . from a brick pavement must needs be very pernicious.' The library which was Fisher's 'very paradise', had a great reputation in spite of porous walls and damp brick floor. There were two long galleries full of books, each one sorted into its own niche. When Fisher had died on Tower Hill and by Margaret Roper's efforts his body lay in the Chapel of St. Peter ad Vincula, his books were seized and packed into thirty great 'fats', or pipes, and the rest scattered and spoiled.

The monks' books had perhaps been kept in an 'armarium' under the vestry, entered from the cloister through a traceried archway now converted into a window. They too were dispersed after 1538, and some ninety volumes, marked 'Liber de Claustro Roffensi', are now in the British Museum. The most famous of Rochester manuscripts, the *Textus Roffensis*, comprising the monastery's earliest records, had incredible adventures. One borrower, Dr. Harris the historian, needed it for his book on Kent, and had it packed off to London by water.

There was a shipwreck, and the *Textus* lay immersed fo
hours in Thames mud, and was with difficulty rescued.
William and Elizabeth Elstob, the Saxonists, had a ' delicate '
transcript made, by a ten-year-old page-boy of theirs called
James Smith, who ' imitated the Saxon and other antique
hands to a wonder '. Elizabeth seems also to have made a
copy in her fine script, which she placed, unbeknownst, in
Lord Treasurer Harley's library.

v

Rochester Pageant, in June 1931, stands high among the
many pageants by which of late years the dwellers in historic
places have given their civic glories artistic expression. It
owed much to a marvellous setting on the spaces of green turf
before Corboil's splendid castle. I have the book of words on
my shelf and would not lightly part with the pleasure it recalls.
There was the fanciful prologue, where the Spirit of Rochester,
in stone-grey diaphanous gown,

> On her head a high embattled crown,

passed with her train, the ethereal hours, colours voices,
emotions of an unforgotten past. We spectators attended at
the City's foundation; entered her gates with Ethelbert, Augustine and Bishop Justus; chanted at the dedication of St.
Andrew's nave; with Geoffrey Chaucer crossed over Rochester
Bridge; watched with Elizabeth and Mr. Richard Watts the
masque of Medway's Spousals; and with a happy crowd tossed
flowers along the Merry Monarch's path. I remember as if it
were yesterday the floating out of gauzy scarves, the tossing of
plume and banner in the breezes at play that summer afternoon. I remember the silver flight of the castle pigeons, un-
rehearsed, across the sky. The people of Rochester created
their pageant and played it out : high and low, rich and poor
took part. ' What becomes of any profits that are made ? ' a

townswoman was asked, as she described the joy of it all, the unity it had brought about. 'We shall use it to advertise our city,' she said quietly. 'People do not know Rochester as it deserves. They just pass by it, on their way to Canterbury.' And as she spoke Bishop Laurence seemed to stand beside her, pointing at St. William's Shrine.

The pageant's climax came perhaps in the final episode. At the centre of the green plain sits a tiny figure in an arm-chair, Charles Dickens, genius of Rochester. Presently the stage is peopled with those other citizens born of his fancy to the place. There are Datchery and the Deputy and Jasper from Edwin Drood; David Copperfield and the Chatham second-hand clothes dealer. You will remember how David opened that interview:

'I wanted to know,' trembling, 'if you would buy a jacket.'

'Oh, let's see the jacket! Oh, my heart on fire, show the jacket to us! Oh, my eyes and limbs, bring the jacket out! Oh! how much for the jacket? Oh—goroo—how much for the jacket?'

'Half-a-crown.'

'Oh, my lungs and liver, no! Oh, my eyes, no! Oh, my limbs, no! Eighteenpence, goroo!'

And now the Micawbers arrive on our green stage; surely there is an opening for a man of Mr. Micawber's talent in the Medway coal trade. Next a real coach drives up, with Pickwick, Tupman, Snodgrass, Winkle and Jingle seated inside. And that famous bit of dialogue between Dickens and the little boy he once was, that also finds an echo.

He is driving along the road to Canterbury, you will remember, when there crosses it a vision of his former self.

'It was midway between Gravesend and Rochester and the widening river was bearing the ships, white-sailed or black-smoked, out to sea, when I noticed by the wayside a very queer small boy . . . I took him up in a moment and went on. Presently the very queer small boy says, "This is Gadshill we are coming to, where Falstaff went out to rob those travellers and ran away." '

And then Dickens confides to his readers how a small-boyish ambition fulfilled brought joy into his life.

' Do let us stop at the top of the hill and look at the house there, if you please! '

' You admire that house? ' said I.

' Bless you, sir,' said the very queer small boy. " When I was not more than half as old as nine, it used to be a treat for me to be brought to look at it. And ever since I can recollect, my father, seeing me so fond of it, has often said to me, If you were to be very persevering and were to work hard, you might some day come to live in it! Though that's impossible! " said the very queer small boy, drawing a low breath.'

That ' noble fancy ', Falstaff's marching orders, Dickens hung up, illuminated and framed, on the first-floor landing, when he was master of Gadshill : ' My lads, my lads, to-morrow morning by four o'clock, early at Gadshill! There are pilgrims going to Canterbury with rich offerings, and traders riding to London with fat purses. I have vizards for you all : you have horses for yourselves.'

The house was built in 1780 by one Stevens, an ostler who married mine host's widow and became a brewer and ' mare ' of Rochester. The novelist bought the place, meaning to improve and relet it, but he grew so fond of it—deep-set as it was in his childish consciousness—that in 1860 he made it his home. Originally it had been ' a plain two-storey brick-built country house, with a bell-turret on the roof, and . . . a quaint neat wooden porch with pillars and seats '. Dickens built on a drawing-room, and dug a passage under the road to the Shrubbery. In a Swiss chalet sent by a friend and re-erected among the trees, he worked during the summer, while the five mirrors hung around the walls refracted ' the leaves quivering at the windows and the great fields of waving corn and the sail-dotted river '. ' My room,' he added, ' is up among the branches of the trees, and the birds and the butterflies fly in and out . . . and the lights and shadows of the clouds come and go with the rest of the company.'

When his friends, from England and America, came to visit him he rushed them about, picnicking amongst cherry-orchards and hop-gardens, or sightseeing at Canterbury.

'They saw', he wrote of Longfellow's visit with his wife, 'all the neighbouring country that could be shown in so short a time. I turned out a couple of postilions in the old red jackets of the old red royal Dover road for our ride, and it was like a holiday ride in England fifty years ago.'

Dickens was a walker of the old-fashioned sort; he thought the seven miles between Maidstone and Rochester some of the most beautiful scenery in England. Near or far, the Satis House of Mr. Richard Watts, the Six Poor Travellers' Alms-house; Cobham's and Pickwick's Leather Bottel; or, away among the marshes, the dozen small tombstones in Cooling churchyard, reached from Higham across stubble fields; all these things belong to him as inseparably as they belong to Rochester and its country-side. For ten zestful years he was identified with Rochester. On June 6th 1870 for the last time he 'walked with his letters' into the city. The last page he ever wrote, before that broken conclusion of Edwin Drood, describes the old town on a brilliant morning: 'Changes of glorious light from moving boughs, songs of birds, scents from gardens, woods and fields . . . penetrate into the Cathedral, subdue its earthly odour and preach the Resurrection and the Life. The cold stone tombs of centuries ago grow warm; and flecks of brightness dart into the sternest marble corners of the building fluttering there like wings.'

When, three days later, he lay dying, he wished to rest in the little graveyard at the foot of the castle wall, or at Chatham or Shorne. All these were closed, and so, as the nation wished, he was buried in Westminster Abbey.

## VI

When the nineteenth century began, save for the numerous 'machines' passing along the High Street between Dover and London, Rochester was a country town, no more than 'agreeably populous', with rural walks on the Medway bank; the greatest excitements it could offer its genteel residents were assembly- and coffee-rooms and a circulating library. In 1830, despite its situation 'on one of the finest rivers in Europe', a local historian declares, 'it does not appear that it ever enjoyed the benefit of any manufacture'.

Dickens's Rochester of the nightingale and unclouded skies evidently altered rapidly in the years immediately following his death. When Dean Hole penned his popular *Book about Roses* at the end of the nineteenth century (a twenty-second impression dated 1905 lies before me), the Deanery by the main street was 'in proximity to countless chimneys, long and short, polluting the atmosphere, discolouring the flowers and accompanied from time to time by an offensive odour of cement'. Even in such surroundings that 'brave brother of the Rose' succeeded, with infinite pains and liberal manure, in producing abundance of beautiful roses.

### CHATHAM AND NEIGHBOURING PLACES

#### I

Chatham Dockyard goes back to the days of Queen Bess and the menace of Spain, when it was the source of much national pride and complacency. On the Queen's visit in 1573, Camden declared that it was 'the best appointed arsenal the sun ever saw'. It stood on the site afterwards called the Ordnance Wharf or Old Dock. Charles I enlarged the area, made storehouses and new docks, into which ships could float with the tide. Charles II, soon after the Restoration, visited his new

warship, the *Royal Sovereign*. Then came that terrible blow
to English prestige, de Ruyter's attack on the Medway, which
filled Pepys's heart with rage, though never with despair. He
was constantly at Chatham, on business of 'the Chest', the
benevolent fund founded by Drake and Frobisher for neces-
sitous seamen. Sometimes he dined with the officers, inspected
a new gun, 'the best of all devices I ever saw, and very serviceable, and not a bauble', or took a look round the yard. No
detail escaped that critical scrutiny. In October 1665 he surveyed in company with Commissioner Pett; 'and among other
things a team of four horses came close by us . . . drawing
a piece of timber that I am confident one man could easily have
carried upon his back. I made the horses be taken away and
a man or two to take the timber away with their hands.'

How invaluable he would have been to-day on a commission
for National Economy!

In the eighteenth century the Dockyard, a 'splendid and
commodious place', extended for a mile along the south-east
side of the river. Some day, when vessels, driven by electricity
or other yet undiscovered force, are building there, to be
manned perhaps by an international naval police, our sons will
read of its activities in 1933 as curiously as we read Denne's
description of 1772 : 'Spacious storehouses (one of which is
660 feet in length) . . . manifest their prodigious contents.
. . . In the magazines are deposited amazing quantities of
sails, rigging, hemp, flax, pitch, tar, rosin, oil and every in-
gredient necessary for the equipping of ships. . . . In this yard
are four deep and wide docks, for docking and repairing large
ships; the *Victory* was built in one . . . the largest ship in the
universe carrying 110 guns.'

Has any poem or anthology in prose or verse been made, I
wonder, of the ghost-ships lying in the Medway which a lover
of sail and spar might hail from the quay? Elizabeth's ships,
whose names Lambarde set out like a proud chorus to his
praises of the arsenal; the *White Beare, Merhonora, Garlande*,

*Rainbowe*, *Swallow*, *Foresight*, *Quittance*, and *Tramontane*.
The ships in which Charles put his trust, till de Ruyter sent
them up in flame, chiefly the *Royal Oak* fiercely burning, and
its captain who would not save himself. ' It was never known ',
said that intrepid Highlander, 'that a Douglas left his post
without orders.' The *Victory* of course is there; Andersen the
Danish historian saw it at daybreak, 'a most beautiful but
small vessel of her class : she carries 110 guns and is upwards
of forty years old; yet in point of strength, she is probably a
new vessel. Her stern is very elegant, and built in a style of
great simplicity. . . . Her head . . . displays His Majesty's
arms, tastefully emblazoned and supported by angels. She was
at that time painted in checker, which gives a most tremendous
appearance to men of war when at sea.' On that same journey
to Chatham in a Sheerness passage boat, under a moonlit sky,
Andersen had seen the *Leyden* of sixty guns lying in Long
Reach. Suddenly her bell struck on board and men's voices
proclaimed, ' All's Well.' ' The harmony of this midnight
chorus ', he wrote, ' rent the solemn air; a tremor pierced my
soul and a sigh escaped, succeeded by the wish that " All's
well " might be heard without terror in every part of the
world.'

II

As the train dives in and out through the tunnels between
Chatham and Gillingham one catches brief glimpses of the
close-packed ' skin ' of brown dwellings and steeply mounting
streets drawn over the surrounding hills. What a splendid bit
of downland scenery, climbing up from the Medway brim, this
must once have been. Building began with the enlargement of
the Dockyard. About 1635 people were flocking into Chatham
parish, and there came the first enlargement of the old church
and the erection of a steeple. The whole ' village of Brompton '
was built between 1695 and 1772; ' near four hundred houses
erected on this pleasant ascent within the memory of persons

living'. The first house in the new village was an inn, called 'The Sun in the Wood'—the fast-vanishing wood.

Dickens's earliest youth, between four and nine, belongs rather to Chatham than to Rochester. His father was a clerk in the Dockyard, and his home a whitewashed plaster-fronted house in St. Mary's Place, once known as the Brook. With his sister Fanny the small Charles attended a day-school for little boys and girls, over a dyer's shop in Rome Place. He remembered the 'puffy pug-dog' in the narrow entry, which snapped at the scholars' bare legs and grinned with moist black muzzle and white teeth. At seven years old this school was exchanged for one in Clover Lane, where his master was a young Baptist minister, Mr. William Giles. A railway-station eventually swallowed up the school play-field, hawthorn-trees and buttercup turf. Nothing could take from Chatham the glory of having been 'the birthplace of Dickens's fancy'. There he learned to know certain famous books, which, like David Copperfield, he read over and over again. There too the variety of the changing scene impressed his child's mind: 'the gay bright regiments always going and coming . . . the sham sieges, the plays in the Ordnance-hospital, the ships floating out in the Medway'.

That modern tale of Chatham and Rochester, *The Mystery of Angelina Frood*, lends them no glamour but that which hangs about the detective and his quarry. The scene-painting is realistic, to the point of squalor; it has its muddy foreshores, haunted with odours indescribable; turbid water eddying between the barges; little alleys bordered by ruinous timber houses; children who play around rubbish-heaps and dabble in grey slime. Chatham High Street, adjacent to the Medway, presents 'a feature characteristic of old riverside towns, in the multitude of communications between street and shore. Some of these are undisguised entrances to wharves; some are . . . small thoroughfares lined with houses and leading to landing-stages; while others are mere passages or flights of steps,

opening . . . inconspicuously on the street . . . suggesting the
burrows of some human water-rat.' In this warren and along
those shores Dr. Strangeways and Bundy the body-snatcher
track down vestiges of the missing Angelina Frood. They
find a hand-bag, a coat-button, a shoe. Others had searched
those purlieus before them—for traces of Edwin Drood : 'All
the livelong day that search went on; upon the river, with
barge and pole and drag and net; upon the muddy and rushy
shore, with jack-boots, hatchet, spade, rope, dogs and all
imaginable appliances. Even at night the river was specked
with lanterns and lurid with fires; far-off creeks . . . had their
knots of watchers, listening to the lapping of the stream and
looking out for any burden it might bear. . . .' And at the
Weir, two miles away, Mr. Crisparkle dived into the icy water
to bring up a gold watch and chain. Mystery it seems cannot
keep away from Medway-side; coincidence haunts its muddy
creeks. Angelina's reached a complete solution; for Edwin
Drood's an unfinished sentence was the inevitable close.


### III

Towards the end of the fourteenth century the Beaufitz
family came from Acton in Charing to occupy Twydall Manor
between Gillingham and Rainham. The first Beaufitz was
buried in Gillingham chancel in 1380, the last, William Beaufitz, in November 1433. In half a century the family adorned
St. Mary's Church with a series of memorial windows among
the most extensive and most beautiful in the county. They
certainly survived the Reformation, but whether their destruction lies at the door of the sectaries, or of time and neglect
alone, is hard to say. A serviceable parish clerk, Baptist
Tufton, a model for his order, wrote in 1621 a description of
the church monuments under his care, and especially of nine
windows, wholly or partially filled with 'pictures'. The
general scheme required a scene from Holy Writ in the upper

part of the light, and beneath 'a lyvely pourtraiture' of the donor, with coats of arms, especially the bend with three bells of the Beaufitz shield. Thus the first window contained the Blessed Virgin enthroned, with the Holy Child, and a picture of Robert Beaufitz. The second depicted the Magi, the manger at Bethlehem, 'John Beaufitz, the younger, esquier, with a garland of roses upon his head'. In another window the figure of St. John Baptist, with various panels of Herod and Herodias, was paired with 'St. Christopher, carrying Christe upon his shoulder over a great water, his staffe in the meane tyme flourishing with leaves and flowers'.

There was a splendid Ancient of Days, like that on the Black Prince's tester; a St. James carrying pilgrim's hat and staff; St. Agnes with fair locks hanging about her, St. Cecily with rose garlands. . . .

IV

To return for a moment to Strangeways and Angelina Frood. Both have the Dickensian characteristic of being great walkers. This feature is less inevitable in detective stories than the use of the telephone and the swift car. The doctor visits the Poor Travellers' house, and the cathedral, where he meets Dr. Jervis, just as Datchery encountered the Princess Puffer; he tramps along the London road to Gad's Hill, stopping on Rochester Bridge, 'to watch a barge . . . just passed under and . . . rehoisting her lowered mast'. The heroine follows Watling Street as far as Cobham, and wanders freely about Chatham and Gillingham. Rochester she avoids for fear of making acquaintances; we, who by this time have made acquaintance enough, old and new, may now climb the hill, as she did, from Strood towards Frindsbury Church.

Lambarde calls the place Frendsbury, and adds that in some Saxon documents the name is 'Freondesbyrig, or Friends' Court', a pleasant if doubtful bit of etymology. The best-authenticated legend of Frindsbury is belligerent as well can

be.  Once upon a time the neighbourhood suffered severely
from drought; the public-spirited monks of St. Andrew's
agreed to the exertion of a processional march to Frindsbury
heights to pray for rain.  This was doubly magnanimous since,
without the march, the weather-wise might have discerned
symptoms of a falling glass.  Here is Lambarde, vivid and
picturesque as ever : 'Because the day of . . . their appointed
iorney, happened to be vehemently boisterous with the winde,
the which would not onely have blowne out their lightes and
tossed their banners, but also have stopped the mouthes of their
Synging-men, and have toiled themselves in that their heavie
and masking attire; they desired lycence of the Maister of
Stroud Hospitall to passe through the Orchyarde of his house,
whereby they might . . . save the glorie of their shewe; which
otherwise through the iniure of the weather, must needs have
been greatly blemished.'

On they went through the sheltered orchard, 'merily chant-
ing their latine Letanie '.  Unluckily the master had allowed
their passage without first consulting his brethren.  To show
their resentment these pleasant gentlemen hired a company of
ribalds from the villages who fell suddenly upon the visitors
unsuspicious of anything more unkindly than wind and
weather.  The monks put up a stalwart fight.  Some used the
staves of their crosses, others made pikes of their banner-poles.
One drove a brother of Strood into a deep ditch; one, ' as big
as any Bull of Basan, espied at the length the posterne of the
Orchyarde, whereat he ran so vehemently with his head and
shoulders that he bare it cleane down before him, and so . . .
made the way for the rest of his fellowes . . .' who, shaking
their ears, fell afresh to their orisons.  Thus the rain came; but
the monks compelled the men of Frindsbury, for ever after,
to bring their clubs to Rochester on Whit-Monday as a penance.
And on May Day the boys of Rochester and Strood, for excellent but forgotten reasons, skirmished upon Rochester Bridge.

The situation of Frindsbury Church high on a cliff above

the Medway is magnificent. A lime avenue approaches it from
the main street, where village and suburban life struggle together; here and there a cottage stands up in a summer riot of
snapdragons, as if to keep change at bay with a rampart of
flowers. From the public garden on the cliff panoramas confront you of Rochester and the Medway basin. The bridge
spans the river, and from a huddle of houses on the south shore
rise the castle and the pointed cathedral spire. Little bundles
of verdure are packed in among the brown roofs. The curve
of the Downs embraces row upon row of little slate-roofed
dwellings, reaching ever farther back into 'hither green'
meadows. Opposite, on the north shore, long roads wind up
the hills, hurrying away from the crowded riverside quarter.
Along the Medway margin, barges lie in rows with sails
furled, or they float on her broad stream with brown wings
outspread; and in their company are tugs with sloping funnels
or gaily painted steamers. South-west of the church cement
factories whitened with dust have encamped their chimneys tall
and short, and there are gas-drums and unsightly hollows of
worked-out chalk-pits. The river rounds into the southern
promontory, so hurriedly occupied that forgotten interspaces
of rough greenery still flourish, and elder-bushes blossom and
fruit. Behind All Saints' Church something remotely like a
lane travels back into the chalk-hills. There are rose-cupped
convolvuli on the road margin, and the scent of pinks in some
allotment-garden floats over the hedge.

v

Topographers concur in choosing the most deterrent adjec-
tives to describe the 'dreary, depressing, unattractive, featureless' peninsula between Thames and Medway, with the Isle
of Grain at its toe. The Hoo's, St. Werburgh, All Hallows,
and St. Mary are 'devoid of interest', though St. Werburgh
Church is allowed 'an imposing exterior' and its tower is a

landmark to sailors on the Medway. Yet there are redeeming features; the historian of ancient manors at least finds rich material for his studies. To begin with, after leaving Frindsbury there is Upnor Castle, which Queen Elizabeth constructed in 1560 to defend her dockyard. When Hasted wrote, for many years ' there had not been a gun mounted in it for service, nor yet a platform '. From a military standpoint it was as derelict as the other forts of its command, which guarded creek and marsh and are now forgotten; the Swamp or Birds-nest, where ' the embrasures of earth long since mouldered away '; Cockham Wood Fort, 'with all the guns . . . thrown by on the ground'; Hooness Fort or the Folly. Let us pass to the problem of Wainscot, a hamlet farther east along the main road. It had an alternative description, ' Parlabiens' Yoke ', from the Parlabien family, owners under Edward II, who passed the manor on to the Colepepers of Aylesford. The *Oxford Dictionary* says the substantive Wainscot probably derives from ' wagon-schot ', as applied to foreign oak used for fine panelwork, which came into England in the mid-fourteenth century, The earliest example they give is dated 1353. The Fabric Rolls of Rochester Castle relate that in 1367 John Pomfret provided 400 ' estrichbords called Wainscot' for interior decoration at twenty-six shillings a hundred. What is the connexion, if any, between Wainscot Manor, alias Parlabiens' Yoke, and the importation of foreign oak? Were the Parlabiens overseas merchants, and did their manor godfather the oak? It is a pretty problem, though a simple solution may be known to my readers. Away north from Wainscot is Cliffe-at-Hoo, with a noble church dedicated to St. Helen, mother of Constantine the Great. Cliffe is supposed to be the Saxon ' Cloveshoo ', where seven great councils were held between 742 and 824, and notable canons drawn up for better church government. Through a rude doorway still traceable in the north wall of the north chapel the councillors may even have passed from prayer to debate. Most attractive fragments of stained glass are in the north aisle, the Mother with her Holy Child, wearing a little red robe, and a golden ship, floating on waves where slender fishes swim to and fro. The ship carries a golden pennon and thick golden cables, and over the stern is an ark-like deck-cabin.

Cowling or Cooling Castle—was it really 'so-called from its bleak situation'—is another of the melancholy promontory's attractions. The gatehouse with two forty-foot towers, the great curtain-wall and moat are evidence of a brave man's desire to protect his country-side against the ravages of Frenchman and Spaniard. John de Cobham thus fortified his manor-house in 1380, and to make his intention plain, he affixed to the eastern tower a tablet in enamelled copper, imitating a charter, black-lettered on a white ground, with coloured seal and cord. The English inscription bears the testimony of Cowling Castle to succeeding generations :

> Knowyth that beeth and schal be
> That I am mad in help of the cuntre;
> In knowyng of whyche thyng
> Thys is chartre and wytnessyng.

John de Cobham's granddaughter, Joan, married Sir John Oldcastle, the Lollard leader, as her third husband and to Cowling Castle Archbishop Arundel 'sent forth his chief summoner with a very sharp citation'; but he dared not enter the gates to confront so noble a man. Sir Thomas Wyatt took the castle by assault during the short-lived success of his rebellion in 1554.

Out of a perverse wish to 'find beauty in an undesired face', I determined to visit the Isle of Grain, 'the dreariest parish in Kent'. An omnibus from Hoo robs the expedition of wild adventure, and follows a pleasant uphill road between orchards with glimpses of the river-barges. The road, much winding, next passes Upper and Lower Stoke and their church with low, unfinished tower, befitting such a windswept place. After Stoke the country grows more bare; fewer elms stand in the hedgerows. Fields of blue-grey mangels and of cut corn slope to a belt of unmistakable marshland. Into these creeks the salt water floods up with every tide. Here is the broken barrier, 'the Stray', which separates the Isle of Grain from the Hundred of Hoo. The northern mouth next the Thames is called the Yenlet, the same old English name as Genlade of the Thanet strait. The Medway entrance is the Colemouth; it passes through salt-marshes where salt-works used to occupy the islanders.

'The Isle of Grain', says Hasted, 'lies very flat and low; the greatest part of it consists of pasture and marshes; the vast tracts of marsh and the bad water make it very unwholesome.' But as I followed the road along its backbone Grain seemed to me to justify its name; it really was a granary of an island; abundant cornfields reappeared and stretched almost to where St. James's Church stands by the meeting-place of Thames and Medway. Nowadays a huge petroleum station has squatted on the marsh, and a colony of people live around it in green huts. It must be very bleak in winter, but to-day the soft colours, the fresh, strong airs make it hard to credit one is in so dismal a locality. The motor-bus has helped to bring it release from perdition; before me lies the picture of a pleasant sea-shore, with paddling children and little rowboats, labelled 'Medway Beach, Isle of Grain'. Grain is three and a half miles long by two and a half wide. There are fragments of history in its garners. Ralph de Wydegate once presented the nuns of Davington with twelve shillings and two geese of annual rent in the island; but it had a more ancient title to fame. In exchange for the coveted manor of Lambeth on Thames-side Archbishop Baldwin gave to the Monks of Rochester a sheep-walk in the 'Isle of Gren', on the north side of Medway.

### OLD MAIDSTONE

#### I

The genius of Maidstone of Mid-Kent is quite other than Canterbury's of the East. It is the busy town of the merchant, the craftsman, the master of the laden hoy. Churchmen indeed gave it the buildings which are its pride; All Saints' Church of Simon Islip, the palace, the college of Archbishop Courtenay; but the arbiter of its destiny has been 'the great ryver called Medeway water'. For its river the place was named; it is 'Medwegestun'—Medway's town—the form found in Saxon documents. The mysterious maid or maids came quickly enough on the scene; Medway's name slurred on the lips of familiar friends, led strangers, like the *Domesday* surveyors, to mistake it for 'Maegdestane'—Maidstone, in fact; the Law Repors of Edward I spell it so—'Maydenstan'. On the silver seal of the Corporation stands, precariously, a long-haired maid 'naked, on a spherical stone, holding in her right hand a stone ball, and in her left a branch'.

Labouring folk for the most part made the town what it is. More than five centuries ago it was stirred up to share in the Peasants' Rising, that tragic awakening of the English craftsman from his long servitude.

The historian Fuller, who held the 'clerkly' view that 'this rabble of Rebells . . . endeavoured the rooting out of all penknives and all appearance of learning', was at pains to rhyme into English John Gower's mocking summons to the flag of revolt. Gower had a conviction that times were disjointed, though scant sympathy with the peasant. And yet, if the vanished paintings on his tomb in Southwark Cathedral were indeed—as is averred—figures of Charity, Mercy, and Pity, intended to symbolize each one volume of his works, then Love must belong to the *Confessio Amantis*; and Mercy, God's mercy for the sinful soul, to the lost *Speculum Meditantis*; but

Pity remains the appropriate symbol of his *Vox Clamantis*, the voice of one that crieth in a distracted world. Here begins Fuller's version of that ragged roll-call of Kentish men, and women too :

> Tom comes thereat when called by Wat, and Simm as forward we finde
>
> Bet calls as quick to Gibb and to Hykk that neither would tarry behinde;
>
> Gibb, a good whelp of that litter, doth help mad Coll more mischief to do;
>
> And Will he doth vow the time is come now, he'l joyn with their company too . . .

' Men without sir-names,' comments the translator, ' so obscure they were, and inconsiderable.'

On that June day 1381 Wat and Gibb and Larkin slew the grazing beasts in Sudbury's park, and released the prisoners, John Ball among them, from the archbishop's prison at Maidstone. But their struggle brought no paradise on earth; within seventy years rebellion again raised its head—this time the better sort, the gentry, with the mayors of Kent towns, found a leader in the Irishman Jack Cade—'John Mortimer' so called—who signalled a general rising near Ashford on the 24th of May. Many a Maidstone trader followed him, whether or not he rode through the town as through London streets, carrying a naked sword, with a gilt helmet and gown of blue velvet, ' as he hadde be a lord or a knyght, and yit was he but a knave '.

Maidstone was pardoned for this outburst, and the rank and file of Cade's followers were condoned. So for a century the land had rest, till Sir Thomas Wyatt came along in 1554 from Alington Castle, where his poet-father lived, calling for stout arms to place ' Queen Jane ' on the throne. A local schoolmaster, John Proctor, was so concerned about ' the notable infamy sprung of this Rebellion to the whole county of Kent ' that he made diligent investigation, hoping to justify the loyal subjects of Queen Mary. From his pages we learn what happened in Maidstone market-place that January day, after Wyatt had ridden in, with many another gentleman of Kent. Amid rounds of applause he unrolled his parchment and in a great voice gave out his proclamation. It 'so wrought in the hearts of the people that divers (which before hated him and he them) were now . . . mutually reconciled; and said unto him "Sir, is your quarrel only . . . to advance Liberty; and not against the Queen?" "No," quod Wyat, "we mind nothing less than anywise to touch her Grace; but to serve her and honour her, according to our duties." "Well," quod they, "give us then your hand. We will stick to you to death in this quarrel."' The tide of insurrection then flowed away from Maidstone to other Kent towns, till the day so few weeks later when Wyatt's adherents returned where his standard was first displayed, to suffer death on confession of treason.

## II

Queen Elizabeth gave the townsmen of Maidstone the liberties of Medway water from East Farleigh Bridge downstream to 'Hawkewood beneath Burham Barne'. Yearly in summer-time the mayor and a little company of four jurats and six freeholders passed along the reach to claim their privileges. In June 1621 the river was so low the party must needs turn back at Gernans Forstall; 'and for want of water, being lett to passe further, did returne and passe fishing'. The expedition was a pleasant picnic: boats laden with men and women accompanied the officials; there was a cheerful supper in an ordinary at a shilling a head; and the Chamber stood wine and music; except that 'a competent some (sum)—6s. 8d.—was collected for the Musicians'. Fishing rights in the river were sternly guarded. No one might fish with a net between 'Colledge bredge and Caryng Style', unless the mayor or his deputy were present—what leisure on their parts is implied!

The mayor's perquisites were certain profits, from oysters and
'Risshes'; the Corporation kept swans within their liberty,
used their own swan-mark and appropriated masterless white
swans.

### III

Camden, towards the end of the seventeenth century, describes Maidstone as a 'neat and populous town stretched out
into a great length'. It straggled up on to the hill-sides, and
the 'high towne' must have been, as it is to-day, the pleasantest
quarter. Perhaps it was there Camden gained his impression
of neatness; it is hard to reconcile the epithet with the condition of the old riverside lanes. Poor folk were preponderant
in a population of two to three thousand; to eke out meagre
incomes they kept hordes of pigs, which roamed the streets by
day, and at night shared their owner's abode. Attempts were
made to cleanse the town; pray do not overlook them. A
householder threw his pailful of two gallons of water into
the gutter, daily at eleven, from March till September; paved
streets were tidied on a Saturday afternoon, and the rubbish
concealed in backyards—anywhere, in fact, so long as the great
river, the River Medway, was not polluted. But such futilities
were frustrated by the roving pigs, until the marauders were
officially forbidden to be abroad without a driver. The
authorities had no doubt of the salubrity of their climate:
'Forasmuche', their order ran, 'as this Towne, beinge . . .
placed in a sweete and wholesome ayer, hath greatly bene
pestered with divers infeccious and dangerous savours . . . by
occasion of the goinge and runninge of hogges and swyne in
the streets,' and so forth.

From 1544 onwards, plague was endemic in the town. It
haunted the by-ways so persistently that at one time the civic
fathers were evidently panic-stricken; they forced the old alms-
men and women to act as nurses for the plague-victims—'they
to do their true endevour . . . for the comforte, helpp, and

succour of the syck ', on pain, if they shirked the unwelcome task, of being driven from charity's shelter, their alms-houses in the town. The poor old bodies with ' the letter P. of redd and blew cloth affixt uppon the sleeve of the lefte arme ', lest next week's relief should be forfeit, had little enough of strength or skill to wrestle with the foe; the annual death-roll mounted up to forty, fifty, sixty of the townsfolk; in 1665 it was over ten per cent.

The onus of infection was always upon London; it was imported, not home-bred; borne in letters or in ' vittalls ', or in some other mysterious fashion. Accordingly in 1593 it was ordered ' that no hoye, nor foote or horse post shall during the infeccion at London, viz : until Mychaelmas next, carry or recarrie any goodes from this Towne to London . . . except the Kinges goodes ', which were, of course, germ-proof. Parcels already on their way must be opened in the fields and dried by the hoymen for fourteen days before delivery.

Yet in spite of ravaging pestilence, of a sternness that branded poverty with its P., draped the unmarried mother in a parti-coloured hood, ordained the vile whip, the hideous gallows on Penenden Heath, the town had freedom of heart enough for merriment. The King's (or Queen's) Mead, beside the river, was the ' common sporting place '. (Incidentally, the Marian martyrs burned there, and there too under George II a deserter met his fate.)

From time immemorial the Mead had been ' wholly enjoyed ' for a shooting place and for other pastimes. Shooting ' with longe bowes at prickes or rovers '—stationary or moving targets —was also allowed in Mistress Astley's Park, beyond the river. There was general indignation when carriages began to take a short-cut across the Mead and cattle were turned in to graze. Presently a space was fenced off by the chamber to make a handsome bowling-green, longbows being by now a bit out of date. The Puritans looked askance at such joys. A useful shop was erected where once the Maypole had stood and child-players, in gay frocks, had kept Queen Bess's coronation day. Two houses next intruded, though floods often threatened their foundations. At last in 1825 the common sporting place fell under Macadam's ugly spell.

IV

Before the Acts of 1628 and 1664 introduced locks and a towing-path the navigation of hoys in the Medway was difficult enough; 'the banks were broken and irregular, and . . . the movements of vessels depended entirely on the state of the tide'. But the Maidstone of Elizabeth was a little place, with a population under 3,000; in 1565 the town owned but four smallish hoys manned by crews numbering twenty-two; while four wharfs sufficed for all traffic. Under James I trade began to expand and tolls upon incoming vessels to figure in the Corporation's budget. One might make a pedigree of the successive industries of busy Maidstone from the early Stone Age to the toffee and canned soups of to-day. The first fortunes were carved out of the surrounding hills. The local stone—hardstone, or freestone, or more familiarly, ragstone, 'from its breaking in a ragged . . . manner'—was used for building peaceful homes and for destructive weapons. 'With the shot formed from rough slabs unearthed in the Medway valley,' says one writer, 'the walls of many a hostile fortress were doubtless razed and Prince Hal was enabled to triumph in the fields of France. . . . John Louth and John Bennett owned quarries here, and in 1418 . . . received an order from the Crown for seven thousand cannon balls.' The influx of strangers from the Netherlands about 1567 brought in the weaving industry, although for some two centuries already Flemings and other clothworkers had been settled in the Weald. The immigrants took kindly to Maidstone, and the Corporation allotted St. Faith's Chapel for their worship. The 'Doche people' made the 'grogreyn, and mockadoes' of for-

gotten fashions, 'sackclothes, wollen clothe and such lyke ware'. Surprisingly soon the trade had been 'learned and taken from the Strangers by the Kinges borne subjectes inhabitinge within the Towne'.

After the loom, the hop-garden, perhaps even prior to it, in small and unpopular beginnings; for to the Walloons under Henry VIII the import of the 'unwholesome weed called an hopp' was possibly due. Not till Charles I was the prejudice against putting 'that wicked weed' into beer, 'to make people melancholy', finally overcome. Then the hop-gardens of Maidstone began to weave rich garlands over the hill-sides. The local cloth trade was declining, and the twisting of linen thread, serviceable and many coloured, now found scope in the making of hop-bags. Flax for the thread-twisters was locally produced; Pepys, that tireless observer, has a little thumb-nail sketch of its preparation for the wheel. He visited Maidstone on March 24th 1669, 'and walked all up and down the town, and up to the top of the steeple, and had a noble view and then down again. In the town did see an old man beating of flax, and did step into the barn and give him money, and saw that piece of husbandry, which I never saw; and it is very pretty.' Can his barn have been the roomy place still standing opposite the palace, the archbishop's huge tithe barn, now an agricultural museum for ploughs that have drawn their last furrow, and outworn reaping-hooks?

v

The hop-garden found a laureate in Christopher Smart, who was born in 1722 at Shipbourne, near Tonbridge, and after his family moved to Barming attended the Grammar School in Maidstone. His descriptions, overlaid with classical bric-à-brac, do convey a sense of that 'dignified' scenery about his home; the poem has besides some small value in the history of hop-culture. There is this, for example, of the river and the Kent hills :

The Apennine
Of a free Italy, whose chalky sides
With verdant shrubs dissimilarly gay,
Still captivate the eye, while at his feet
The silver Medway glides . . .

Or this again of woods and orchards, rich furniture of the Medway Valley :

. . . Ceres there
Shines in her golden vesture . . .
. . . Nor are you
Pomona, absent; you 'midst hoary leaves
Swell the vermilion cherry; and on yon trees
Suspend the pippin's palatable gold.

So the boy-poet rambles on towards his chosen theme, the hop plant itself :

. . . select the choicest hop t'insert
Fresh in the opening glebe . . .
. . . the noblest species is by Kentish wights
The Master-hop yclep'd.  Nature to him
Has giv'n a stouter stalk, patient of cold
Or Phoebus, ev'n in youth; . . .
. . . the next
Is arid, fetid, infecund and gross
Significantly styl'd the Fryar; the last
Is call'd the Savage, who in ev'ry wood
And ev'ry hedge unintroduc'd intrudes. . . .

And thus, having planted and tended, the poet bids his hearers to the picking :

. . . yonder hill,
Where stand the loaded hop-poles, claims your care.

Already in his day local labour was supplemented by a crowd of Londoners :

See! from the great metropolis they rush,
Th'industrious vulgar.  They like prudent bees,
In Kent's wide garden roam; expert to crop
The flow'ry hop, and provident to work
Ere winter numb their sunburnt hands, and winds
Engaol them, murmuring, in their gloomy cells. . . .

O'er twice three pickers and no more extend
The bin-man's sway; unless thy ears can bear
The crack of poles continual, and thine eyes

Behold unmoved the hurrying peasant tear
Thy wealth, and throw it on the thankless ground.

So many hop-gardens have been grubbed since 1914, so many hoppers' huts stand empty, that Smart's word-pictures may some day be regarded as historical monuments of old Kent.

### TONBRIDGE AND TUNBRIDGE WELLS

#### I

To learn the opinions bygone folk have held of our own particular town or village—how it shaped to their consciousness and was well remembered—what an appeal this makes! To run one's finger down the index—but no! in the best sort of musty volume there is no index—to turn the pages leisurely until the name of Dumbledown or Cherry-cum-Merry catches the eye! . . . Tunbridge Wells is a quarry easily driven to earth; here—at random on my bookshelves—is Mrs. Montagu writing from this strange place, where 'one has neither business nor leisure, so many glasses of water are to be drank . . . so many turns on the walk to be taken . . . so much pains to be well, so much attention to be civil'. It is, she declares, the 'parliament of the world'—no less. 'Pick-pockets, come to the top of their profession, play with noble dukes at brag.'

The fame of Tonbridge, compared with its modish neighbour, became almost as tattered as its great Norman keep, which the Parliament dismantled in the Civil War. Enough of the ruins remained to 'surprise' Horace Walpole when he lay at Tonbridge town during his tour in Kent: 'The gateway is perfect, and the inclosure formed into a vineyard by a Mr. Hooker to whom it belongs, and the walls spread with fruit, and the mount on which the keep stood planted in the same way. The prospect is charming, and a breach in the wall opens below to a pretty Gothic bridge of three arches.'

It made Walpole long to add a crowning touch of romance :

' We honoured the man for his taste—not but that we wished the committee at Strawberry Hill were to sit upon it and stick cypresses among the hollows.' Mrs. Montagu, on the other hand, when she rode to Tonbridge on a milk-white steed and stole the parson's golden pippins, criticized Mr. Hooker for cutting down some fine trees 'almost co-temporary with the castle ' to make room for his vinery.

The apotheosis of the Wells came as James I's reign drew to an end. Lord North's poor young daughter, ill of ' a spotted fever akin to the plague ', was sent, all in vain, ' for the sake of the waters to Tunbridge Wells '. There speaks your contemporary letter-writer! At first the resort was but dull—so dull that my Lord of Dunluce lost to Sir John Suckling almost £2,000 at ninepins, having nothing better there to pass the time. The Parliament allowed certain prisoners like Sir Thomas Peyton and Lieutenant-General David Leslie to go to the Wells from the Tower for their health, provided they returned after fifteen days' stay. Poor captives! they might easily find it an improvement on their prison-house. Dullness was still a drawback when Queen Catherine of Braganza went there, and was exact in observing medical rules. Her ladies took the water too, as ' some diversion in that place, dull but for the company '; for the rest one may consult the Comte de Grammont's *Memoirs*. With Waller's lines, written at Penshurst, the Wells made a very early appearance in English verse. The poet reproaches his lady-love :

> . . . the rock,
> That cloven rock produced thee,[1]
> . . . by whose side
> Nature, to recompense the fatal pride
> Of such stern beauty plac'd *those healing springs*
> Which not more *help* than that *destruction* brings. . . .

## II

The art of advertisement was in its infancy. Anthony

[1] Sacharissa, that is, of the stony heart.

Hamilton said there was no more rustic place, nor a simpler, in all Europe than Tunbridge Wells; and thirty years later than the *Memoirs*, when in 1693 Metellus wrote his *Dialogue containing a Relation of a Journey to Tunbridge Wells*, the accommodation was still primitive and the amenities 'undeveloped'. The scarcity of this little book leads me to browse over its pages in your good company.

Metellus, a gentleman-commoner of Christchurch—his real name was Lewkenor—went to the Wells with four companions : Acer, 'a Divine of a sharp Wit and eloquent', incidentally a misogynist; Curio, 'a Civilian and an eloquent Man'; Laelius, 'a witty young Gentleman, but a Deist'; and Aesculape, their Physician, something of an Epicure. Metellus and Curio had little amiss with their health; they needed no other treatment 'But to take Air and then to take our ease'. The Doctor also rode, pairing off with Laelius : Acer the Divine,

> To whom Minerva still was kind
> Yet Fortune frown'd,

preferred to travel by stage-coach. Curio, sitting on a raw-boned steed and 'fierce in his riding-weed', declared that his friend was the laziest of men :

> Thou'lt bitterly repent it before Night.
> You'll meet with Company, I hope, anon,
> Will make you wish you'd been more early, Man.

His prophecy unhappily fulfilled itself.

By diverse ways the party arrived at the Wells and began to look for lodgings. To their townbred eyes the place seemed a wilderness; but there were some 'pretty houses' about, and the Doctor and the witty Laelius, who had no turn for bookish seclusion,

> an airy place
> Soon found; which airy Company did grace.

The other three, being as much in love with their own society as any 'hikers' (and one may remember they too were a post-

war generation), presently, in an outlying part of the Heath,
came upon an isolated cottage :

> The greatest Plot that was in all that wild
> And spacious Heath; and the most undefil'd. . . .
> This is the Desert then, said Acer, we
> In such a Cottage, Curio, may be free. . . .

It was certainly a 'pleasant place'; behind it a meadow;
sweet springs close at hand; a wood on one side; a cornfield
still waving green; before them the ample Heath; from every
quarter the breath of purer air than towns enjoy.

The cottage stood among ferns and shrubs, and

> . . . taller Trees were nigh.

In one of these, a well-grown ash, the owner had contrived a
bower, clearly designed for higher uses than mere shelter :

> For we, soon as we saw it, thought it fit
> In such a Solitude to shelter Wit.

In answer to their knock a tidy old dame came to the cottage
door, and said, politely enough :

> 'Las Sirs, 'tis late, and we're all going to bed.
> We see no Gallants here, nor entertain
> Such Men as you; we scarce think't worth our pain;
> Nor have I Linen clean, nor can I give
> You dainty Meats; on hardest Fare we live.

She had good reason for her reluctance; not long since ill-
fortune had come to her through entertaining well-dressed
strangers, at just such a late hour; she would take no risks.
However, our trio reassured her of their honest intentions; if
'verbal motives' could not prevail, what about a handful of
gold pieces?

> For thee, Gold, what won't Woman undertake?

The good Dame :

> Fixing her Eyes upon the golden Gift

immediately asked them inside.

This ' Sylvestrian Dame' was mother of a daughter (or

possibly daughter-in-law; the point is obscure), and of a brawny
son, a married man, and also mistress of a maid. Her cottage
larder was not ill-plenished; there was:

> A piece of Pye of Hare, her Son had caught,
> With fatter Mutton bak'd, which she had bought.

The whole family waited at table:

> They wait like Servants and they look like Friends.

Acer now related at some length his journey by coach. His
fickle goddess had unluckily,

> Damn'd him for a day into the Jaws
> Of modern Furies.

Horrible to relate, his only fellow-passengers in the vehicle
were three women: 'a Northern Lady, Madam God knows
who, Bonny and blithe; Her brisk Companion too'; together
with a scheming old maid. These all set their caps at Acer, or
so he was pleased to imagine, while the driver, who must have
many lineal descendants on the road to-day,

> . . . like a Rhadamanthus sate;
> Hurried us downward at such Devilish rate
> And uncontroulable, the Plea Hold, Hold,
> Signify'd nothing; he was hot and bold. . . .

So long a journey obliged a halt for dinner at an inn in Sevenoaks. Mine host appeared and offered the travellers a tantaliz-
ing bill of fare; but to Acer's dismay:

> Northern Madam and her Dames, afraid
> The Burden of a Dinner would be laid
> Too hard on them, who had no Gallant there,
> In Wisdom thought it safest to forbear
> Their Hunger then; cry'd, 'tis too late to eat;
> What should they do with all that greasie Meat.

The landlord is in despair; the coachman swears he must 'eat
or dy'; Acer in a hungry rage 'conjures down the host of
squeamish fairies', and orders the cloth to be laid. Before
leaving Sevenoaks they meet the 'Tunbridge Fairies', who,
like modern advertisements of a hotel or garage, begin their
importunity betimes, haunt every coach and tout for custom:

> There first, fair Dippers, who come fourteen Mile
> To get a Promise or a hopeful Smile
> Of any Lady or of some fine Man
> To dip their Water for 'em, if they can.

No description of Tunbridge Wells is complete without a
pretty compliment to the wild herbs abounding on the Heath,
which scented the air with health-giving fragrance.  Acer took
them as a sign of his journey's end,

> . . . A little farther, shelter'd with the Green
> And Shady Wood, some rarer Herbs are seen.
> Wood-Sorrel, wholesome Betony, does grow,
> Which has more Vertues than Physicians know.

Another hint that Tunbridge was at hand gives a modern turn
to his observations,

> Just by the side of this so pleasant Way,
> Some Pyebald Houses stand, and strangely gay . . .
> As slight as if built only for one Day.

They were five-roomed houses, with no fire-place, meant for
summer-time uses :

> Sure the wise Founder hardly could suppose
> 'Twould still be Summer there, when he built those
> Fine Bowers for Houses, but hop'd he might make
> A Twelve-month's Rent in Three; so save his Stake.

The speculator's rent proving higher for one week than
London rents for a month, our travellers left,

> the dainty House
> For splendid Castle to the Country Mouse;
> We hasten thence, and not a hundred yards
> But we see more fair Houses, still—of Cards . . .
> We praise 'em yet, and, for most fine and fair
> Dwellings, commend 'em to the Birds of th'Air.

Yet these frail-seeming little houses had already been many
years in fashion!  Anthony Hamilton talks of them about
1666, clean and comfortable, and scattered over the country
half a mile from the wells; and they or their successors were
still on view when Mrs. Montagu took the waters in 1749;
small houses, rural and romantic, mingled among the trees.

So much for the outskirts; meanwhile Curio and his companions have explored the town itself.

> That little place of so great fame,

hitherto of rustic simplicity, is only now ' beginning to be fine '.
There is the shady Upper Walk, and the shops suggesting
Cheapside in the country :

> Midst of the Trees Apollo has a Quire;

music being as essential to the cure as the waters themselves,
or the sweet-smelling herbage :

> Our Bodies Crystal Springs would cleanse in vain
> To little purpose purifie the Brain,
> Did not these Harmonies of Phoebus do
> With them still, some part of the wonder too,

and all for the small sacrifice of half a crown.

Parallel to the Upper runs the Under Walk,

> But something lower, and of lower Bliss.

Here

> The lady without wetting of her Shooe
> May chuse her Dinner, while her Gallants wooe.

Here she may accept their offerings, the Tunbridge Bisket or
the country cake, or, better still, a basket of choice fruit :

> Under the fragrant Leaves of Yonder Trees
> You ready gather'd find fresh strawberries;
> With odoriferous Rasps; beneath that Tree
> Shaded with Poplar Leaves, you Cherries see. . . .

As for the spring itself :

> In midst of Rocks, within that sandy space,
> Fam'd Well, the ancient Mother of that place,
> Nature has plac'd . . .

Here Nature works the wonders which give fame to her
fountains :

> Plac'd with her Back to the wide Heath and Hills,
> As conscious that her Business were our Ills.

Throngs of patients gather round; the dippers glass in hand,
deal out her bounty to the sufferers. Why indeed was the dis-

covery of this saving fountain so long postponed? The reason
is evident :

> The World devolv'd is to an Age of Spleen
> Beyond that so-long-talkt-of Iron Age;
> A Time that brings forth such a rusty Rage
> As none of the known Medicines can asswage.

Marvellous indeed were the effects of a glass or two of Tunbridge water :

> Like ghosts at first we here the living meet . . .
> When on a suddain a strange Change is made;
> They flourish all who did so lately fade.

Heart and head alike are renewed; the power of enjoyment
revives :

> Here Friend meets his old Friend; the amo'rous Lad,
> Fond lover, finds his Mistress, and is glad.
> Under that Oak contemplating we see
> Some great Improver of Philosophy . . .
> Near these, great Heroes of a higher Fate
> Settle in Solitude Affairs of State;
> Having laid down the Burden of ill Health,
> Now with Delight support the Commonwealth;
> Free from that Throng of Clients, and alone,
> Their Time and Health here first can call their own.

Yet even in this Elysium is room for improvement; here are
but the beginnings of a town,

> Which thus, unbuilt, bring such a concourse down. . . .
> The place thus urges thee, where can thy Wealth
> Be better spent than where 't's repay'd with Health? . . .

And with this hint to the capitalist and a delicious incon-
sequence, Metellus calls upon Acer to translate for him the
Fourth Book of Virgil.

### ON VISITING PENSHURST

Passing Speldhurst the Medway comes on into Kent, making a way through green meadows and beneath wooded and
hop-garlanded hills. Presently, under an old bridge, it flows

through a pool of yellow lilies; across the water Penshurst Place stands watching among the great oaks, and the pinnacles of Penshurst Church are close at hand. The Sidneys came to the old stone house under Edward VI, who ' gave this House of Pencester . . . unto his trustye and welbeloved servant, Syr William Sydney . . . serving him from the tyme of his Birth unto his Coronation in the Offices of Chamberlayn and Steward of his Household . . .'

In the next generation Philip Sidney was born, on November 30th 1554, in a year grief-shadowed for his mother, Lady Mary. For in the course of it her father the Duke of Northumberland, her brother Lord Guildford Dudley, and sister-in-law the tragic Lady Jane Grey, had perished on the scaffold. Philip was ' named for ' Philip, King of Spain, whom Sir Henry escorted to England for his marriage with Queen Mary. What Englishman is not aware how the child became in after years ' the great glory of his family, the great hope of mankind, the most lively pattern of virtue, the glory of the world '. A tree was set in the park to mark so happy an event. You may see ' Sir Philip Sidney's Oak ' when you go to Penshurst, hoping to stand under the dedicated branches. But that oak was well on in years when the heir of the Sidneys was born. The veritable tree, Ben Jonson's

> taller tree, which of a nut was set
> At his great birth where all the Muses met,

was probably a chestnut; the chestnut indeed which formerly stood a little away from the oak and was either blown or (inconceivably) cut down at the end of the eighteenth century. The poet Waller wrote of it, and some other vanished Penshurst trees, the lofty avenue of beeches known as ' Sacharissa's Walk '. It pleased him to imagine on that hallowed stem the carven secret of his own love :

> Go boy, and carve this passion on the bark
> Of yonder tree, which stands the sacred mark
> Of noble Sidney's birth.

The Penshurst of Sir Philip's boyhood was the grey-stone predecessor of the present house, still in part embodied with it. He remembered its look and air when he wrote in *Arcadia* of a house 'built of fair and strong stone, not affecting so much any extraordinary kind of fineness as an honourable representing of a firm stateliness'.

The originator of 'Pencester' was Sir John de Pulteney, who bought the manor from the heirs of Sir Stephen de Penchester, and so succeeded to an ownership dating from the Conquest. In 1341 he had licence to strengthen his new residence 'with walls of chalk and stone and to embattle it'. The Regent Bedford purchased Penshurst in the early fifteenth century and added, beyond the upper end of Sir John's Great Hall, 'a building with a steep gabled roof and walls of great thickness', afterwards known as the Buckingham Building. Even when Sir Henry Sidney had made yet further additions the house remained a place of no great magnificence. Ben Jonson characterized it to perfection:

> Thou art not, Penshurst, built to envious show
> Of touch or marble: nor canst boast a row
> Of polish'd pillars, or a roof of gold:
> Thou hast no lantern whereof tales are told;
> Or stair, or courts; but stand'st an ancient pile,
> And—these grudg'd at—art reverenced the while.
> Thou joy'st in better marks, of soil, of air,
> Of wood, of water; therein thou art fair.

Game was plentiful in the park to serve a very hospitable table; the 'purpled pheasant with the speckled side', 'the painted partridge willing to be killed', carp and pike in the ponds. In the orchards fruit ripened in proper Kent abundance:

> The early cherry with the later plum,
> Fig, grape and quince, each in his time doth come:
> The blushing apricot and woolly peach
> Hang on thy walls, that every child may reach.

Sir Henry Sidney built as well as the Gatehouse 'the whole façade looking north and west, as far as the Buckingham Building'. The house now formed three sides of a quadrangle 'called the President's Court, from the inscription dated 1571 on the tower at the end', which gives Sir Henry his title of 'Lorde President of Wales and the Marches of the same'.

Penshurst is, above all, a place to be visited after the mind has been well stored with reading, not of Sir Philip Sidney alone, nor his *Astrophel and Stella*, nor even *Arcadia*, and there an end. Some closer friendship must be sought with Sir Henry, whose name was overshadowed by his famous son, and with his wife the Lady Mary, her fair face cruelly disfigured by the small-pox; with Robert Sidney, Earl of Leicester, and his lady, Barbara Gamage, heiress of Coity Castle; with Mary Sidney, Countess of Pembroke, 'subject of all verse' (and the Urania of Spenser's in particular) and of Aubrey's commendation, 'a beautiful lady, and had an excellent wit, and had the best breeding that that age could afford'.

Barbara Gamage entertained King James at Penshurst when he was hunting with Prince Henry. Her marriage to Robert Sidney was all but forbidden by Queen Elizabeth, had Raleigh's messenger not arrived a few hours too late. By the next reign she had become a capable châtelaine. When the royal guests arrived 'they saw the fires, Shine bright on every hearth'. A room in the Gatehouse which bears King James's name may have given him good repose. Ben Jonson pronounced the encomium on his hostess:

> . . . What praise was heap'd
> On thy good lady then! Who therein reap'd
> The just reward of her high huswifry,
> To have her linen, plate and all things nigh
> When she was far; and not a room but drest
> As if it had expected such a guest. . . .

Then, too, the visitor to Penshurst should prepare to meet there the orphaned children of Charles I, placed by the Parliament with Lord and Lady Leicester. Princess Elizabeth, that pathetic child, left her diamond necklace in their keeping when she went away to die at Carisbrooke Castle. . . . He should be aware also of the tragedy and greatness of Algernon Sidney :

> Unconquer'd patriot! formed by ancient lore,
> The love of ancient Freedom to restore. . . .

So 'compassed about with a great cloud of witnesses' our traveller may open the door, lifting the worn handle initialled for Barbara and Robert Sidney, and pass through the court-yard to the Hall.

The Great Hall of Sir John de Pulteney has an open oak-timbered roof, and the spars rest on grotesquely carved figures, which the guide will identify as Pontius Pilate, or Salome, or the Witch of Endor. The furniture of long old tables, the leathern helmets of Roundhead times, fill in a picture of life well-lived within its walls.

Then in the upper rooms what a treasury, and yet a sweet homeliness never lacking. The cabinets, Dutch, Italian, Indian; the portraits, Lady Jane Grey; the lovely Barbara Gamage and her daughter; the Princess Elizabeth; the Countess of Pembroke too, painted by Marc Gheeraert. Personal relics there are at every turn. The *Historical Guide* enumerates 'a few letters, some signatures to bonds and bills, a lock of hair of a reddish-brown tint' belonging to Sir Philip Sidney. I was shown also a cracked mirror in a wooden frame, said to have been his shaving-glass. I pictured his face, as Zucchero painted it, with the dark eyes, and arched brows, reflected there, and asked my informant if the glass had not been re-mounted. 'Indeed no,' she told me indignantly, 'it is just as it came from the battle-field. . . .'

But enough; go yourself, and knowledgeably, to Penshurst; walk its long galleries full of recollection.

## SEVENOAKS

### I

A CAREFUL particularity about the name Sevenoaks calls for questioning; a delightful name, but not to be taken for granted—'Sennocke,' says Lambarde, '(as some call it) Sevenoke, of a number of trees as they coniecture. . . .' The shortening, like a nickname of affection, was plainly in ordinary use when he wrote. Hasted too says that in his day, two hundred years later, the place was 'commonly called Sennok'.

The sixteenth century is more cautious than the eighteenth about those ancestral oaks. Lambarde asserts nothing, while Hasted says boldly they were seven 'large' trees, and stood on the hill 'at the time of first building'. After all, the name might well commemorate seven mighty trees felled to provide beams for the first Saxon settlers on the spot, seven tough giants which turned the edge of the primeval axe. We all agree that oaks abounded on the wild hill-ridges, and that the seven must have been specially distinguished among the great forest of trees.

The village, remote in the woodlands, was so little interrupted in its solitude that (unlike recent historians) I do not hesitate to picture its first hero laid secretly as a puling, nameless waif 'in the streetes at Sennocke'. I do not share their fears that he might have been crushed under some wagon-wheel or cruel hoof; nor with them do I banish his finding to the greater solitude of Sevenoaks Common. Rather I am surprised—incredulous even—that under Edward III Sennocke possessed 'streets' in the plural.

In the track of that deserted baby sounds of the great world

presently came into the village : having no name of his own
Sennocke lent him hers to make famous.

William Sennocke, again says Lambarde, ' this orphan, was
by the helpe of some charitable persons . . . nourtured in
suche wise that being made an Apprentise to a Grocer in
London he arose . . . (in course of time) to be Maior and
Chiefe Magistrate of that Citie.' He was, in fact, Sir Richard
Whittington's immediate forerunner in the mayoralty, his
friend and colleague, so that there can be no question of a
borrowed legend; indeed, William of Sevenoaks is a substantial figure in civic history and beyond it.

He earned his freedom of the city in 1394, and became a
member of the Grocers' Company. His shield, which bore,
' on azure ', for the sky, ' seven golden acorns, by two, three,
two ', hung ' at the upper ende of Grocers' Hall until the Great
Fire '. Stow has an engraving of it.

As a prominent and wealthy merchant he was active in
organizing the defence of merchant ships at sea, sorely harassed
by French and Breton pirates; for the trade of London went far
afield, ' to Bordeaux and other places for wine and merchandise '.

Sevenoake himself, if Richard Johnson's stirring tale may be
relied on, came face to face with the Frenchman at Agincourt,
fought single-handed with the Dauphin, and took his place
among the ' Nine Worthies of London '. Thus it befell in a
moment's lull of battle he lay down to rest, when ' a comely
knight disguised ' came on him and reproached him for ' a
layzie swain '.

> I, knowing that he was mine enemie,
> A bragging Frenchman, (for we term'd them so)
> Ill-brookt the proud disgrace he gave to me,
> And therefore lent the Dolphyne such a blow
> As warmed his courage well to lay about
> Till he was breathless, though he were so stout.
> At last the noble prince did ask my name,
> My birth, my calling and my fortunes past,
> With admiration he did heare the same,
> And so a bagge of crowns to me he cast,

> And when he went away he said to me
> 'Sevenoake be proud, the Dolphyne fought with thee.'

One hardly dare overshadow such a tale of doughty combat between hedgerow child and royal son of France, with the faintest suspicion; indeed, it may make it the more remarkable that William was a man over forty at the date of Agincourt. On the very day of battle he was alderman either of Bishopsgate or Tower Ward; though why should not an alderman go forth to war?

## II

Sevenoake was evidently a parishioner of 'St. Dunstan-in-le-Est', for he was churchwarden and trustee of endowments belonging to its chantry chapel of the Holy Trinity. But he never lost touch with his birthplace, where a property now known as Panthurst was given him by the owner, William Panter. And when he died in 1432 and was buried in St. Martin's, Ludgate Hill, one of his five extant wills ordered his executors to maintain in Sevenoaks 'for ever, one Master, an honest man . . . which may keep a Grammar School in some convenient House within the said town . . . that he may teach and instruct poor children whatsoever, coming thither to be taught, taking nothing of them of their parents or friends for the teaching . . . them'. Sevenoaks Grammar School lately kept its quincentenary. The little history published in celebration by Mrs. J. T. Lennox records the benefactors who followed Sevenoake, particularly Sir Ralph Bosvile of Bradbourne, its second founder under Queen Elizabeth, and his daughter Margaret, wife of Sir William Boswell, Secretary at The Hague, who was the first Lady Governor and established two scholarships at Jesus College, Cambridge. The buildings have also their record down to the present time, when a fine school-hall has been built by Mr. Charles Plumptre Johnson.

I notice that two of the long line of head masters have a title to literary fame. William Paynter, compiler of *The Palace of Pleasure*, succeeded his father in office for a brief year. (Were

they kinsmen of Sevenoake's friend Panter?) And then there
was Elijah Fenton, of whom Dr. Johnson said 'that the
elegance of his poetry entitled him to the company of the wits
. . . and the amiableness of his manners made him loved
wherever he was known'. The Earl of Orrery was his patron,
Pope his admiring friend; 'Fenton is gone,' he wrote to Johnson, 'I must tell you he has done you many a good office and
set your character in the fairest light to some who either mis-
took you or knew you not. I doubt not he has done the same
for me.' Fenton was head master for four years only (1706–10),
and so busy improving the school's reputation that his Muse
rested on her laurels. From Kent he wrote to Southerne, the
actor, perhaps foreshadowing his own retirement:

> . . . My genius sinks, and hardly knows
> To make a couplet tinkle in the close.
> Yet when you next to Medway shall repair
> And quit the town to breathe a purer air;
> Retiring from the crowd to steal the sweet
> Of easy life in Twysden's calm retreat . . .
> Where Lambarde form'd for business and to please,
> By sharing will improve your happiness . . .
> With bright ideas there inspir'd anew,
> By them excited and inform'd by you,
> I may with happier skill essay to sing
> Sublimer notes and strike a bolder string.

The Twysden 'retreat' was probably at Bradbourne. Mr.
Thomas Lambarde lived in a house on the site of Park Grange,
and to him Fenton addressed the verses which Dr. Johnson
held to be 'no disagreeable specimen of epistolary poetry'.
The 'Epistle' contains a description which might apply to
Fenton himself:

> Him no vain hopes attract, no fear appals,
> Nor the gay servitude of courts enthralls,
> Unknowing how to mask concerted guile
> With a false cringe or undermining smile,
> His manners pure, from affectation free
> And prudence, shine through clear simplicity.

As to pupils of celebrity, Grote the historian of Greece was
at Sevenoaks School, and the two Wordsworths, nephews of

the poet, Charles and Christopher, afterwards Bishop of Lincoln. To another sphere belong the two great soldiers Henry, Viscount Hardinge, Governor-General of India, who succeeded the Duke of Wellington (in 1852) as Commander-in-Chief of the British Army; and his school-friend, General John Woodgate of Peninsular renown.

I wonder what Sevenoaks School said about it when news went round in 1636 that Dr. Thomas Farnaby was moving to their town, from London, his seminary for the sons of noblemen and gentlemen to the number of some 300. At any rate, the two schools flourished side by side until Civil War planted on poor Farnaby the suspicion of malignancy, and he was imprisoned and threatened with exile to America. He founded a family who were long settled at Kippington, now turned into a modern building estate. The old pedagogue rests in Sevenoaks Church, which stands in the line of the village street, high on the ridge between the Weald and Holmesdale. From this vantage it has watched the invasion of the forest slopes by a myriad villas and the armies of stucco and bricks.

### III

A memory of Sevenoaks that pleases me belongs to the old mill at Greatness, a hamlet on the eastern edge of the town. It has its parallel in Canterbury stories of Huguenot flight. At the time the Edict of Nantes was revoked the little eight-year-old daughter of a Huguenot couple of good family was smuggled into England for her safety. She never saw her parents again, but was brought up by a merchant of Kensington, who became her guardian. She married another refugee, by name Ourcel, and one of her descendants married also into a Huguenot family, the Nouailles. In the eighteenth century these people started at Greatness a factory for silk thread. At Canterbury their compatriots had long been weaving fine brocades of silk patterned with gold and silver tinsel. At Greatness many foreigners were employed and the mills

flourished for upwards of a century. Peter Nouaille was the
last to work them; he lived in a house on St. John's Hill at
Sevenoaks, and his only daughter, Anne Nouaille, survived
there to the great age of eighty-nine and died in 1897.

The mill-houses were probably on the pattern of some in the
Stour valley, which tower up with huge white wooden walls
on a framework of heavy timber. At the height of their prosperity, about 1760, one Thomas Mills was foreman and had as
apprentice a lad of fourteen named Harrison, who worked on
there for forty years. One of Harrison's sons sought his fortune
in other fields; and when he returned home in 1833 found the
mills that almost seemed his father's razed to the ground. Remembrance and regret inspired him to compose an ode, of 500
lines, on the silk mills at Greatness. They may be set beside
Churchyard's earlier verses on the Spilman Mills at Dartford,
and are scarcely better poetry. Yet I had pleasure in reading
them in Richards' *Old Sevenoaks*, where they are reprinted
from the scarce original.

Here is Harrison's picture of the finale to so much industry
and enterprise :

> At length the mill was altogether stayed,
> The year's returns the outlay ne'er defrayed :
> And where t'was bustle, and where wheels went round,
> Suspended was the long accustomed sound,
> The mill was shortly razed to the ground.
> Then bidders were invited to attend,
> To make their purchases, and so to send
> Away from Greatness all the cogs and wheels,
> Bobbins and wicker baskets, spindles, reels.
> Thus when I visited the place I found
> No vestige left, but spaces in the ground
> In which the water-wheel was used to play
> That when a child I looked on with dismay. . . .
> Thus is obliterated all that man
> Would wish to have remembered. . . .

IV

Who could write of Sevenoaks without a word of the Vine,

most famous of cricket grounds? It had a ducal origin, its Duke being an ardent cricketer up to the age of forty, a sportsman and a tree-planter to boot. John Frederick, third Duke of Dorset, gave the ground to Sevenoaks between 1770–80. He employed the best players of the day, and stakes were heavy when his team took the field.

In a three-day match, played in June 1780, the Duke's men made 93 and 92, while their opponents put up 105 and 81 for three wickets. That defeat cost the Duke 500 guineas. Another famous match the following year was played between his team and Sir Horace Mann's; this time the 500 guineas stayed at home.

The Vine Cricket Club was formed in the late eighteenth century, and its Cricket Week rivalled Canterbury's in popularity. The owners of Knole kept the ground in order, and in 1850 Earl Amherst, owner of Montreal, close to Sevenoaks, built a pavilion and rented it to the club. A century ago that sward so exquisitely smooth was cut with a scythe and sheep fed on it at intervals. To the wicket, when play began, strange-looking figures followed in their order; a high hat and Wellington boots were *de rigueur*; the bat had a crook in it and (Advance Australia!) low stumps and slow under-hand and round-arm bowling were the order of the day.

The earliest recorded maker of cricket bats, crooked or straight, was William Pett of Sevenoaks. 'In the year 1773,' says a writer in *The Times*, 'Mrs. Rishton wrote to Fanny Burney, "Mrs. Rishton begs Miss Burney to buy Mrs. Rishton 2 cricket batts made by Mr. Pett of 7 oakes. You will get them at any of the great Toy Shopes, the maker's name always stamp'd upon them."' Mrs. Rishton preferred the 'very best' at four shillings or four and sixpence each. The Duke of Dorset also patronized 'Father William Pett', but his price—for a quantity perhaps—was half a crown a piece for eleven 'cricket batts' and three and sixpence for a ball.

## KNOLE

### I

I read on its first publication, and have lately re-read, *Knole and the Sackvilles* by V. Sackville-West. In the interval of the two readings I visited Sevenoaks and went through the Park gates. Who would not envy as well as admire the author of that book? To have such a 'hero', and to write of 'him' with intimate affection and a poet's pen withal. For in spite of the family notes which occupy many delightful pages, Knole itself —the rag-stone pile, courts, galleries, garden, wilderness—is the inspiration of this perfect record. If Knole were to crumble to dust, here the essence of its charm would remain, distilled into a lover's library. Here the author is in and of the pictures she makes for us. She has seen the scarlet creeper ablaze on the Green Court walls, and the coolness of its stripped stones, with a little moulding drawn across them, shaped to the towers. In the banqueting-hall it is she who meets that puzzled yet still dignified intruder, a stag, strayed in from the park. As a child she is the appointed guide to show strangers the house; to acquaint them with her favourite mermaids and dolphins in the ballroom frieze, though not every one enjoys their oddity as she does. For all her familiarity with 'four acres of building' she confesses to involuntary pauses 'to think out the shortest route from one room to another'. She has failed, she confesses, to verify the old conceit that the seven courts of Knole correspond to the days of the week; fifty-two stairways to the weeks of the year; three hundred and sixty-five rooms to the days. Her knowledge is of another, a more sensitive, kind. The colour of the Cartoon Gallery, 'with the sunset flaming through the west window . . . has often taken my breath away'. The greens and pinks of the Venetian Ambassador's Bedroom, now dusty and tarnished, give it 'a bloom like the bloom on a bowl of grapes and figs': she cannot keep the

simile out of mind, standing there beside the Burgundian
garden-tapestry and the rosy Persian rug. The old musty
smell in the galleries too, 'whenever I met it would bring back
Knole'; in part it is the powdery fragrance of a Georgian
potpourri always made after the recipe of the Lady Betty
Germaine. Above all, the poet of *The Land* is conscious that
her Knole is also England's. 'Of whatever English county I
spoke, I still should be aware of the relationship between the
English soil and that most English house.' Or, again : 'It has
the tone of England; it melts into the green of the garden turf,
into the tawnier green of the park beyond, into the blue of the
pale English sky.' What other guide to Knole can we, the
strangers, desire?

## II

And there is much more to the book than its colour and
atmosphere; the writer has had 'the free run of the Knole
manuscripts'; she makes her readers free of the same liberty.
The clearness of her topographical descriptions will be appreciated when they visit Knole. There is the north side, where the
sombre pile looks 'like a medieval village'; and the garden
side, with its mullions, Tudor gables, heraldic leopards. The
grey entrance reached along a tree-shaded approach is plain
and severe; a gatehouse between two square towers each
furnished with a wing. Horace Walpole found about that
entrance 'a beautiful decent simplicity which charms one'.
Through the wicket a great courtyard is first entered; the side
facing you is enriched with a Tudor oriel window, surmounted
by machicolation and an archway crowned with battlements;
a pagoda-like clock-tower overtopping the pile. The machicolation so oddly placed is a reminder of the days when great houses
might have to defend themselves; it was put there by Archbishop Bourchier; and the Tudor window was added by Archbishop Morton, as much as to say, 'We can now look out upon
a world at peace.' The greater part of Knole, setting aside a

possible Roman foundation and the certain ownership of the
Pembrokes and the Lords Say and Sele, was built in Tudor
times.  The Tudor archbishops were the first considerable
adapters, though their exact shares, beyond Bourchier's Brown
Gallery, Great Hall and Solar (now the Ball-room), are not
easily assigned.  Cranmer resigned his house perforce to
Henry VIII, and in 1586 Queen Elizabeth gave it with more
graciousness to her cousin Thomas Sackville.  'The galleries,'
says our guide, 'are perhaps the most characteristic rooms in
such a house.  Long and narrow, with dark shining floors,
armorial glass in the windows, rich plaster-work ceilings and
portraits on the walls, they are splendidly sombre and sump-
tuous.'  In the Leicester Gallery, 'dark and mysterious,
furnished with red velvet Cromwellian farthingale chairs and
sofas, dark as wine', is hung perhaps the most suggestive
portrait of the collection—Catherine Fitzgerald, Countess of
Desmond, in extreme old age.  She lived for somewhere about
140 years; all the pageant of English history from Edward IV
to Charles I passed before those strange, unseeing eyes.  Time
has put out their spark, yet still they seem to look on and on
into Time-without-end, asking what more there can yet be
for them to gaze upon of human vicissitude.  The picture
haunted me for days.  I read of it in the book of Knole as
'rather a frightening portrait'; it suggested to the author a
grim wandering through the galleries after nightfall by candlelight, creaks and sighs and swaying tapestries.

It is a relief to turn into the garden, half formal, half wilderness, secluded by the archbishops' rag-stone wall.  Or indeed
into the garden pages of our book, where we may envisage the
green walks, little orchards of gnarled apple-trees, borders of
sweet old-fashioned flowers.  In 1543 Henry VIII paid Sir
Richard Longe for making his garden at Knole; and its lay-out
has altered little since the seventeenth century.  A gardener's
bill for seeds, dated 1692, with its 'sweet yerbs, pawsley, sorrell,
spinnig, spruts, leeks, sallet, horse-ridish, jerusalem hawty-

chorks ', reminds me of Archbishop Reynolds's account for his fourteenth-century Lambeth garden : ' Littuce, spynnach, Caboche, Isope, Bourrage ', and the rest; so constant is fashion in the kitchen plot. The beauty of the trees in Knole Park passed into a proverb long before Mrs. Radcliffe pronounced their panegyric. (Did she enjoy a candlelight parade of those ghostly galleries?) When Henry Oxinden in 1640 describes, in Arcadian phrase, the beauty of Leeds Abbey, he talks of the hills ' which garnish their proude heights with Knolle-like trees '.

III

Having revitalized the old house by a kind of poetic sun-light, our writer brings to life those ten generations of Sack-villes whose portraits adorn the walls. Just as Knole is for her the typical great house of England, so, she declares, her ancestors derive significance from being ' so representative '. ' From generation to generation they might stand, fully equipped, as portraits from English history.' And this claim to a great extent she justifies. The recipient of Elizabeth's gracious present, Thomas Sackville, Lord Buckhurst and Earl of Dorset, was the youthful author of *Gorboduc*, the *Induction* to the *Mirror for Magistrates* and the *Complaint of Bucking-ham*, to which his poetic descendant pays her tribute. In later life, as a grave statesman, he was asked by the Queen to enter-tain the Huguenot exile, Odet de Coligny, Cardinal de Châtil-lon; he acceded, but displeased his sovereign for that his hospitality had not been ' in better sort '. It did not adequately set off her queenly gift. She sent messengers to protest, who were shown just how simply the household lived at Knole; no plate, coarse glass, no damask, but plain linen for napery. The emissaries took exception to Sackville's square-shaped dinner-table, and were displeased to learn my Lady's waiting-women had slept on the ground to leave bedsteads for the Cardinal's servants. I shall remember the episode when next I stand by that ungainly mound in Canterbury Cathedral where lies the Cardinal in no state at all.

The three years' diary (1616-19) of the Lady Anne Clifford is one of the most attractive of Sackville documents. She was left at fifteen sole heiress to her father, George, Earl of Cumberland, and at nineteen married Richard Sackville, third Earl of Dorset. She prefaced the diary with a flattering pen-picture of her own childish beauty, a pardonable vanity at sixty-three, when her loveliness was no more than a memory. The painting of her as a young woman by Mytens shows the thick, dark locks, peaked on her forehead, the black eyes and graceful shape, which the old dame (who shaved her head and smoked a pipe) so wistfully remembered. Her white hands, the fingers very long and slender, Mytens has artfully set against the blackness of her velvet gown.

There are glimpses of Knole in the fragmentary record. Lady Anne goes out of an evening with 'the Child', her little daughter Margaret, riding a piebald nag, fastened, poor child, into a 'pair of whalebone bodice'. She solaces her loneliness with books; Exodus, and Turkish history, and Chaucer; with games too; 'Glecko' with the steward, or 'Burley Break' upon the lawn. Yet for all these distractions she is 'extremely melancholy', and tiffs with her lord unceasingly over those northern castles he would have her sell against her will to replenish his empty purse. . . .

So we tread the portrait gallery through more than two centuries, until Knole's historian brings us face to face with that 'queer silent old man', Lionel, second Lord Sackville, who stands 'conformably, at the end of the long line of his ancestors'. She is there with him on the last page, a child, clasping her knees, staring absorbed while he tells her stories of the past. He feasts her too on the reddest cherries, the bluest grapes, the ripest peach, picked out for her enjoyment, and to his guests' perplexity, from the dinner-table in the Great Hall.

*Bethersden to Benenden—Goudhurst to Brenchley*

### BETHERSDEN TO BENENDEN

#### I

A SPECIAL charm belongs to places like Andredsweald, which are Nature's 'Wild', marsh, forest, moorland; there through ages unchallenged she has gathered her harvests and on the labours of man still lays her domination. The story of the Weald begins in the seventh century with the rough justice meted out to the royal murderer Sigebert, a fugitive 'amidst the recesses of wild beasts', until, says Lambarde, 'a poore Hogheard found him and knowing him to be the same that had slaine his Master, slue him also, without all manner of mercy'.

Already hogs rooted in the forest, which stretched its dark shadow for 120 miles length and 30 miles breadth over four counties. Two rivers flowed from its depths—the Limen and the Rother; in Caesar's day forest and river together made the inland boundary of the Kentish tribes. In Andredsweald the kingly oak was the king's; but at the proper season a freeman of Kent could drive his hogs to feast on the acorn mast. Little by little a law of the forest shaped itself from the conflicting privilege of king, churchman and peasant. The population of the country-side increased, with its flocks and herds, struggling to be fed. The king perforce resigned his claim to all except the choicest of the shady 'denes' where flocks could best find cover. A royal grant of Kentish soil was not complete without its 'shake-time', a share of pannage or hog-feed in a wealden

valley. Each owner gave his dene a distinctive name, sometimes his own name; this was the ancestry of Frittenden,
Tenterden, Bethersden, Smarden, and many another 'den'
upon the ordnance map. Boundaries were marked by a cross,
an oak, or a stone. The 'Drofmen', or drovers of the annual
migration, at times took their wages in a portion of land; here
and there one settled himself upon it. A ploughman who
found some acre in the Wild where corn would thrive, sought
leave to live there, sow and reap: so arose a thin, scattered
and wildish population. Eight Wealden places are named in
*Domesday*; four of them already had a church. The estate to
which a dene belonged now became the manor of the feudal
lord. The nearer manors, like Ashford, Charing, Lenham,
on the Wealden border, could make good use of their denes;
the distant manor found it profitable to let to tenants, only
reserving jealously all timber rights. Not indeed until after
the Reformation severed the age-old connexion between Church
and Weald was it customary to agree upon an extra rental for
leave to cut the growing timber. Even to-day no tithe is pay-
able on woodland in the Weald. The number of its inhabitants
increased but slowly. ' It was a great while togither ', says
Lambarde, 'in manner nothing els but a desart and waste
Wildernesse, not planted with Townes or peopled with men
as the outsides of the shyre were, but stored and stuffed with
heards of Deere and droves of Hogs only.' Each of the Kent
historians has a dissertation, and usually a difference, on the
proper boundaries of the Kent Weald.

Broadly speaking, it bounds on the west to Surrey, on the
south to Sussex. Northward is the wooded range which it is
now the fashion to call the Greensand hills. Their older, if
illogical, name was the Red Hills—red by contrast with the
White Hills, the chalk downs. Wealdish men spoke of 'The
Hill', simply, as of some far mountain where dwelt outlandish
people. On the north, then, the 'Red Hills' run from Well
Street, past Ide-hill and River-hill, with a break for the Med-

way passage at Teston, as far as Boughton Malherbe. A chain
of hill-top churches carries on the line to the east—Egerton,
Pluckley, Great Chart and Kingsnorth; thence, below Orle-
stone, touching Warehorne Church, and below Kenardington
Church falling to Appledore on the Marsh, and so again downstream to the Sussex border. One reason of the slow peopling
of the Weald was no doubt the stubbornness of the soil. '. . . It
will grow to frith or wood', wrote Gervase Markham in the
seventeenth century, 'if it be not continually manured and
laboured with the plough and kept under by tillage. . . . It
is throughout (except in very few places adjoyning to Brooks
or Rivers) of a very barren nature . . . until that it be holpen
by some manner of comfort, as dung, marle . . . fodder ashes,
or such other refreshings.' Even with modern methods his
words are still substantially true; passing a field close to Bid-
denden I have seen the labourers fling the rough grass swathes
as they were mown on to a bonfire; later the spread ashes no
doubt would 'comfort' the unfruitful soil. Still 'it will grow
to frith or wood'; the wide vistas which are the glory of the
Weald always keep their woodland character. It is composed
of innumerable bushy hedgerows fencing little pastures, of
great oaks captive by the roadside, of hazel-copses, or bosks of
oak, ash, and the rarer beech, intermingling with the greenery
of orchard or hop-garden.

II

Great Chart is a good gate of entrance, its church being one
of the eastern boundary marks. First comes a sweep of flattish
pastureland; next the road leaps down by broad stages; then
it climbs again to Bethersden Church, where the granite War
Cross faces you in an angle of the churchyard, stark against
sapphire distances. At Bethersden I hoped to visit the marble
quarries from which a new Chair of St. Augustine was probably hewn out in 1220 to grace Becket's Translation. Luckily
its grudging church door which I could not open brought to

my help, from an overhung cottage, close by, a guide able to satisfy every curiosity.

'I read somewhere that Bethersden Church was made of the local marble,' I began, when the door gave way to firm handling and we entered together.

'Well, no,' he replied, and his good Kent accent must be imagined, 'the tower and walls are all rag-stone, and, so far as I know the church, man and boy, there's no marble here at all.'

'Is the marble still in working?'

'What's left crumbles up; it doesn't hold; there's nothing, as you might say, worth the taking out.'

'And where were the principal quarries?'

'Chiefly on the old Ashford road, close to what they call Daniel's Water. But there's nothing much to be seen, only a little roughness in the ground.'

We proceeded round the church. My companion's father, according to the village chronicle, had lowered the old pews and relaid the pavement. He himself—he stopped beside the brass effigy of a Lovelace fastened to the north wall—had taken that monument from the floor and hung it there for safety. Oddly enough he found that the inscription, on a separate slip of brass, had writing on both sides.

Bethersden (sometimes written Beatrichesden) was the seat of the Lovelace family—Bethersden-Lovelace. The Cavalier poet was at home on these Kentish uplands. For some generations his family lived in an old mansion, now represented only by a wall and some oak panelling at a farmhouse close to the school. When Richard Lovelace came of age, having seen service with the royal army in Scotland, he retired to his Kentish estates. Was it of a Wealden grasshopper and Wealden acorns that he wove his snatch of rural poetry?

> O thou that swing'st upon the waving hair
>   Of some well-filled oaten beard,
> Drunk every night with a delicious tear
>   Dropt thee from heaven, where thou wert rear'd.
> The joys of earth and air are thine entire

That with thy feet and wings dost hop and fly :
And when thy poppy works, thou dost retire
To thy carved acorn-bed to lie.

In April 1642 he delivered to both Houses the Kent Petition
in the King's behalf, well knowing the reward of such
temerity; on April 30th he was committed to the Gatehouse
prison, and on Midsummer Day bailed out on a security of
twenty pounds. In the meantime he had written an immortal
song, 'Stone Walls do not a Prison make, nor Iron Bars a
Cage.' The sale of sixty good acres to Richard Hulse of Great
Chart paid the price of this adventure. After the ruinous
second imprisonment in Peterhouse he sold Lovelace Place to
the same purchaser, 'grew very melancholy, became very poor
in body and purse . . . went in ragged clothes'. Lovelace
Chapel contains no other mention of the family than the name
of their old home on a memorial tablet to little Cicely Hulse;
she lived a while at Lovelace Place, and 'in 1679 returned to
Heaven, in the tenth year of her age, as hopeful in respect of
virtue, witt and beauty as her yeares could admit of or her
parents wish '.

The great storm of 1822 blew in the windows and robbed
Bethersden Church of much ancient glass, leaving but a few
scraps of grisaille and a little delicate canopy work in red and
blue.

### III

'The chief glory of Halden Church', says its historian,
Canon Livett, 'is the timber tower'; its steeple pricks through
the hill-top woods, a landmark for the country-side. 'The
tower', continues Canon Livett, proclaiming the skill of the
medieval craftsman; 'the tower consists of two stages. The
upper stage is square, covered with shingles and surmounted
by an octagonal shingle-covered spire . . . the lower stage
spreads out to an octagonal shape, the sides being formed of
wooden walls, made up of numerous posts and panels of nearly

equal width, and . . . tiled lean-to roofs.' He dates the building in the late thirteenth or early fourteenth century. Within
it hung five bells which local pride has named 'The Nightingales of Kent'. Four were made by the famous seventeenth-
century bell-founder Joseph Hatch, and two display his trade-
mark a medallion bearing three bells.

Like Halden, Tenterden's pride is its tower—a century
younger and how differently conceived. Grey-stoned and
battlemented, its four octagonal corner-turrets richly pinnacled,
it is so magnificent a steeple that one could forgive the jealousy
of less favoured villages had it not shaped itself into a spiteful
tale. Old Latimer made great play with the idle legend which
fifteenth-century mothers, pointing to the lovely skyward pile,
must first have babbled to their children.

Tenterden is the only corporate town in the Weald, and a
limb of the royal borough of Rye. When Henry VI gave it
a charter the sea touched the parish boundary at Smallhythe.
The building fashions of successive generations make up the
charm of Tenterden street. The houses are as varied as the
creepers which adorn them are various in flower and leaf. How
were they ever fitted into one harmonious whole; houses of
the Henrys, Elizabeth, James or George; old red-brick or stone,
framed or timbered houses, cheek by jowl, neighbourly as their
inmates? Farther towards Rolvenden, where the cottages are
well set back, shady grass plots make a green border for the
high road.

One might know much more of Tenterden's history had not
some prisoners confined in the chamber above the Town Hall,
as is supposed, set the place alight on March 19th 1661. Nearly
all the records and all but one charter of King Charles were
burnt to ashes, and the loss was the more distressing because
the Tenterden Corporation had taken pains to protect its muni-
ments. Under James I an enlightened resolution reads to the
effect that: 'Itt is att this assembly decreed . . . that all the
records . . . of the Towne . . . of Tenterden shalbe presently

. . . laid in the presse provided for that purpose. Except the Charters and Customall which shall remayne in the custody of the Maior. . . .'

Only an old record book of Queen Mary (1557–8), now remained with a register of the Corporation Court, begun only twenty years before and the Civic Roll from 27 Hen. VI. This roll contains from time to time a note of contemporary happenings; for instance : 'This yeare aboute Barthilmewe tide the Queen's Ma^{tie} was at Rie, Hempsted and Sussynghurste.' 'This yeare the Spanyshe fleete came for Ingland aboute Saint James tide 1588.'

After so great a disaster the poor remnants of the town records were best committed to the church's care; they were placed in a chest which still stands under the tower. St. Mildred the Virgin is patron saint of borough and church alike, and her figure with coronet, staff, and book, is on the reverse of the Common Seal.

In the long list of Tenterden's vicars some names stand out. One Magister John Moeer (1479–89), perhaps a kinsman of Sir Thomas More, was a scholar with a large library. He bequeathed his books to Eton and Christchurch, St. Augustine's Abbey, Magdalen at Oxford, and other places of learning. To Thomas Linacre, scholar and physician, he also left books and the sum of ten pounds.

### IV

The road through High Halden, and on to Tenterden, Rolvenden and Benenden is gloriously free and wind-swept. It twists and turns around the ghosts of great oaks that long ago hampered its passage.

Rolvenden stands high on this broken ridge, a large, compact village as yet unspoilt. Is it still, as in Hasted's day, 'universally called . . . Rounden'?

The houses, mostly of framed timber, have boards so clean-painted, window-frames so gaily green, tiles of such a cosy rust

and crimson, that the vista of the village street is the most
homelike imaginable. Running north and south, it makes an
avenue to the great church. The west side is built right
up; some houses abut on the roadways, with a little shop
or two; some stand back, leaving their rose-gardens to
parley with passers-by. On the east side the dwellings give
place to a green meadow, before the street halts at the lich-
gate.

The massive upstanding church has a fine western steeple
and five eastward gables. The nave arcading, as in so many
of the Wealden churches, modelled perhaps on Canterbury
Choir, has columns alternately octagonal and rounded; there
are king-posts, black with age in the roof, which some day
may be stripped of its disfiguring plaster. Most of the high
pews were taken away near the close of last century; the candles
perched on alternate pews were apt to gutter tallow tears down
the neck of the occupant as the sermon drew to a close. In the
south chapel a little stairway climbs into a square panelled
gallery or pen, neatly curtained, and furnished with a fine set
of chippendale chairs. An old octagonal table in the centre
suggests cards, and is said to have come from Hole Park. Overhead is a piece of dark coving, the ribs still brightly coloured
red and blue; this once canopied a side altar, though now it
roofs a family pew. The north chapel is also a 'reserved
compartment' belonging to Maytham Hall. There the east
window is blocked by the huge monument which records the
coming of James Monypenny into Kent, 'of an ancient family
at Pitmilli in the Shire of Fife'. In 1721 the adventurous James
married Mary Gybbon of Rolvenden, and thenceforward the
kinship of Monypennys, Gybbons, and Phillips owned much
surrounding property and both the 'big houses'; Maytham and
'The Hole' (said to be a corruption of 'The Holy Well', in
the grounds, which still provides healing waters). Present-day
occupants prefer to call it Hole Park.

Another Monypenny union perpetuated in the family the

Christian name of 'Silvestra'. What could be more appropriate to the Weald, though, indeed, the original Silvestra was the daughter of a rector of St. Clement Danes. She adopted Kent with thoroughness, surviving her husband almost half a century and dying in her ninety-first year. Her great-granddaughter (was it?), another Silvestra, married her name with that of 'Le Touzel'; Silvestra le Touzel, what romance clings about it!

Rolvenden, on its eminence, has marshes to the south and east. You cross the upper level, pierced by Hexden Channel, on the road to Newenden, which then rises to a little ridge and falls, lower still, to the Rother level. On a holiday cars race perpetually from Sussex into Kent over Newenden Bridge—an ancient bridge, with grey cut-waters, but no bays for a luckless foot-passenger. Under it the slow-moving Rother glides, and an old broken boat or two is stranded on the bank. Some fishermen go by—on motor-cycles of course; how have they patience to angle by such a lounging stream!

The cottages of Newenden, framed in wood and old red brick and rose-bowered, are strung along the Rother bank, sheltered by the ridge behind them; they gaze over marshlands bordered with river-flowers and overflown by many swallows, to the Sussex hills. St. Peter's Church has lately acquired a remarkable new chancel; the roof-beams are curved like rounded ribs of a ship or the ark of God. Its treasures are the ancient font sculptured with a splendid lion and dragon, and a fine perpendicular screen adorned with painted escutcheons enclosing the south chapel; there is one gap, where a thief put his hand. The churchyard is a flowery paradise—fuchsias, antirrhinums, ramblers covering even the old gravestones. The church itself is raised above the road and is quiet enough in winter; in summer ' the doors must be shut if we are to hear the service '.

Nowadays to learn your Weald afoot you had best follow byroads. About a mile from Benenden a finger-post hands one to Hawkhurst; and next a rough farmway plunges on the right, downhill between thick copses. A name on the ordnance map lured me along this track. What whimsical fancy christened those hill-side farmsteads? The lane went swaying into hollows and out of them again, between a hazel copse and a hedge sprayed with lovely purple vetches, like fairy grapes. A signboard encouraged me: 'This road leads only to Great Nineveh Farm.' But it led also to the dogs, loud and vociferous; and to this day I can picture in my ignorance either a Nineveh weeping among the Kent hills or another smiling and rose-crowned. Still the lane beckoned on, up and down, up and down, linking the homes among the hills. This Forest Farm, its grey face chequered with grey oaken beams, has never been cajoled, modernized, into anything other than it is. The old lean-to is still entered by a half-door from the living-room; you must stoop under the lintel and descend a ladder into it. The chimney-stack holds two roomy fire-places, back to back, a huge chamfered beam stretched across. The brick ovens must be heated by two faggots to a white heat before they are ready for the bake. There are oak doors, oak planking, heavily beamed ceilings up the steep stair; on the ground a pattern of criss-cross bricks notably polished. The girl-child of the place trudges three miles and a half to Benenden School, starting out along the track where *Planta genista* grows as thickly as in the Welsh hills.

But of all the valley farms give me Attwater's, near the foot of the next rise. A long, low building, roof and walls cherry-red, windows diamond-paned, rose-red blown curtains; hay-stacks at hand, and a wagon with tilted shafts; neighbourly great trees, an oak, a Spanish chestnut gold-fruited; hills close at the back, and hills to look upon; a sheltered place, ripe with years.

A long stretch to cover now, and heavy rain begins to fall. I reach a cross-roads and more buildings.

'What is this farm?' after scrutinizing a wet map, I ask a

lad standing near me, taking cover for the sake of his Sunday
elegance.

'Four Wents,' he said, and pointing to the finger-post, ''cos
o' this, I s'pose.' One finger mercifully told me I was right
for Cranbrook, but kept the mileage secret.

The rain was now a torrent. I joined Sunday Suit and his
best friend under their copse. Just as our boughs began to drip
the sun came out and I resumed my lonely road, shining now
with great pools. One other wayfarer was upon it; a young
partridge, weighted by its sodden plumage, peered from the
long hedge-grasses with bright, mournful eyes. Then I heard
a familiar hoot, and suddenly my by-road reached its goal.

### GOUDHURST TO BRENCHLEY

#### I

Goudhurst and Horsmonden occupy the wooded ridges
which border the River Teise.

From the Vine Inn at Goudhurst—'Goodhirst' of old—
steep Clayhill falls some 200 feet to Hope Mill, by the station,
which has a bathing-pool close at hand. Goudhurst lies on the
right bank, Horsmonden on the left, but both choose southern
slopes and are full of sunshine.

Sir Robert de Crevecoeur gave Goudhurst Church in the
twelfth century to the canons of Leeds Abbey in return for
their prayers. Henry VIII granted the advowson to Rochester
Chapter, who still take the great tithe. But long before this
Goudhurst had tired of its canons, and demanded a resident
vicar. Archbishop Stratford, in 1341, gave the villagers their
desire, but endowed the vicarage with an all-embracing tithe
upon their ' lambs, wool, cows, chickens, pigs, ducks, apples,
pears, onions, mills and hay '. They built the nave and arcading of the church under the stimulus of their independence; the
north aisle and rood-loft were added a century and a half later.

Some say that the screen-bases were carved by the same hand as the woodwork in Henry VII's Chapel. The west tower was last erected, and has lost by lightning one storey and its spire. These high Wealden churches have suffered much by storm: the *Tenterden Recorder* notes in 1672, 'Dec. 29th, Benenden Steeple and Church and 5 houses burnt, set first on fire by lightning.'

Grooves in the base-moulding of Goudhurst Tower are said to show where the village archers sharpened their arrows; perhaps (as Canon Raikes's history suggests) before they followed Sir John, the last Bedgebury of Bedgebury, to Agincourt; his brass effigy lies on the South Chapel floor. His sister and heiress, Agnes, carried Bedgebury in dower to the Colepepers, of Bayhall, who now became the lordly family of Goudhurst.

Having grown into 'Culpeppers', they entertained Queen Elizabeth for one day in her Kent Progress of 1573, and vanished from Bedgebury in 1688 with the death of the last Thomas Colepeper. There followed a series of owners, beginning with Sir John Hayes, second husband of Lettice, Lady Falkland, who rebuilt the house, and ending with the Beresford-Hopes, in whose hands it grew into 'an imposing specimen of Louis XIV Architecture without and of Louis XIV decoration within'. Bedgebury was the birthplace of the Peelite *Morning Chronicle*, to which Lord Salisbury and Sir William Vernon Harcourt contributed in their young days: later on the *Saturday Review* was planned there. The extensive Elizabethan park long since shrank to an estate of some 1,500 acres; the mansion, like so many country houses of our time, has become a girls' school.

II

The early pages of G. P. R. James's novel *The Smuggler* introduces a lurid episode in Wealden history. 'Of all counties,' he writes, 'the most favoured by nature and by art for the very pleasant sport of smuggling was the county of

Kent.' The levels of Romney Marsh, the flats of Sandwich and Pevensey Bay, the cliffs around Folkestone, the broken country behind Sandgate—all were unrivalled for the landing and secret keeping of contraband. Think, too, inland, of the dense undergrowth and untrodden park-lands; the roads of felled trees or broad stones laid side by side, such as only horses or men afoot could traverse; the unfrequented 'minnis' or moor; here was a wild paradise for the spirit of adventure. Nor was the population less accommodating than Nature herself. Everywhere there was half-humorous tolerance for the smuggler, readiness to benefit by his risky trafficking. 'The county magistrates when called upon to aid in his pursuit looked grave, and swore-in constables at their leisure; they . . . ordered . . . the butler to *send the sheep to the wood*, an intimation not lost upon those for whom it was intended.' The main road of access to the Weald 'perversely pursued its way up and down the hills on the north boundary till it thought fit to descend to Ashford'. But for this highway on its outer rim, century after century it was served by tracks notoriously vile. Queen Elizabeth has 'a hard beginning of her Progress in the Wild of Kent, where surely were more dangerous rocks and valleys and worse ground than was in the Peak'. A seventeenth-century traveller, Samuel Jeake of Rye, finds 'good weather overhead but dreadful and dangerous ways from Appledore to Ashford'. In the eighteenth century the fastidious Walpole, after sleeping at a Tonbridge inn full of farmers and tobacco, can hire no horses to escape to Penshurst, 'the only man in the town who had two would not let us have them because . . . the roads were so bad'. The engineer Rennie, surveying the Weald for a projected canal, still finds 'the country almost destitute of practicable roads . . . the interior untraversed except by bands of smugglers'. So G. P. R. James chose a stage befitting his adventurous tale, and constructed it with so intimate a knowledge of the district that its course can be followed step by step upon the map. Radford, the Hythe shopkeeper turned land-owner, and his reckless son Richard, the gentleman-smuggler, fill the villains' parts, and the heroes are Sir Robert Croyland and Captain Osborne, a baronet incognito. Osborne puts up at the Hythe inn; the landlord cocks an eyebrow when asked for a private apartment and promises his guest one snug enough, with two doors, ' so that *they* can come in by the one and go it through the other '. In the moonlit ruins of Saltwood Castle Radford and Harding, smuggler-in-chief, plot how to run a cargo of Indian shawls, painted silks, bales of lace, enough to lade a hundred horse. But Little Starlight, grandson to Galley Ray the witch, turns traitor for a few crowns, and Mowle the customs officer, hidden in an ivied tower, ' listens in ' to the conspirators. . . .

## III

Goudhurst was the historic scene of the most famous of Wealden smuggling episodes. Indeed, the newspaper report is here wilder than the romance. It tells how a desperate gang had long terrorized the neighbourhood : they rode openly into the town, plundered houses, inflicted death, torture, and outrage. Trade was at a standstill; none stirred out after nightfall, scarce even in broad daylight. One Mr. Ballard of Tunbridge Wells, passing through at noon, was ' robbed of thirty-nine pounds, his watch and ring, and so cruelly beaten that on being carried home he lived but four hours'. Then arose a champion in Israel. A young soldier called Sturt, of a marching regiment, where he was ' in high esteem by his officers, from his perfectness in the manuals and every art of war ', returned home on his discharge. Possessing initiative which army routine could not destroy, he no sooner learnt of the town's wretched plight than he collected a band of young men pledged to the public service, and was appointed general officer of ' the Goudhurst Militia '. The test of endurance did not long delay. A militiaman was captured, and under long torture revealed the secret of the new association. Very ill-advisedly the smugglers let their prisoner go, with a bombastic message that they were coming in force to plunder Goudhurst and set it ablaze. Little did they know their man; Sturt harangued his troop and set them to cast bullets and assemble powder and fire-arms. He chose his battle-field at the upper end of the village and there entrenched his forces. Presently along came the smugglers at a gallop, ' every one stripped to his shirt, with a handkerchief bound about his head and furnished with a carbine and brace of pistols'. Like any ogre Fee-fo-fum, Richard Kingsmill, the leader, roared out that he had been at the killing of forty of the royal troops and ' would yet broil four townsmen's hearts and eat them for his supper'. The first shots were exchanged; a smuggler fell, then two others; many were wounded, the rest, in spite of bravado un-prepared for resistance, took to their heels. Kingsmill's end is recorded in the parish register : ' the leader of the scoundrels fell, Killed by the discharge of a bullet of lead'. Two others were hanged at Tyburn and their bodies removed in chains, as a fearful warning, to gibbets on Horsmonden Green and Goud-hurst Gore. All this happened in 1796; and smuggling lasted on for many years to come.

There are innumerable historic houses in and around Goud-hurst, many of which have charming names. ' Bockingfold' the fierce Bartholomew de Badlesmere once held ' by the service of one pair of Clove Gilliflowers every year'; the dark and fragrant gilliflower still blooms profusely in cottage gardens round about. The history of ' Finchcocks' begins in 1255; then there is Combwell Abbey; Pattenden, where Sir Maurice Berkeley, standard-bearer to three successive kings died in 1581; Triggs, Twyssenden, Twysden, and many another.

IV

After the high road has dropped below the Vine Inn and

bent west along the hill-side through a convenient gate, you may gaze over the lovely Teise valley and its slanted wood-lands. This is the surest way of discovering just where Hors-monden Church stands. One would naturally go first to Horsmonden to find it. Already I had been there, on an Easter Bank Holiday. The village Green was besieged by heavy charabancs from poorer London. It was a sunny day and we were all ' avin ' a picnic in the country, and enjoyin' of ourselves. Family parties bordered the grass. South London mamas sat solidly on their brown mantles, releasing from many a newspaper the midday meal. The tin receptacles for waste had long since overflowed; whatever could one do with the rest but spread it liberally on the green? Father was cheerful too, smoking, legs outstretched, chatting loud-voiced with a pal a group or two away. Except the trees, the only uprights were the smaller children : they trotted to and fro introducing their grubby little selves by a long stare, a snatched toy, a pull at somebody's crust. The general shop was doing a roaring trade in sweets, buns, cheap toys; otherwise the houses on the Green showed blank faces, enduring rather than enjoying their visitors. They are not among the prettiest of Kent cottages, but date from a prosaic period when beauty had been a while forgotten.

There seemed no natives about on that Bank Holiday. At least I repeatedly asked my way to the church, until I knew beforehand the reply. ' Sorry, but a stranger.' At last I found a sandwich-and-coffee bar improvised for the invaders' benefit : the owner told me to take the left-hand road and ask again. ' It's a good step,' he added, ' two and a half miles at the least.'

My guide-book was ambiguous : ' The village surrounds a green called the Heath, about a mile from the River Teise. Near to the river stands the church.' In the optimism of a morning start I had read these words literally. I now stepped out by the left-hand road and met almost at once two girls—country girls—holiday clad. It was weak-minded to ask again within five minutes, but ask I did, for some obscure psychological reason.

'I am right, am I not, for Horsmonden Church?'

The elder girl stared. 'Why, you're walking right away from it,' she said. 'It's back behind you, close to the station.'

'It's the *old* church I am looking for.'

'The old church? I never heard of more than one church in Horsmonden, did you?' turning to her companion.

'No, I never did; anyway, there's no church along this road,' and off they went with a giggle.

They were so confident that I actually turned back and followed them towards the Green. Then I thought better of it, pulled out my map, kept to the left-hand road. It was shady walking for nearly a mile to the first cross-roads. The finger-post being silent on the point of St. Margaret's, Horsmonden, I was justified in taking counsel, but of whom? I waited until a youth came cycling by, and put my question while he was still yards away. He dismounted and said politely he was sorry he couldn't direct me, but there was a young lady living in the next cottage. . . . I clicked the little gate and knocked gently at the door. No reply. 'She's in the garden behind,' called out my cyclist, waiting to see his instructions obeyed. Yes, there she was; her little foot on a spade digging among the cabbages, like any—— Who is the goddess of lady-gardeners? Her directions were calm and clear; only a mile or so to go now. Yet she seemed, I felt, sceptical of my bump of locality. And, oh, may she never read this record! I walked and walked; I passed, with a glow of triumph, the tower which a rector of Horsmonden built in memory of Sir Walter Scott. I rounded the fence, expecting, like Childe Roland, to come to my other tower, dark now with longing and mysterious. I dropped down a steep hill, far down, into a maze of lanes—farther, farther. I reached a turning labelled Goudhurst, and there, irrationally, altered my objective from a steeple to an omnibus. When next day, not owning defeat, I began the search all over again, suddenly, below the Vine Inn, Horsmonden Church peered from a leafy screen across the valley. The new way was a walker's way, down the hill by a steep pack-track, across the Teise by a little bridge, over the railway, up the opposite hill. Here, past a comfortable farmstead, one enters the domain surrounding Horsmonden Rectory. Even then, with the choice of several avenues, I was again embarrassed and again rescued, by a lady cyclist pushing her wheel up the hill. There were two churches, she explained, but the old one, close by now, really was a church; as for the temp'rary, near the Heath, 'There ain't no burials there; you know what I mean; it don't seem like a church if you ain't got *them* outside.'

Between ranks of splendid oak-trees I went, and past the beech, with gnarled roots. The wood-pigeons were cooing; a 'plane high up droned on its way. To the very latest moment that church hides itself: its last screens, after the chestnut copse, are a farm and an oast across the neck of the promontory on which it stands. Those graves—hart's-tongue fern growing in their crevices—are on the hill-side which falls away from the church walls. There the dead sleep, as they had lived, under the shadow of great trees. Their awakened eyes might look across the valley to the hop-garden, orchard, or cornfield where in life they laboured. No road is near, except the park-like road of approach. By the churchyard gate a huge old walnut-tree, a decrepit giant, bravely clings to life. The grey-stepped mounting block, that has served many a rider to Sunday prayers, is close at hand. . . . Inside, the church is well restored and well maintained. The magnificent brass on the chancel step is a memorial to Henry de Grofh'erst who served for fifty years (1311–61) the altar before which he lies. One could believe the face to be an attempt at portraiture, not a conventional image. The eyes, open and downcast, are set rather close; the mouth is a little open, as if still uttering prayers and praise.

I noticed the following item of parish history on a board under the belfry tower : 'To celebrate the signing of the Peace Treaty, a Peal Solo changes was rung on these bells in three hours, on St. Margaret's day, July 20th 1919.' The ringers' names come next, and then : 'This board was taken from a branch that fell from the old yew-tree in the churchyard during a snowstorm, April 27th 1919.'

### V

The meadows around Horsmonden are miniature parks, where the magnificent trees stand apart and reign each over a little province of verdure sheltered by wide-spread branches. The valley-sides are clothed with slanted hop-gardens, lovely as any vineyard. A pleasant if roundabout way to reach Brenchley on foot from the Heath is to climb by Furnace Hill to the ridge of Castle Hill (an inn and a ruined castle dispute the honour of the name). Here the prospect north and south over the Weald is magnificent. I saw winged clouds empty themselves in torrents of rain upon Paddock Wood far below, but the high lands were tempest-free. Brenchley is an enchanting place—the heart of it, that is. The guide-book calls it 'large and populous', but though its newer features may be sketched in commonplace along the high road, the cluster round All Saints' Church still is—enchanting. Old-world and unworldly too, may be, when on a Bank Holiday the village shop produces no other sustenance than a chocolate biscuit and a Lyons tartlet, both highly recommended. That 'Kentish people do not buy apples' explains the absence of fruit, even a banana; but I think of the coffee-bar on Horsmonden Heath, and with a grace of thanksgiving nibble my biscuit, sitting on a tree-trunk in an unfrequented meadow. In Brenchley graveyard an avenue of huge pyramidal clipped yew-trees leads up to the north porch. A man is hard at work shaping one of them; he tells me they are clipped once a year,

always in the last week of July. They are, he says, 'growing
out too fur up top'. Wonderful at an age well over 300 years
to be soaring still. Here are two churchyard epitaphs worth
recording; one of them, on the north side, is from a two-
horned grey stone to the memory of one Thorn. Thus it runs :

> This world is like a city, 'tis full of crooked streets,
> Death is the market place where all poor mortals meet.
> If life were only merchandise that men could sell or buy
> The rich alone would live, and the poor alone could die.

This other remark, brief and incisive, concludes an epitaph
to Alexander Wimshurst in commercial style :

> 'Item, left issue, one son (viz.) Adam.'

One feature of Brenchley Church delighted me. Two finely
carved angel figures lean out from beams in the chancel roof.
They are clearly the last left of a company of six, bearing the
instruments of the Passion. Again and again I have met such
angel-companies in France, carved, painted, or in tapestry, but
never, I think, in England.

My hospitable biscuit shop is part of the former mansion-
house of the Roberts family, a timbered building of Elizabethan
date. George Roberts of Moatlands was buried in All Saints'
Church, and the property came to his daughter Margaret, who
married Walter Roberts of Glassenbury in Cranbrook. He and
his Margaret were the 'most deare cousins, Mr. W. and M. R.',
of Phineas Fletcher; their wedding inspired his poem called
'An Hymen' :

> Heark, how our Kentish woods with Hymen ring
> While all the nymphs and all the shepherds sing,
> Hymen, oh Hymen, here thy saffron garment·bring . . .
> See where he goes, how all the troop he cheereth
> Clad with a saffron coat, in's hand a light;
> In all his brow not one sad cloud appeareth;
> His coat all pure, his torch all burning bright. . . .

Another Sir Walter, son of the first, and his wife Barbara
clasp hands on a monument in the north transept. Both have
flowing curls and she wears a slender low-bosomed gown like

a Lely picture. The inscription is almost illegible and the flooring at that point seemed ready to crumble under foot, so that long scrutiny was inadvisable. An inscription in the east chancel remembers Elizabeth Fane, who came from Corshorne in Cranbrook, was twice wedded, and the mother of many children. She survived her second husband, George Fane of Badsell, almost half a century and spent her widowhood in the Old Parsonage at the west end of Brenchley. There she exercised a ' memorable hospitalitie ', which her household saw no reason to complain of, for they never left her although her doors stood always ' open, to entertaine the rich and relieve the poore '. How well one can picture ' company ' joyfully arriving at the Old Parsonage, now a large black and white house with careful modern additions. The straight front, with the two ground-floor rooms it conceals, were Madam Fane's. In the parlour the oak panelling is of an unusual linen-fold pattern; the open Tudor fire-place has plain little shields at the corners of the chamfer, and the initials E. F.

The windows of these rooms look on to a green court, where flagged paths lead to a handsome arched gateway dated 1522; Elizabeth Fane must have found it in place with its Doric columns, frieze and pediment. The house is said to stand ' on the verge of . . . an ancient chase '; and to the left of it there leans a huge ruinous oak of patriarchal age. Beyond the gate the garden-path is flower-bordered, and a triple door-way can be seen in a dark rampart of clipped yew. Nowadays houses are close up to the old garden : once it must have lain among green fields, aside from the village stir.

I know one story of Brenchley during Elizabeth Fane's time. In 1581 Margaret Simons was arraigned at Rochester Assizes on a charge of witchcraft, her accuser being the vicar, John Ferrall.

' His sonne ', so Reynold Scot relates, '(being an ungratious boie) passed on a daie by Margaret's house; at whome by chance hir little dog barked—which thing the boie taking in evill part drewe his knife, and pursued him there-with, even to hir doore; whom she rebuked with some such words as the boie disdained . . . At the last he returned to his maister's house, and within five or six daies fell sicke. Then was called to mind the fraie betwixt the dog and the boie; insomuch as the vicar . . . did so calculate . . . partlie through his owne judgment, and partlie by the relation of other witches, that his sonne was by hir bewitched. Yet, he also told me that this his sonne (being as it were past all cure) received perfect health at the hands of another witch.'

Mistress Fane, I hope, did not offer frequent hospitality to Master Ferrall. One pictures more pleasantly the boy Phineas Fletcher in her society. He loved Brenchley and would not unwillingly have come to live there. So he assures us:

> . . . Would my luckie fortune so much grace me
> As in low Cranebrook or high Brenchly's hill,
> Or in some cabin neare thy dwelling place me;
> There would I gladly sport and sing my fill. .

*Chapter XII: ON THE RED HILLS*

*Boughton Monchelsea, Ulcombe and Boughton Malherbe—*
*Little Chart, Pluckley and Great Chart*

## BOUGHTON MONCHELSEA, ULCOMBE AND BOUGHTON MALHERBE

### I

WHEN Spenser in the seventh Aeglogue of the Shepheard's Calender wrote about the holy hills,

> . . . sacred unto saints they stond
> And of them hav theyr name,

he gave two examples, one familiar, the other forgotten by most :

> St. Michel's Mount who does not know,
> That wardes the Westerne coste;
> And of *St. Bridget's bowre* I trow
> All Kent can rightly boaste.

It is strange to find St. Bridget in Kent, but lamentable that her bower's whereabouts has apparently passed from mind. Some writers suggest the fanciful name belonged to the stern ridge of the North Downs; others bestow it on the ' Red Hills ', the north boundary of the Weald. On a day when the wide distance was dimmed by the smoke of weed-fires, I came first upon Boughton Monchelsea Church, standing on the wooded ridge, well south of its village, with central tower square, solid and low, and a nave in the north aisle. A schoolboy of tender age guided me along the lane, stopping by hedgerow gates to shout to his relatives at work in the fields that he was on his way home, and affably explaining which side of the roadway

I had best take to avoid death from a descending motor. This Boughton of the many Kent Boughtons, says Hasted, 'has the addition of Monchensie (pronounced Monchelsea) from the family of that name', magnificently Latinized as 'de Monte Canisio'. Their ownership began after Bishop Odo's disgrace; they were gone, in favour of the Houghams, before the end of Henry III. One member of the family belongs to the romance of medieval education. The first French grammar extant in England or France was written for the Lady Dionysia de Monchensie by Walter of Bibbesworth. She was the only daughter, some say born out of wedlock, of William de Monchensie, and married Hugh de Vere, third son of Robert, Earl of Oxford. She was childless, and the heir of her lands at Boughton and Swanscombe was her cousin Aymer de Valence, Earl of Pembroke.

Was ever a more instructive grammar than the little Dionysia's! She might learn the French for peeling an apple and tying on her bib; the names of wild flowers; of orchard-trees, cherry, pear and bullace; of nightingale and merle, sheldrake and woodlark; above all pretty tales about the wren. As befitted a country maid, she could describe hay-time and harvest and every implement of toil. She watched in French the table laid with spotless napery, the bread cut, the parings thrown into the alms-basket, the boar's head carried in, garlanded, for the feast. Was Dionysia still dimly remembered after two centuries, when a namesake, Dionysia Woldeham, held land in Boughton Monchensie?

Boughton has, or had, another surname, 'Boughton *Quarry*, from the large quarries of stone within the bounds of it'. Some deeds belonging to the Kent Archaeological Society illustrate the working of these famous quarries in days gone by. For instance, in 1486 Richard Clerke of 'Bocton Monchensie', yeoman, sells to William Crompe the younger of Otham, 'two days workys of quarry in the quarry called Bocton quarry'.

Evidently the owners of quarry land hired it out by portions, measured against the days' work required to quarry so much stone as the purchaser had need of.

Boughton stone ready wrought at the quarry was used for 'newels, coping-stones, drip-stones, cornices', and so forth in the building of Rochester castle. And a manuscript agreement of 1610 records that Sir Francis Fane arranged with Henry Stace and Henry Peeke of Boughton, masons, 'for the making of two rownde windowes and one flatt windowe of the best Stone in Boughton quarryes, for the newe greate Chamber at Merworthe'. So has Boughton stone travelled from its hill-side all over Kent.

The church is much restored, and a fire in 1832 destroyed many interesting monuments. Part of one wrought by Nicholas Stone is skied in the north aisle. Stone made these effigies of Sir Francis and Lady Barnham to Sir Francis's order in 1633, and duly received an impress of forty pounds on his estimate of ninety-five pounds, from 'Mr. Pearcs, Screvenor'. Lady Barnham had already died in 1631, the mother of fifteen children: the inscription says that after her departure her husband 'existed but did not live', till he followed her in 1646. On a grandiose erection at the west end Sir Christopher Powell of Wierton, M.P., reclines in a toga, with his wife and mother draped as Roman matrons mourning over him. Mrs. Esdaile tells us that these exotic garments symbolize the robe of an immortal soul.

II

The view from Ulcombe churchyard, 350 feet above sea-level, is, if possible, even more entrancing than Boughton's landscape of the Weald. Twin giants, yew-trees of huge dimensions, reign among the gravestones, coeval perhaps with the church's Saxon foundation; for *Domesday* records of 'Ole-combe', 'there is a church here'. The yew at the south-west angle has a girth of 28 ft. 4 in. and is 43 ft. high; its ancient fellow at the south-east measures 28 ft. 10 in. round about,

and 50 ft. high. There was great slaughter amongst churchyard trees in the unsettled days after the Reformation. An ash
at Boughton Monchensie was 'ridd upp by the Rotes' and
exchanged by the vicar for other timber. At Teynham a great
elm fell to the clerical axe, and at Newenden a yew-tree, 'a
defence unto their churche and chauncell'. Perhaps the
Ulcombe yews were too solid to be trifled with, and continued
as before to provide sprigs of 'palm' for the Lenten procession.
The 'Palm-Tree' of sundry Kent inns, one in Elham valley,
for instance, is the homely yew.

All Saints, Ulcombe, was once a collegiate church, like
Wingham or Wye; its tiny college included an arch-presbyter,
two canons, one deacon and one clerk, who together served
the upland parish. The college existed before 1293 and lasted
at least till January 1425. The title of archpriest was still in
use by Thomas Welles, a Wykehamist, Prior of St. Gregory's,
Canterbury, Bishop of Sidon, beneficed at Chartham and Adis-
ham until 1512, when he exchanged his office for a canonry
at South Malling. His chaplaincy to Archbishop Warham
perhaps brought him first to Ulcombe, for the lord of the
manor, Sir Anthony St. Leger, married Agnes Warham, the
archbishop's niece. Welles's title will recall to some the 'Archpriest' of France, Froissart's Arnold de Cervoles, companion
of Du Guesclin, who fought at Poitiers. Was it by some
collegian's hand that Ulcombe Church walls were adorned
with so many paintings—of the crucifix? Under the most
striking the war memorial is placed. The reformers complained (in 1562) that the tabernacle was still standing at
Ulcombe and that an aumbry remained near the altar, where
the books were wont to lie. This omission to destroy has never
been repaired; there are still two niches in the east wall; though
the 'iii seats for priest, deacon and sub-deacon' have vanished.
Not long ago a stone altar-slab, with consecration crosses, was
found in front of the Wandesforde Chapel door, and reverently
restored to its ancient use. The vandalism which threw it

aside was not uncommon in village churches. One reads in the Visitation Records of 1550 at Pluckley : ' Item for drinke to ym that had out the altare stones ijɗ.'

The St. Leger (Sellinger) family lived in the ancient mansion east of the churchyard. They left two splendid brasses to commemorate Ralph and Anne, she wearing a butterfly head-dress; a monument also to Sir Anthony St. Leger, K.G., thrice Lord Deputy of Ireland. ' By whose meanes,' runs the epitaph, ' in his first government, the Nobilitie and Commons were induced . . . . to geve unto Henrie the Eight, King of England, in that province allso . . . the title and scepter of Kinge . . . whose praedecessors before were intituled only Lordes of Ireland.' The lines do scant justice to his remarkable administration of that distressful country. He travelled into remote places, ' where . . . none of your Grace's Deputies cam this hundreth yeris before ', and showed unwonted understanding of the Irish character. He was ' the Deputy that made no noise ', mainly because, for the first time the wheels of his government ran smooth. The plottings of jealousy brought him into trouble at last, and he was under a shadow when he died.

Thus a chapter of Irish history is recorded in remote English Ulcombe. The home of Joseph Hatch, the bell-founder, has been identified in Roses Farm on the boundary of Broomfield and Ulcombe parishes. No less than 155 of his bells remain in Kent steeples; indeed, one questions whether the three bells, dated 1632, of the six in Ulcombe belfry are not his; especially as a 1640 bell—he died in 1639—bears the inscription ' William Hatch made me ', William being Joseph's nephew and successor.

III

Let us follow now along the line of the hills, to Boughton Malherbe, the haunt of illustrious memories. Boughton Court, as it is called to-day—Bocton or Boughton Hall, Place, or Palace of the seventeenth century, stands a stone's throw from St.

Nicholas Church. Izãak Walton knew it as 'an ancient and goodly structure, beautifying and being beautified by the Parish Church . . . adjoining unto it, both seated within a fair park of the Wottons, on the brow of a hill'. To the Wottons he gave a perfect epitaph, for they seemed, he said, 'to be a family beloved of God'. Still church and house are beautified each by the neighbourhood of the other, and the remembrance of Nicholas Wotton and his long line of noble sons lives again for each visitor to their home. The first Nicholas settled in Kent under Elizabeth after a prosperous city career. He was a member of the Drapers' Company, alderman, twice Lord Mayor, and married to a Kent heiress, Joan Corbye. Her family had owned Boughton Place under Edward III, who permitted Sir Robert Corbye 'krennellare et turrettare' the house. The Corbyes inherited through the female line, from the de Deanes, and behind them from the de Gattons, and as far back as Henry III from the Malherbes, after whom the place is surnamed.

Thus the citizen husband stepped into a knightly line, and quartered his arms 'argent, a cross patee, fitched at the foot, sable', with the Corbyes' 'Saltire, ingrailed sable, on a silver ground'. He went to live in the ancestral house, making large additions and perhaps changing its military aspect, before he died in 1448. His family lived on there; first another Nicholas, whose brass is in the church; next Sir Robert, Lieutenant of Guisnes and Comptroller of Calais, under Edward IV; and next again his son, Sir Edward also Treasurer of Calais and Privy Councillor, who refused Henry the Eighth's offer to make him Lord Chancellor 'out of a virtuous modesty'. Sir Edward's celebrated brother was Nicholas, Dean of Canterbury and York, to whose proud memory he erected the lifelike portrait in alabaster which kneels in St. Thomas's Chapel; the head, it is said, was made in Rome. To a dream of the Dean's when he was Ambassador in France, the next heir owed his ability to reign at Boughton—he dreamed that his nephew was on the brink of some ruinous project, and without delay wrote off to Queen Mary begging that Thomas, on some colourable pretext, might be committed at once to jail. To prison the young man went; afterwards it transpired he had intended to join his neighbour Sir Thomas Wyatt in fatal rebellion. Thus providentially Thomas Wotton lived to succeed his father; became sheriff of Kent in 1558; in 1573 entertained Elizabeth when she arrived at Boughton from Sissinghurst. In the good tradition he too refused knighthood and the high office she pressed on him; 'being a man of great modesty, of a most plain and single heart, of an ancient freedom and integrity of mind'. In the next year at Boughton Malherbe, Mildred Norrington, Pythoness of Westwell, was tried before two discreet justices, Thomas Wotton and his neighbour George Darell, of Calehill.

This girl was servant in William Sponer's household and, like the Nun of Kent, a ventriloquist. To listen to her one might suppose those quiet hamlets given over to the evil one. She raved, wrestled with demons, accused her neighbours of witchcraft. Two local parsons exorcized her, noting solemnly on a scrap of paper that 'Sathan's voice did differ much from the maid's voice'. But here at Boughton, face to face with the law, the Pythoness came to her senses. Being neither tortured, flattered, nor tricked into confession, confronted only by two honest and determined gentlemen, she owned up; and in Master Wotton's house, before a large audience, gave a display of her illusions and trances, like the most up-to-date medium.

James I raised Thomas's eldest son Edward to the peerage as Baron Wotton of Marly, and it was he who acquired St. Augustine's Palace, in the ruins of the abbey, from the Cecils, and employed John Tradescant to fill the garden borders with white and purple Canterbury bells.

There were but three holders of the Wotton title: Thomas, the second Baron, died early in 1630. His widow, Mary

Throckmorton, Lady Wotton, lived on through the Civil War.
Her house at St. Augustine's was 'twice plundered by the
populace, at which the Mayor assisted and encouraged their
outrage', and in 1642 Sir John Seaton and Colonel Edwin
Sandys visited her to search for arms. Tradition attributes
her death to terror and the soldiers' ill-usage, but she survived
till 1658, and is buried at Boughton, leaving her name to Lady
Wotton's Green before St. Augustine's Gate. A devoted
servant and kinsman of hers, Edmond Sandford, has a little
brass tablet in the aisle of Boughton Church. No other record
of him remains, but as a young man he may have supported
her in face of her enemies. She 'laid over him this tombe stone
for continuance of his memory, precious as a perfumed oynt-
ment for the constancy of his profession of religion and the
fidelity of his service'.

IV

The Boughton estates now passed to Lord Wotton's eldest
daughter, Katherine, married first to Henry, Lord Stanhope.
He died before succeeding to the Earldom of Chesterfield, but
in 1660 his lady was created Countess in her own right. Before that time came she had lived through so many adventures
as to make her perhaps the most romantic figure of all the
Wottons of Boughton. As a young widow she was courted by
Lord Treasurer Cottington and Sir Anthony Van Dyck, but
refused them both, the painter because he had charged too
much for her portrait. Presently there came along to negotiate
the marriage of the Prince of Orange with the child-princess
Mary, a Dutch nobleman, John Polyander a Kerkhoven, Lord
of Heenvliet. He succeeded where others had failed, and in
Mary's bridal train, he carried his bride back to the Netherlands. Heenvliet became Superintendent of the Household,
Lady Chesterfield acted as Princess Mary's governess. Even
yet her adventures were not over, for on Heenvliet's death in
1660, she entered the service of the Duchess of York, and

married as her third spouse, the Royalist soldier and postmaster Daniel O'Neill, 'as honest a man as ever lived'. Him too she outlived, and he lies in Boughton Church under a pyramid of black marble. The memorial, says Hasted, 'placed injudiciously, just within the altar rails, fills up almost the whole space'; . . . modern taste has banished it to the vestry. Lady Chesterfield presented to Boughton Church a gilt baluster-stemmed cup and paten of Dutch workmanship in memory of her parents. Her only son, Charles Henry Kerkhoven, Baron Wotton of Boughton Malherbe and Earl of Bellamont, was buried in Canterbury Cathedral January 11th 1683. After him the Boughton estates went away to the Earls of Chesterfield, and Philip, the famous Georgian statesman and wit, sold them all to Galfridus Mann of London. When Hasted wrote in 1782 only enough of the house was left to serve as a farmstead. The west front is still full of interest. A beautiful oriel window of sixteen lights projects on the upper and lower storeys; part, it may be, of the first Nicholas Wotton's additions. There is a later Dutch gable at the northern end. Inside, the lofty chambers have been repartitioned, and new floors inserted, so that a fragment of the domed and painted drawing-room ceiling remains in a top attic. A lithograph, perhaps a century old, representing part of this room, gives some idea of the rich panelling, with gilded ornament and slender fluted pilasters, which has now journeyed to the States. The banqueting-hall once had panelling also carved with stylized vine-clusters of great richness. Under an old cotttage adjoining the mansion is a mysterious cavern, where the Pythoness might have held her séance, though it probably housed a store of hospitable wine. . . .

And, just before a farewell to Boughton Place, I shall set the name of its greatest lover, Sir Henry Wotton, only child of that romantic second marriage of Thomas Wotton's to the mourning widow, Mrs. Eleanor Morton, on which Izaak Walton delightfully commented : 'The tears of Lovers or Beauty dressed in sadness have a charming eloquence.'

Sir Henry's story, his life in Italy, his retirement to Eton College, his wit, learning and piety are written down by that perfect biographer. 'He usually went', one rejoices to learn, 'once a year, if not oftener, to the beloved Bocton Hall, where he would say He found a cure for all cares by the cheerful company which he called the living furniture of that place; and a restoration of his strength by the connaturalness of . . . his genial air.' By his will he left to Dean Bargrave of Canterbury his Italian books and the viol da gamba, 'which hath twice been with me in Italy'. He rests in Eton College Chapel.

In character Sir Henry was the epitome of his race; the portrait of their great qualities he has himself set out in noble verse :

> Whose passions not his masters are,
> Whose soul is still prepared for death,
> Untied unto the world by care
> Of public fame or private breath . . .
> . . . This man is freed from servile bands
> Of hope to rise or fear to fall,
> Lord of himself though not of lands
> And having nothing, yet hath all . . .

### LITTLE CHART, PLUCKLEY AND GREAT CHART

#### I

It is hard to leave Boughton Malherbe with Chilston Park, a little to the north, unvisited, and memories of the Hales family and their connexion with Stuart misfortunes unrecalled. John Evelyn did better—he went, in May 1666, 'To visit my cousin Hales at a sweetly-watered place, at Chilston near Bocton', and noted it in his *Diary*.

The way towards Pluckley lies east along the ridge, and leaves unsaluted Queen Elizabeth's oak in its little enclosure. The lane is at first so high up it looks over the Weald to the right and to the left across the gault valley. The Red hills curve a little southward towards Pluckley; but the lane after passing between Surrenden Dering woods and Little Chart drops to the valley of the Stour, that western branch flowing from the chalk.

The Derings and the Darells of Calehill were neighbours for generations. Sir Edward Dering did his best to get John Darell knighted as the Civil War was about to begin. 'I doubt', he wrote from London to his wife, 'John Darell hath but a dullnesse of soul in anything but frugality, and if there be too much of that, that is a dullnesse too. If he had not preferred his twelv'th market (which every yeare he hath) before a knighthood (which no man in the world takes above ones in his life), he had been knighted on twelvth day. If he had kept time and promise to be heere on Saterday night, itt had been done (the queen was moved again) on Sunday . . . the issue is that the King about two of the clocke went suddenly out of towne with the Queen and prince. . . . Thus Mr. Darell is like to be Mr. Darell.' He was at last in time for the accolade, and soon after married Bridget Denne of Dennehill as his second wife. They had no children, and Calehill passed to the heirs of Major Nathaniel Darell, to whom belongs the scaling-ladder hung on the church wall at Little Chart, and taken 'in a bold sally' from Admiral de Ruyter. In this north chancel of the Darells the old rites were celebrated for some time after the Reformation, although it is part of the parish church, divided only by an open screen. St. Katherine's chancel is crowded with Darell monuments; the earlier brasses, the alabaster tomb of a Sir John who died in 1509. His effigy wears the collar of SS., and a tiny bedesman leans against the sole of the right foot, head on hand, as if worn out with long supplication. There is a great helmet too, a funeral trophy made from the halves of two head-pieces; the front, part of a tilting heaume, the back, of a bascinet; the whole surmounted by the Darell crest, a Saracen's head, boldly carved and turbaned.

The view of the Weald from Pluckley is seen by blue
glimpses of distance caught between the dwellings built along
the ridge. The village green is surrounded by brick cottages
with mullioned windows of special Dering design : the church,
with square tower and shingled spire, and the old inn, called
the Black Horse, excellently hospitable, help to make up the
old-world scene. The elder Derings left many fine brasses in
the church pavement, now a knight with his war-horse, now a
lady with butterfly head-dress. One Nicholas Dering of
Rolvenden wished to be buried ' in the church of St. Nicholas
àt Plukley, before the picture of Seynt Blase there '. Here
as elsewhere the village cloth-makers reverenced their patron
of the woolcomb. This is a digression from the monuments
in Pluckley Church. *Revenons!* but to a duller age. For
modern Derings affixed their marble tablets, sternly un-
romantic, to the east wall of the family chapel. Sir Edward
Dering, the best known of them all, lived too late for a brass,
but made rash attempts to restore ancestral specimens, here
and elsewhere. ' He was ', says Mr. Ralph Griffin, ' manufac-
turing a pedigree for himself from before the Conquest, and
was out to connect himself with all the great families of
Kent.' A few years since, the Dering heirlooms, and his
treasures with them, were scattered to the winds, and the noble
avenue leading to his old home ruthlessly hewn down. The
Don Quixote of his day, his neighbours found it hard to take
Sir Edward's vagaries seriously. ' Pray God,' Henry Oxinden
wrote of him, ' his much-turning hath not made his head dazie
and that he doth not turne out of his right wits.' Certainly
his heart was better than his head, though he was no mean
scholar.

In the eighteenth century the Derings and the rector supported a charity school in Pluckley for twelve boys and eight
girls. The children all learnt the three R.'s, but beyond this

the benefits were not great. 'The girls are also taught to sow, and knit; the boys work at proper times; always in harvest and hopping time and whenever their parents particularly want them.'

III

The love of wild flowers awoke, many many years ago, in the heart of a London child at finding wild white violets in a hedge close to Great Chart Rectory. Do they grow there still? For no village child could the wonder be as great; that kind of revelation is one of the very few compensations for being reared among chimney-pots.

Long ago the children in Chart Church of a Sunday were solaced through long-drawn services by the brilliant colours shining on them from the windows; images even of their fathers and uncles and granddads gorgeously arrayed; for in the north window of the North Chapel were 'sixteen pourtraitures of men in glasse, all kneeling. . . . Now it goes by tradition, from the father to the sonne, these were the builders of this Church.' Among the laymen were two priests, Richard Medhurst and Walter Wilcock : their names are not on Hasted's list of rectors, which begins in 1460 with Robert Hoo. John de Godington 'was painted in coat-armour, looking up to a crucifix placed above him '; Henry de Singleton also knelt in armour. All had disappeared before Philipot wrote of them in 1659. The outline of the three-light perpendicular tracery belonging to this window, now blocked, can be seen on the outside wall. A little glass is left in the East window of the South or Goldwell Chapel. The 'Gold wells' besprinkle it which made so fascinating a rebus on the family name. Sometimes the wells appear in the armorial coat, 'argent, six escallops azure, on a chief sable, three wells or '; one light has 'the figure of a man, kneeling on an ornamented pavement, clad in a blue gown, and flanked by two gold wells '. There is a woman in the same posture; they are William and Avice

Goldwell of an ancient family which owned Great Chart
Manor from time immemorial, and in the fifteenth century
added to it the manors of Godinton and Wurtin : William died
in 1485. Once the effigy of Bishop James Goldwell of Norwich
(1472–99) was in the same window of this chantry chapel, and
surrounding him ' in every quarry, a golden well or fountaine '.
He was a distinguished ecclesiastic and diplomat and he loved
Chart Church of his forefathers as Kempe had loved Wye,
and Courtenay, for some reason less well-defined, had loved
Meopham. He was also a munificent benefactor of Norwich
Cathedral, where he built, mainly at his own charges, the roof
and flying buttresses of the choir. His tomb can still be
identified.

iv

A great-great-grandson was it, of William and Avice Goldwell, Nicholas Toke, born in 1588 and known as The Captain,
kept an account book of his Godinton estates, which has been
printed in a stout volume of 532 pages, and may carry us right
away from the statesmanlike atmosphere of Boughton Court
into the ordinary life of a country squire.

The account book shows how the labourer's family was employed *en masse*; there are servants aged twelve, while ' Old
James ' remains on, at half a crown a week, ' for keeping the
cherrys '. ' A good many Tokes actually worked on the farm
as regular labourers,' writes the editor, ' one was employed as
butler. They were paid at the normal wage, just as other
labourers were; but apart from the fact that the name is not
apparently found in the county except in connexion with this
one family, there is no doubt of their relationship, as it is often
stated.' Everything is detailed in those many pages : wages,
the expenses of harvest, haymaking, felling timber, hedging
and diking; the purchase of sheep and oxen, washing the lambs,
shoeing the horses, schooling the children; the taxes and the
chimney money :

'March the 22th.

'I sould the woll over the gatehouse to John Shoulder of Canterbury for five pounds the pecke, and all the woll in the greene coorte garrett for five pounds and ten shillings the pecke. . . .'

And the next year :

'Payd Spratt more for a perrewige £1 10 0.'

And again, when the days shorten towards winter :

'October the 5.

'Fennor payed for candles at 5*d.* the dussen, more for sugar, spice and other things.'

And after Toke's fourth marriage with Mary Browne :

'For a red velvet saddle cloath and furnitur for my wife. £5 10.'

The bride, one of five, with a sixth in view when Death claimed the nonagenarian bridegroom, had expensive tastes. In January 1680 Captain Nicholas died, and the last entry is in another hand :

'Payed Blanket for a coffin, £3 10*s.*'

And

'Payed the painter for the scutchions, £6 0 0.'

Nicholas is said to have been a Royalist, but, more fortunate than many Kentish gentlemen, his lands escaped sequestration.

To-day Godinton is one of the most beautiful of old Kent houses, with fine panelling and carving and mantelpieces adorned with incised patterning in Bethersden marble. Outside there are deep embrasures of yew, and opposite the entrance a mighty Domesday oak which, an ancient tree already, saw the Goldwells out and the Tokes take possession. Great Chart Church stands on the last promontory of the Red hills, or the Quarry hills as Hasted calls them here. The village, sloping away from the church down the hill, is full of old cottages. In the churchyard there is a minute dwelling which might have belonged to a pygmy anchorite. Once the churchwardens of Chart were obliged, under a statute of Edward VI, to 'buyld houses for the Pore'; they accordingly sold, for 33*s*. 4*d*., 'one whole sute of old white damask '; 32*s*. 7*d*. they 'bestowed upon' John Welscheman's house; 5*s*. on Margery Vynall's, and 2*s*. 5*d*. on Johanne Longherst's, all poor and impotent persons. These sums do not tally with the proceeds of the 'damask sute', but so their outlay is recorded. Poor Johanne; can it be that 2*s*. 5*d*. sufficed to build that toy house in the churchyard?

## Chapter XIII: IN THE DARENTH VALLEY

*Westerham to Shoreham—Lullingstone to Dartford*

### WESTERHAM TO SHOREHAM

#### I

DARENTH opens in the North Downs' barrier, the most westerly of the three river-gates of Kent. Hitherto from springs àt Westerham it has flowed due east along Holmesdale, hemmed in between chalk escarpment and sandstone hills. At Otford it turns sharply north, and breaks away, past frowning Polhill, along its own straight and lovely valley, a captive, yet for ever escaping, between the white cliffs crowned with beech-woods.

> Holmesdale, the proud valley
> Never wonne nor never shale,

does not, of course, belong exclusively to our county. Lambarde explains its ' extending itselfe a great length into Surrey and Kent also ', and conjectures that it was ' at the first called Holmesdale, by reason that it is . . . a plaine valley, running between two hils that be replenished with stoare of wood '. Every topographer quotes his words; none more apposite could be found; Holmesdale below Westerham is just that, ' a plain valley ', a rift with scant margins between hill boundaries. The high Downs cut it off to the north from the Kent thoroughfare of Watling Street; and its own roadways, for the use of a sparse population, took their course along foot-hills, where the woodland grew less densely. One of them ran from Westerham, following the western river-bank by Otford to Dartford, two fords being thus at its disposal. The natural formation which

is Holmesdale reaches much farther into Kent than does the
name itself. East of Rochester one hears only of the Upland
and the Weald; in West Kent, of the Upland, the Weald, and
the Holmesdale. The sources of the Darenth at Westerham
are chiefly in the grounds of Squerries Court; there are other
springs in the steep meadow below Westerham Church. From
these the river starts out on its thirty-mile journey; the 'clear
water', as Leland has it, and Spenser is at one with him when,
among Thames tributaries, all 'little Rivers, which owe
vassallage to him', he numbers

> . . . the still Darent in whose waters cleane
> Ten thousand fishes play and decke his pleasant streame.

Squerries, as early as Henry III, gave name and seat to a family
who by some play of words bore as their cognizance a squirrel
browsing on a hazel-nut.

At the beginning of the eighteenth century the Earl of Jersey
sold Squerries to John Warde, whose youngest son, George,
was comrade-in-arms to General Wolfe. Wolfe was born at
Westerham Vicarage, the son of Colonel Edward Wolfe and
his wife Henrietta, on January 2nd 1727, and died, according
to the inscription in the church, 'in America, September 13th
1759, Conqueror of Quebec'. His family lived, says Wolfe's
biographer, at 'Quebec House', so-called after the event, 'a
low square mansion . . . in a hollow at the foot of the hill
down which winds the eastern outlet of Westerham, leading
to Brasted and Sevenoaks'.

The hero and his brother were taught in a house standing
near Westfield Grange, Westerham, a small school kept by a
Mr. Lawrence. While they were still children their father
moved to Greenwich. Nowadays a statuesque Wolfe reigns in
Westerham, a bed of scarlet geranium to do him homage, and
close at hand St. George of England, prototype of all heroes,
complete with charger and dragon, on the sign-board of the
Georgian inn.

The shingled spire of Westerham Church peaks out among

the trees at the head of Kentish Holmesdale. Many London citizens and merchants chose this quiet place to lay their bones in : Mannings, Earnings, Aynesworths, Missendens, Hardys, and so forth. One inscription is on record which ran : ' Here lyeth the body of John Earning, son of Anthony Earning merchant, who was unfortunately slaine in the Strand, over against the New Exchange on the 18th of June, 1688, in the 19th year of his age, to the great griefe of his friends.' Whether poor John fell in a duel or was killed by a thunderbolt history does not relate.

From Westerham the Sevenoaks. road, passing through Sundridge, hugs the southern hill-side, and left of it the valley falls steeply to the river. Sundridge used to be the *villeggiatura* of the rectors of Lambeth. They held the two livings together and came and went between the handsome house on the Thames and this hill-side one bordering on the Darenth.

Close to Sundridge Church a mounting road leads to the brow of Ide Hill and that marvellous Wealden prospect which the National Trust has ransomed, to the memory of Miss Octavia Hill, the philanthropist.

Chevening is perhaps the most attractive of the Holmesdale churches, especially if one comes upon it from Knockholt, high on the Downs. There is a hill-side path, where, on the right hand great trees root in a steep slope, and keep sentinel upon a gorge threaded by a yellow road. Presently the slope reddens with beech-leaves, and some old yews press their shadows into the picture. Still downward the path, until the beeches trail along the edge of the escarpment, and at the foot are soft grasses and flowers in little hollows, sweet marjoram and harebells. Where the path levels out the cattle are lying in a green meadow embayed with trees. Chevening Church is on the edge of the park and has a fine west tower, several Elizabethan monuments and a brass or two; but one remembers only one memorial, modern by comparison. When I entered the church its effigy was shrouded and the chapel where Lennards and

Dacres repose securely locked. However, a village lady hurried up with keys and authority to draw off the covering sheet. 'When I'm about my dusting,' she confided to me, 'I often fancy she has come alive,' laying her hand gently on the still, white lady. I could well believe it, as 'she' lay there—her pretty head hollowing the marble pillow in that long sleep— the little babe she carried away clasped in her arms, a snapped lily-stem against her long robe. Chantrey made her, and none, I think, before or since, has contrived a lovelier monument to youth and grief. The inscription gives me her stiff, high-sounding name : 'The Rt. Hon. Lady Frederica Louisa Stanhope.' It adds that she died in childbed, January 14th 1825, aged 25 : 'Her life was all purity and happiness, its pious close like the slumber of a child.'

A charming row of red-brick cottages, their flagged paths bordered with golden-rod—the church-tower framed in lime-trees, backed by the darker rising woods : this is the picture, as one looks back upon Chevening street from the cross-roads.

## II

Otford was 'Otta's Ford', before ever it came into written history in a burst of valour and of miracle. 'This year', says the *Anglo-Saxon Chronicle* A.D. 774, 'there appeared in the heavens a red crucifix after sunset; the Mercians and the Men of Kent fought at Ottanford, and wonderful Serpents were seen in the land of the South Saxons.' Kent lost the fight, but Offa, the Victorious, King of Middle England, gave the battle-field to Christchurch Priory. After the Norman Conquest Lanfranc took Otford Manor for the See of Canterbury, and so the story of the place, as so often in Kent, is written round the great churchmen.

A great lover of Otford, a student of its history, field by field, introduced me to the place. I could only write of it in his company.

I can see his massive figure now, waiting for the pupil-to-be on the Village Green, a small white terrier gay but submissive at his heels. I descend from the Sevenoaks' bus and the lesson begins :

'This is Otford Street, under the old houses. The villagers have called it so from time immemorial. Never heard of the Pilgrims' Way. That is the invention of some eighteenth-century journalist fellow.'

Then, facing round to the grass patch where the roads meet :

'This is Otford Village Green. The Parish Council got hold of it to commemorate George V's Coronation. Had a tremendous beano. Sports, and a maypole and a Manor Court, with oath and fealty and all the rest of it. That copper-beech was planted in remembrance. It's safe now for all time, all but the pond. Some other fellow filched that and fenced it in.' (I am not responsible for my tutor's opinions. He had a blunt and honest tongue.)

'St. Thomas Becket's spiteful miracles at Otford', as Lambarde called them, seemed to my guide too entertaining to pass over, however apochryphal. There was his provision of 'a fit spring to water it', when the 'spite' consisted in his overstocking low-lying Otford with an unwelcome commodity. Somewhere he discovered a really dry patch, struck his staff into it and a plentiful stream appeared. After all, the Darenth was near at hand. . . . Only the well, and the spite along with it, is not Becket's at all : in scholarly opinion this is no other than a Roman bath. It lies between a cornfield and a strawberry field east of the manor ruins, the surface covered with pond-weed, brambles overhanging the old walls.

'There does not seem anything Roman about this masonry,' I remarked to my friend when we stood at the water's edge.

'No more there isn't,' he replied reassuringly. 'The little round building up on Otford Mount was made of hewn stone from the bath. That sportsman old Dicky Russell, Castle Farm, carried it away. He meant to sit in his tower and view

the hunt when he could ride to hounds no longer. To lay his
bones there too, if only he still might voice a ghostly Tally-
ho. . . .'

I heard also about Becket's second curse, but this I give you
in Lambarde's racier English : 'They say that as he walked on
a time in the olde Parke (busie at his praiers) That he was much
hindered in devotion by the sweete note and melodie of a
nightingale that sang in a bush beside him; and that there (in
the might of his holinesse) he injoined from thenceforth no
birde of that kinde should be so bold as to sing thereabout.'
That malediction deservedly withered away; there are June
nightingales in Otford, and the black swifts which also fell
under the saint's displeasure. Was it not time for a Brother
Francis when God's saints could not pray through His nightingale's song? 'Innumerable such toyes,' comments Lambarde
with proper scorn, 'false Priests have devised . . . which, for
the unworthinesse of the things themselves, and for want of
time (wherewith I am streightened), I neither will nor can
presently recount.'

### III

Warham has been criticized for erecting a thirty-thousand-
pound house at Otford when Morton and Bourchier had
already 'liberally builded' at Knole. Lambarde, surveying the
estate in 1573, wrote bitterly that 'William Warham, wishing
to leave to posteritie some glorious monument of his mis-
begotten treasure, determined to have raised a gorgeous palace
for himself'. Yet Warham's personal friends accounted him
the most self-denying of men; Sir Thomas More says that he
died 'incredibly poor'.

Having builded, he spent much time at 'my pouer place
at Otford'; dispatched many letters to his magnificent rival,
Cardinal Wolsey, and accepted from the cardinal a costly jewel
for St. Thomas's Shrine. At Otford also he entertained Cam-
peggio, a two-days' guest, with whom he had ridden from

Sandwich through the Kentish lanes; a host of 1,000 horsemen, harnessed with gold chains over their armour, escorted them, glittering under the midsummer sun. After all, there were calls enough upon the lord archbishop's hospitality to excuse a mighty spending.

The golden age passes by and Cranmer succeeds to Warham's uneasy seat. Secretary Morice was present when he bargained ' with such a Prince as would not be bridled nor gainsaid in any of his Requests '. What a picture of insolent browbeating he has left us!

' . . . I was by when Otford and Knol were given him [Henry VIII]. My Lord, minded to have retained Knol unto himself, said That it was too small an House for his Majesty. Mary, said the King, I had rather have it than this House, meaning Otford : for it standeth on a better Soil. This House standeth low, and is Rheumatick, like until Croiden, where I could never be without Sickness. And as for Knol it standeth on a sound, perfect wholesome Ground. And if I should make abode here, as I do surely mind to do now and then, I will live at Knol and most of my House shall live at Otford. . . .'

Henry secured the manor-house in 1537. He did little more than rename the empty chambers : the ' Pages ' Chamber ', they being heedless of rheumatic pains; the ' Queen's Privy Chamber ', for Anne Boleyn, or some other unhappy spouse; ' My Ladye Mary's Chamber ', for an ill-used daughter; ' My Lady of Southfolk's lodging ', for that Catherine Willoughby whose Spanish mother had been Catherine of Aragon's friend.

The first survey of Otford extant was made by William Hyde in 1549. Already it was in ' great decay '; others' greed had matched Henry's own.

In 1573 another survey was taken, for Elizabeth, on which Lambarde and George Multon were commissioners. The wreckage now extended from the stripped lead to rotten woodwork and falling plaster. Of Warham's great stable ' very lyttle remayneth but the fowndacion'; *locks and keys for two hundred chambers, no less, are missing.* A neighbouring land-owner, Sir Henry Sidney of Penshurst, now offered to pur-chase the property, and those protracted negotiations began to which Elizabeth's servants were well used. The Sidneys pressed their point, they surveyed again in 1596; when the Commissioners subtly reported that Otford, even if repaired, ' wolde not be fytt for Her Majestie to lye in; for that yt standeth in a very wett soyle, uppon springes and vantes of water contynually runninge under yt. And comonly the flowers [floors] and walls thereof in the winter are hoary and mustie.' To Sir Róbert Sidney must mattered little, if the Great Park might be his, with herds of antler deer, ' raskale ' deer, and does; he would even build the Queen at his own charge ' a pretty house . . . so that she may dine there as she passes by '.

More and more ruinous grew the great chambers; more and more determined Her Majesty. In 1601 she still ' utterly re-fused to pass Otford '. Then suddenly, when money ran short for the Irish expedition, she yielded; for £2,000 Sir Robert be-came master of the broken walls and the deer-park. The later ownership is obscure. *Archeologia Cantiana* says that Otford Manor was sold about 1626 for £19,000 to Sir Thomas Smythe, the Customer's son and Prime Undertaker for the Discovery of the North-West Passage. But Sir Thomas had already ' gone west' in 1625, and his widow speedily remarried Robert Sidney, Earl of Leicester, no other. There is confusion here, but one thing is sure : little by little the estate was broken up, and ' the ruins of the ancient Castle and Palace ' were acquired by Earl Amherst in 1844.

And what of to-day? My guide led me along the east front to survey the fish-ponds, overgrown with weeds, which ex-tended under a bridge to form the moat. We identified the eastern gallery, only stone-heaps now, though turrets, a gate-way and a window are discernible. ' You would scarcely be-

lieve,' said my guide, ' the enormous size of the place after
Warham's rebuilding. The ground plan covered 440 by 220
feet, a hollow rectangle, bounded by long galleries, the main
façade facing west. The Great Gatehouse stood on the north
side, and the Great Hall cut the block across into two courtyards. Can't you picture that glorious mass of red-brick, on
its stone plinth, tall towers clustering at each corner; the roof
tiled; a forest of Tudor-pattern twisted chimneys?' He strode
out as he spoke, across the empty site, where only the conduits
remain. They were occupied by a colony of ducklings; I remember he stopped to watch the little creatures, muttering to
himself, 'Such young imps! charming, charming, all such
young imps.' We peered into the shell of the one upstanding
tower, to note the beauty of the brickwork, diversified by stone
quoins and diamonds of darker brick. Till recently there were
people in Otford who remembered the one remaining gallery
complete with linen panelling; it was burnt out and Lord
Amherst added an upper storey and made it into cottages. The
small hall is now a barn; the dove-house preserves old fittings
contrived for the convenience of nesting birds. 'When you
write about all this,' said my guide, ' remember that the Palace
should be bought and the remnant saved for the nation. The
only pity is it wasn't done long ago : but there! of course
Elizabeth didn't want to pay for two hundred new keys.'

## IV

Otford Church was spoiled by Street's over-restoration. He
removed the arcading of oak columns, the oak beams across
the chancel, the old-fashioned oak fittings characteristic of a
Holmesdale church. The escutcheons on the west wall belong
to the Polhill family, connected with Cromwell through his
daughter Elizabeth Ireton. One of the brothers, David Polhill,
inherited a sturdy strain of independence. He signed the
Kentish petition of 1701 against war subsidies and, after a

week's imprisonment, to teach him and his fellow-petitioners manners, was escorted in triumph home to Polhill. . . .

We leapt into a passing omnibus and my guide poured out information as we hurried along the village street. Next the school, see there, 'a fayer mansion-house, called the parsonage'; the Bull Inn, not built for a hostelry, has panelling from the Archbishop's Manor, and roundel portraits above a Tudor fireplace. . . . On we rushed, skirting a field called in Saxon Charters the 'Play-meadow'. Twitton too we passed, the 'between town' of Otford and Shoreham, where Edmund Ironsides defeated the Danes. . . . This kaleidoscope of history belongs to the river level, below the chalk cliffs beech-crowned.

v

At Shoreham we dismounted. It is a stiff climb up the down-shoulder to the great war memorial cross traced flat in the chalk, and visible from the railway. Party after party of scholars my guide had conducted to that vantage-ground, to show them how the fields were cultivated only to a certain height on the valley-sides; which lands had always been meadow and which plough; how the ancient field-names were in use to-day; how corn-mill and fulling-mill had kept their stations. He pointed to the two valley-roads, the older one west of the Darenth, and to the hills, afforested on the eastern range with old oaks, and on the west with beeches. The Down we stood on was sprinkled with a summer-garden of chalk-hill flowers; southwards the lovely country-side spread towards Sevenoaks. 'This valley ought to be saved,' my guide said to me very solemnly, 'for a page of history where children can be brought to study their England. It ought to be saved, not as a memorial to king, warrior, or priest, but to the sons of the soil.'

We lunched at the Old Crown Inn, black beams overhead, and my companion told me tales of old Shoreham. 'Now

about Squib the Malster, who owned this inn early in the nineteenth century. One day smugglers arrived; they knew the
house well enough; they brought a prisoner, a wounded
Spaniard. Squib's daughter nursed him back to health, and
presently the two were married and settled happily in the
village. Not for long. One day the "furriner" went to
London with a wagon-load of hops, was caught by the press-
gang and—disappeared. When his child was born Squib's
daughter died. Years afterwards the Spaniard came back to
Shoreham; in the village he met a man who told him his wife
was dead. At the news he turned round, walked off into the
distance, and was never seen again. His son and descendants
lived on in the neighbourhood, keeping old memories alive by
their dark eyes and southern looks.'

Shoreham houses illustrate the modes of life of many generations. The alms-houses, with little windows under pointed
wooden arches and heavy oak lintels, show how poor folk were
made at home in the fifteenth century. There are Elizabethan
cottages and modern villas built for retired tradesmen. Lord
Milman, during his squirearchy, put up Victorian cottages and
a gabled schoolhouse. As we passed by the children inside
were laughing over their singing-lesson, and falling vigorously
to their 'Hoo, hoo, hoo, ha, ha, ha'. The gardens were full
of phloxes and tall daisies just then; I remember the climbing
roses by the bridge, where the river swishes past under green
boughs.


LULLINGSTONE TO DARTFORD

I

The road to Lullingstone turns right at Otford Green; then
left, through a tract of newly built houses, it narrows to a lane
between high hedges decked with wayfaring berries and waxen
traveller's joy. The lane passes presently, by a beech avenue,

into the loveliest region of the Darenth valley. The lower hill-slopes are covered with marjoram; above are the fringes of heavy woodland; downwards, on your left hand cornfields and oasts and gleams of the river; upwards again the Downs and their feathering beechwoods. Do not be perturbed by a forbidding notice at the gate of Lullingstone Castle, provided you are going to the church. It is just a reminder to enter on private property with courtesy and circumspection. Darenth makes a lake here in the park; there are wild duck on its surface; chestnuts looping down towards their own clear images; all round the embosoming hills; an unforgettable scene.

On our first visit we were astonished to find the church stood on the lawn of the great house; we hesitated to venture—trespass—across the sward. Just then a very old gentleman came slowly out of the house. He appreciated our embarrassment, and called to us to go on, go on, if we wished to visit St. Botolph's Church. This was Sir William Hart-Dyke, Father of the House of Commons, gathered to his rest a year or two ago. St. Botolph's is a Norman building, but so much restored *temp.* Edward III (by John de Rokesle, whose brass is close to the rood-screen) that one might suppose it was originally in the Decorated style. It has a nave, chancel, and little bellcote with one bell; a simple design, but how richly patterned with beautiful accessories. The Manor of Lullingstone was bought from the Rokesles by one of those ubiquitous Londoners, John Peche, some time in the fourteenth century. His great-great-grandson, Sir John by now, lies under a magnificent tomb filling the north side of the little sanctuary. It is a marvel of elaboration, from Sir John's effigy in plate-armour, the surcoat embroidered with fruited peach-trees, to the carved canopy, where the crowned A and roses of Prince Arthur of Wales and the pomegranate of Catherine of Aragon adorn the southern spandrels. Elsewhere there are single peaches, carved with the letter ' é ' to remind us that ' Peché ' has two syllables, and the knightly motto ' Prest à Faire '. The words ' Pecche me fieri fecit' carry us a little way towards the origin of the tomb; the craftsmen have left no signature, but some trace here the master-hand of Torregiano and the artists of Henry VII's tomb at Westminster. The makers must have been at work before the young prince died and Catherine's tragedy began.

Sir John was a brilliant figure in courtly circles. At the jousting, when Prince Henry was created Duke of York in 1494, four challengers rode out of Westminster Hall, their horses trapped in the royal colours, and hung with little bells, silver and gilt. Two of them were earls, and one Sir John Peche himself. So valiantly did Sir John run, that in twenty-four courses he broke fourteen spears before a halt was called. Then came his triumph. 'After the souper began the daunces; whiche doon, ij right noble ladies, maidijns . . . the ladie Anne Persie and the ladie Anne Neuyll presented John Peche to . . . the ladie Margarete, the kyngis oldeste daughter; wiche by thauys of the kyng . . . and of all the ladies, gave him the price [prize], that is to sey a ryng of gold with a ruby. . . .' Remember, standing beside his grave, what a paladin lies here. The tomb of Sir Percyvall Hart and his wife Frideswide is opposite Sir John's, whose grandson he was. Sir Percyvall acted as Knight Harbinger to the Tudor sovereigns. A triptych in the castle hall represents him with his two sons. He 'leans one hand on a gold-headed cane, but his left rests upon an hour-glass, beneath which we read "Expecto horam libertatis meae".'

He waited for that release till his eighty-fifth year. The silver-hilted dagger painted in his girdle is a family treasure, and the suit of clothes which appears in the picture only succumbed to moth in 1832. I should like to see that portrait of the good old man : 'A friend to all, a foe to none, fast to his common-weal. . . .'

The last of the Harts so-named at Lullingstone Castle was that Sir Percyvall who twice represented Kent in Parliament and contested the seat five times. He was a fervent Jacobite, entertained Queen Anne and hung up her portrait in his state drawing-room. These loyalties he bequeathed to his daughter Anne, and she wore the Pretender's miniature in her bosom to her dying day. Through her second marriage to Sir Thomas Dyke, of Horeham, a Sussex baronet, the name of Dyke came to Lullingstone. Anne's son, Sir John Dixon Dyke, had not her feeling for the past; to avoid crossing a bridge every time he entered or left his house he sacrificed the castle gateway and filled up the moat. In his nephew and successor's time the family name established itself as Hart-Dyke. 'Whether called by the name of Peche, or of Hart or of Dyke,' writes a biographer, 'the unbroken descent of the same strain of blood and of feeling finds in Lullingstone Church abundant testimony.'

II

After Lullingstone one feels that romance of this quality can scarcely travel farther up the valley; yet there is Eynsford—I left my visit there for another day and then tried to link it up with the castle by a river-path—but a hiatus intervenes, filled for me by a truly hackneyed adventure. I was walking quietly through a field when I heard violent shouting ahead of me. I looked across; there were waving arms, hurrying figures, frantic gestures. A child broke from the group and as she came within earshot shrieked breathlessly 'the little bull is out, the little bull is out'. I saw a glimpse of black and white approach me sideways; it may only have been the trespasser's conscience; but I ran too—and reached the stile first. Still, the lure of a river-side approach made me try again from the Eynsford end and walk for some distance through the meadows. The Darenth just there is a brook of fairy-tale; that day blue skull-cap and rushes had their turn of flowering on its banks; willows and alders leaned over to watch the twists of the stream, the silver lights netted in its eddies. All the way along it makes a pretty undertone of purling sound, which

never startles the wild duck as a stranger's footfall—my footfall
—does sure enough. The Darenth, when it reaches Eynsford,
blends with the village life. Just there its direction turns a little
north from north-east, to thread the ancient bridge. One bank
is fenced by a line of willows; the other green margin melts
into the village street. The group by the old bridge is charming; there is the church of grey flints and the lich-gate; a chestnut tree; an old frame house, once perhaps a mill; a group of
old cottages with an overhanging storey and tiger-lilies in their
garden plots. And Eynsford folk have bestirred themselves to
beautify their surroundings still more. Their village first celebrated Arbor Day nearly forty years ago when that festival
came into vogue. 'The school-bank', says the local history,
'was planted with a row of trees arranged acrostically to spell
"My Son, be wise", that is successively maple, yew, sycamore,
oak, negundo, birch, elm, weigela, ivy arboreal, sumach, elder
(golden).' I wish I had studied the history of Eynsford before
going there, that I too might have spelt out that leafy proverb.
When Queen Victoria died there was another planting to
record how 'she wrought her people lasting good'; it is a
glorious idea to write history in choice and long-lived trees
round the village green, or, best of all, along the new by-pass
road (judiciously, of course), if it might be to earn forgiveness
of our children's children. Eynsford churchyard used, I have
heard, to be a neglected place, until the beautifying spirit stirred
up a body of young villagers to transform it into a real God's
Acre or garden of those who sleep.

The Sibills came to Eynsford as the fifteenth century closed,
and remained there just a hundred years. Their name is queer
and fascinating : still more their coat of arms. A friend of
mine, who has studied the animal carvings of medieval artists
and interpreted forgotten myth and symbol which they illustrate, explained to me the inwardness of the Sibills' strange
heraldic coat. Strange indeed, for it represents a tiger gazing
into a round mirror, where its reflection is distinctly seen. The

tiger, or, strictly speaking, tigress, and mirror was one of many
subjects borrowed by heraldry from the medieval bestiary. The
tigress, says an English-Latin Bestiary of the thirteenth century,
in the British Museum, as Mr. G. C. Druce translates the
passage : ' The tigress, when it finds its lair empty and its offspring carried off, at once follows on the robber's track, who,
though riding on ever so swift a horse, when he sees that he is
being outstripped by the beast . . . has recourse to a cunning
artifice; when he finds it close to him he throws down a sphere
of glass. The tigress is deceived by her own reflection, and
believes it to be her offspring. She checks her flight, desiring
to recover her cub . . . she paws her empty image and
crouches down as if to suckle her young.'

The ruse is repeated again and again; the animal's pursuit
is retarded; the hunter's escape assured; yet, ' misled by her
zealous maternal care, the tigress loses both her offspring and
her revenge '. One would dearly like to know what led some
ancestral Sibill to pitch on this moving episode to adorn his
family shield? It is carved on two spandrels of a stone fire-
place at Little Mote, the ancient home of the family in Eynsford, but its origin is forgotten and the Sibills are no more.

Soon after passing Eynsford Station the railway line takes
a sharp turn and mounts into the hills on the way to Swanley
Junction. But the Darenth flows on past Farningham, Horton
Kirby, and its namesake village towards Dartford and the
Thames. Farningham has a most interesting fifteenth-century
font in the old church, depicting the course of human life in
relation to the seven sacraments. The bride in the marriage
panel wears a head-dress like the Fair Maid of Kent's in Canterbury crypt; the hair rolled round to frame her face is bound
with a jewelled net; the bridegroom has a large fur hat.

Is Darenth still as rural as when I last saw it in May four
years ago: for this region of Kent is being built over at an
alarming pace. I remember the view from the churchyard,
full of eyebright, nettles, and other flowering weeds; the avenue

of betapered chestnuts; the hill rising behind and the old barn roofs. A pretty green lane then led away towards Dartford. I remember too in South Darenth the paper-mill at a bend of the river; the hedges white with may and trimmed with the 'bride's lace' of wild parsley; and the medley of modern villas and old-time cottages.

Wonderful things are to be seen in Darenth Church, which dates from 940 with a Norman chancel of the early twelfth and restorations of the thirteenth century. It has a priest's chamber, and the east end is strangely lit by a round eyelet and two windows, while a cross-shaped opening is blocked in with flint.

### III

Dartford—'Darentford'—in its hilly cleft has lately received the honour of a charter and a large new history has accordingly been prepared. I have not yet read the book—I dare not before writing this chapter; for which the old books have taught me far more than can be set down in a few pages. Indeed, I can only make choice of those things which are of the essence of the place. I must leave aside the pilgrims and the inns it shares with Canterbury; the riches of the church in so far as its shrines and tapers glow as in other Kent churches; all but a few of its personalities. After this self-denying ordinance I turn at first to the ford.

Soon after the Darenth enters the parish it branches into two streams which unite again—I was about to say at Dartford bridge—at the ford let it be, then it widens, after about a two-mile course receives the tributary Cray into its channel, and empties itself into the Thames. For that last two miles till the eighteenth century it flowed through unploughed marshlands. But the ford : go back some 700 years when there was a ferry here and the steward of Dartford Manor had to provide a ferry-boat. About 1235 a hermit built his cell at the river-side, ready to help persons in danger over the crossing and to gather alms for building a bridge. Many came that way on pilgrimage Kent, and by and by, under Henry IV, the bridge was built.

Attached to the Hermitage, no solitary or selfish retreat, was a chapel of St. Katherine, and some of the hermits' names are preserved in church records. Under Henry VII in the parish church of Bromley, John Colebrant took the hermit's habit and made profession ' to live to the honour of God according to the rule of St. Paul the Hermit'. He wore ' a long hooded gown covering his body, with holes for his arms; a tunic, rosary and girdle of rope. His beard was very long and he often went in rags.' The last of the Dartford hermits was Walter Combes, professed in 1518; in 1509 the official collection of bridge-dues began.

I leave the river-side now and climb steep East Hill, which is in the line of Watling Street and almost of old ' St. Edmund's Weye', to the Upper Churchyard. There were Roman burials on either side of Watling Street, and the chapel on the hill-top may at first have been connected with pagan rites. At any rate, it was rebuilt after King Edmund, murdered in 870, became a saint; and, solidly cased in flint, it remained till 1780.

My great-grandfather, the antiquary A. J. Kempe, opened many ancient graves in Dartford neighbourhood. One was a woman's; her light brown hair was still heaped on her skull and fastened with a brooch of pearl which ' rubbed like soap '. In the coffin was a coin of Constantine and fragments of aromatic gum bearing the impress of her linen cerements. Some of the leaning gravestones in the Upper Churchyard are like little sarcophagi shaped to the perishing body; others are sculptured with cherubs' heads and torches, trumpets, and palms. That slender monument, erected in 1851, is in memory of Christopher Waid, a linen-weaver, burned on Dartford Brent on July 19th 1554, one of the earliest Marian martyrs. He wore the fine white shirt his wife had made and repeated at the stake (says the inscription), these courageous words : ' Show some token upon me for good, that they who hate me

may see it and be ashamed, because Thou Lord hast helped me
and comforted me.'

IV

This digresses at length from the East Hill panorama, which
showed me all Dartford, lining the slopes and crouching below
the hilly walls of the Darenth valley. There was the old church
tower, of Saxon origin with an added stage, in the hollow by
the bridge; the stream too that flows past old houses and under
the town trees. The gabled cottages close to the bridge have a
walk along their façades sunken below the roadway, typical,
I fancied, of old-world Dartford sinking gradually, gradually
out of sight. Of the famous nunnery there seems little trace
beyond the fine entrance gate; indeed, we know more of the
nuns than of their buildings, and that is little enough. Edward
III, when he founded Dartford Priory in 1349, installed the
Dominican sisters, twenty-four, with 200 marks to maintain
them, in the castle buildings, where he had held a great tourna-
ment but a few years before. The Order of 'Sisters Preachers'
had only recently arrived in England (1345). St. Dominic,
their founder (1206), laid on them the duty of educating in
religion 'girls of noble but reduced families in Southern
France', and in this country too they were teachers of youth.
About 1527 one of the sisters was allowed 'a preceptor in
grammar and the Latin tongue', and she and other gentle-
women took their lesson in the convent parlour. Local girls
were veiled in this nunnery near at hand, for there was no
great strictness of enclosure, and they had intercourse with their
relatives, who left them small legacies and personal possessions.
Sister Jone Stokton (whose people lived in Overy Street, leading northward from the town) inherited twenty pence, and
Sister Jone Mores twenty pence and a candlestick. The nuns
had a kind friend in John Groverste, an influential townsman
and the occupant of a large house with arched doorway and
shop adjoining at the east corner of Bullis Lane. The sisters

were evidently allowed to visit the Groverstes, friends perhaps of their girlhood, and in return worked a set of tapestry for their host's domestic chapel. Their broidery adorned the 'Blue Room' until about 1817, and though no fragment remains the subject is remembered. It was borrowed from those romances not wholly forbidden within convent walls, and portrayed, in brilliant coloured wools, Hector in armour and Andromache, life-size, and in the background an army with banners. Ten houses belonged to the convent of that picturesque row, standing on the west bank of the Waterside, which looked on to the Cranpit flowing down the middle of the street, and saw the citizens pick their way upon stepping-blocks banded with iron across the shallow stream.

v

Modern industrial Dartford surveyed from that Upper Churchyard has added bold but unbeautiful features to the landscape—a gasometer, many chimneys, much smoke. Not that the past held no history of industry; the stone-cutting, which ate out the gaping chasms characteristic of this North Kent region, must have been its earliest chapter. An interesting contribution was made by Sir John Spilman, who acquired Bicknor Manor, close to the bridge, with its wheat and malt mills. This personage, 'Her Majesties Juiler or gouldesmith of her Juelles', built on his property a mill for making writing paper, said to be the first of its kind in England. On February 17th 1589 Queen Elizabeth gave him a licence; I mention the date from the original document, because one of Dartford's historians renders it 'February 31st 1558', the year being 31 Eliz. It granted John Spilman leave 'for the gathering of all maner of linen ragges, skrolles or scrappes of parchement, peaces of Lyme, Leather, Shreddes and Slippinges of Cardes and oulde fishinge Nettes, fitte and necessarie for the makinge of anie sorte of white wrightinge paper'. The poetaster,

'body of steel, made as of purpose for his never-resting in-
defatigable spirit'.

.		.		.		.		.		.		.		.

The mention of Dartford Heath recalls another camp, less
stern than Cromwell's, and the famous manœuvres in July
1780 'to effect the passage of the Thames'. 'Eight thousand
troops were marched to Gravesend and in three divisions con-
veyed across the river, backwards and forwards in less than
eight hours,' by the use of three moving platforms or causeways
roped on to barges. The troops and the populace amused themselves with rough horse-play; but the belles of the neighbourhood had the time of their lives. There they all are, the
daughters of county families, more or less, the Miss Dykes of
Lullingstone Castle, Miss Mumford of Sutton-at-Hone; last,
but not least, the Misses Catherine and Ethelinda Thorpe of
Bexley. How merrily they forgather with officers and their
wives at the mess; 'partake of the military mania', and—can
you believe it?—'dressed *en militaire*, parade the camp'.
Ethelinda, gayest of the gay, was an authoress; her *Moonshine*,
published after she had become Mrs. Potts, can be perused in
the British Museum, though not much to be recommended :

> . . . a kind of hobbling prose
> That limps along and tinkles in the close.

But those grand manœuvres—youth in the blood—high spirits
in the ascendant, combined for once to inspire her rather better
than her wont. Thus she immortalized the scene :

> Behold in epauleted scarlet, Belles advance,
> Like heroines painted in some old romance;
> Who, thus accoutred, may with due disdain
> View the subaltern beauties of the plain :—
> By beaux protected, slowly march the groups,
> In all the pomp of flounces, silks and hoops,
> By silken trains the wide parade is swept,
> In silken fetters rebel gauzes kept.

## AN EPILOGUE

HOW changes come about! Hardly have I finished writing of present-day Canterbury before its familiar landscape is suddenly altered and disfigured by a small flame in a handful of old hay. In the Precincts a little group stands awestruck, watching a fierce glow in the northern sky, a dense column of smoke, lit by the spurt of fire, which climbs, climbs frantically, behind the silver roof of the cathedral nave.

'Denne's Mill is burning!' The news passes to each fresh arrival. Down by the mill, a furnace now, terrific to behold, the city congregates; the streets are empty, trade at a standstill. Through the narrow converging lanes the citizens flock excitedly, eager spectators at the greatest holocaust most of them will ever see. Nothing can be done, even with the Stour, for so long a serviceable ally, flowing close at hand, with fire-engines rushed in from the country-side; nothing can be done to save the old mill. There is too much garnered here to feed the monstrous flame; six storeys of heavily painted wood; 400 tons of grain, stocks of flour and cereals. The mill, good old servant, is doomed! It has stood almost for a century and a half, one in a succession of mills reaching back to the Abbot's Mill, and without doubt the most imposing of them all. Next to the cathedral, we tell each other sadly, it was the chief landmark in our city; we shall miss it like an old friend's familiar shape. The mill was built in 1792 of such a vast size after the design of John Smeaton, engineer of the third Eddystone Lighthouse, to serve as a granary in the event of Napoleonic invasion, a bulwark against famine; how real the dread of an invaded England must have been, closer than our dread of renewed war. . . . Yes, the mill is doomed. There! one side of it crashes, flaring defiantly into the stream, exposing the burning floors within.  The roof will go next; it is gone—with a terrific release of fire to the morning air.  All is over; there is a gap against the sky which the black roof, curved like a mighty cupola—the black cap set on tall white shoulders—has filled time out of mind.  Nothing remains but the blackened water-wheel, a few gaunt girders, and those heaps of scorching corn.  For weeks to come they will smoulder and glow, and the wind will scatter loose grains as if to sow them somehow, somewhere, over the city, until at last the funeral pyre is exhausted and fallen to ashes.  One hears talk of the future, of rebuilding and street widening. . . . But 'The fire will never be forgotten,' say the townsfolk.  Before our eyes a new incident has written itself into our history.

And so long, I think, as I can walk about the city, turning the sharp corner of Mill Lane where the old bridge crosses St. Radigund's, the ghost of vanished scenes will take shape; the laden wagons stand of a morning about the entrance, under the mill's great shadow; the men shout to one another from floor to floor and hoist up the heavy sacks; the horses nuzzle into their feeding-bags and the children stop to pat their brown noses as they pass by them on the way to school.

# BIBLIOGRAPHY

## I. KENT HISTORY AND TOPOGRAPHY

*Archaeologia Cantiana.* Vols. I–XLIV.

HASTED: *History of Kent.* 4 vols. (1790.)

LAMBARDE: *Perambulation of Kent.* (1570.)

SOMNER, ed. BATTELY: *The Antiquities of Canterbury.* (1703.)

G. S.: *Chronological History of Canterbury Cathedral* (with reprint of *Cathedrall Newes from Canterbury*). (1883.)

GARDINER, DOROTHY: *Canterbury: Story of the English Towns.* (2nd Ed., 1934.)

STONE: *Chronicle of John,* ed. G. W. SEARLE. Cambridge Antiquarian Society. (1902.)

LEWIS, J.: *History and Antiquities of the Isle of Tenet in Kent.* (1723.)

PLANCHÉ, J. R.: *A Corner of Kent: some Account of the Parish of Ash-next-Sandwich.* (1864.)

HUSSEY: *Chronicles of Wingham.* (1896.)

BOYS, JOHN: *General View of Agriculture.* (2nd Ed., 1813.)

PEARMAN, A. J.: *Ashford: its Church, Vicars, College.* (1886.)

ORWIN, C. S., and WILLIAMS, S.: *A History of Wye Church and Wye College.* (1912.)

BOLTON, ARTHUR T.: *Chilham Castle.* (1912.)

*Faversham: Extracts from Wills and other Documents, Containing Benefactions to the Town of.* (1844.)

CULMER, G. G.: *Davington Church and Priory.* (1933.)

*Historical MSS. Commission, Reports* IV and V. (Corporations of Lydd and New Romney.)

GERARDE, JOHN: *Herball.*

SHRUBSOLE and DEANE: *History of Rochester.* (1772.)

BECKER, M. JANET: *Rochester Bridge, 1387–1856.* (1930.)

ANDERSEN, J. A.: *A Dane's Excursions in Britain.* (1809.)

RUSSELL, J. M.: *History of Maidstone.* (1881.)

RICHARDS, F.: *Old Sevenoaks.* (1901.)

SACKVILLE-WEST, V.: *Knole and the Sackvilles.*

RAIKES: *Records of Goudhurst.*

MARKHAM, GERVASE: *The Inrichment of the Weald of Kent.* (1675.)

LODGE, E. C.: *Account Book of a Kentish Estate.* (1616–1704.)

HESKETH, C.: *History of Otford.* (1924.)

DUNKIN, J.: *History of Dartford.* (1844.)

PACKE, CHRISTOPHER: *Ancographia sive Convallium Descriptio, or an Explanation of the plan of A New Philosophico-Chronographical Chart of East Kent.*


## II. BIOGRAPHY AND LETTERS

HOLLAND, SIBYLLA: *Letters of,* ed. BERNARD HOLLAND.

BARHAM, R. H.: *Life and Letters of.* (1870.)

FORSTER, JOHN: *Life of Charles Dickens.* (1870–74.)

CARTER, Mrs. ELIZABETH: *Letters to Catherine Talbot.* (2 vols., 1808.)

—— *Letters to Mrs. Montagu.* (3 vols., 1817.)

PENNINGTON, MONTAGU: *Memoirs of Mrs. Elizabeth Carter.* (1808.)

ROSSETTI, W. M.: *Life of Dante Gabriel Rossetti.*

WRIGHT, R.: *Life of General James Wolfe.* (1864.)

PAIN, E. C.: *The Last of our Luggers and the Men who Sailed them.*

MONTAGU, Mrs. ELIZABETH: *Letters of,* ed. by MATTHEW MONTAGU. Vol. I. (1810.)

AUSTEN, JANE: *Letters of,* ed. EDWARD, LORD BRABOURNE. (1884.)

SCOT, REYNOLD: *Discovery of Witchcraft.* (1654.)

SCULL, G. B.: *Dorothea Scott and History of Eggarton House.*

PECK: *Desiderata Curiosa.* Vol. II. (Richard Plantagenet.)

WALPOLE, HORACE: *Letters of.* Vol. II, ed. PETER CUNNINGHAM. (1877.)

WALTON, IZAAK: *Life of Sir Henry Wotton.* (1825.)

CANTERBURIENSIS: *Life and Adventures of Sir William Courtenay.* (1838.)

BRYDGES, SIR S. EGERTON: *Autobiography.* (1834.)

FAUSSETT, BRYAN: *Inventorium Sepulchrale.* (1836.)


## III. POETRY AND MISCELLANEOUS

CHALMERS' POETS (1810): *Works of Michael Drayton, Richard Lovelace, Christopher Smart, Elijah Fenton, Paul Whitehead.*

GROSART, A. B.: *Poems of Phineas Fletcher.*
—— *Arden of Feversham.*
—— *Tale of Beryn.*
CHAUCER: *Chanoun Yeoman's Tale.*
MARLOWE, CHRISTOPHER: *Plays of.*
ROSSETTI, D. G.: *Poems.*
*Kentish Garland*, ed. JULIA DE VAYNES. (1872.)
METELLUS: *His Dialogue, containing a Relation of a Journey to Tunbridge Wells.* (1693.)
BARHAM, R. H.: *The Ingoldsby Legends.*
HINDLEY, C.: *John Taylor, the Water Poet.* (1872.)

## IV.  FICTION

DICKENS, CHARLES: *David Copperfield; Mystery of Edwin Drood,* etc.
WALPOLE, HUGH: *The Cathedral.*
KAYE-SMITH, SHEILA: *Joanna Godden.*
JAMES, G. P. R.: *The Smuggler.* (1845.)
FREEMAN, R. AUSTIN: *Mystery of Angelina Frood.*
AINSWORTH, W. HARRISON: *Rookwood.* (1850.)
KNATCHBULL-HUGESSEN, E. H. (Lord Brabourne): *Moonshine Fairy Stories.* (1872.)
POTTS, E. M.: *Moonshine.* (2nd. Ed. 1832.)

Thomas Churchyard in Armada year addressed a pamphlet
to Sir Walter Raleigh, describing 'a Paper-Mill . . . of late
set up neere the Town of Darthford, by an High German
called M. Spilman'. It is but a doggerel rhyme, setting out
with the praise of paper :

> . . . It shoes new bookes and keepes old workes awake. . . .
> It flies from friend and foe in letter-wise,
> And serves a state and kingdome sundry wayes. . . .

Then follows a lively word-picture of the mill, surely one of
the earliest poetic accounts of machinery.

> The hammers thump and make as lowde a noyse
> As fuller doth, that beates his wollen cloth,
> In open shewe; then sundry secrete toyes,
> Make rotten ragges to yeelde a thickened froth :
> Then is it stampt, and washed as white as snowe;
> Then flong on frame, and hang'd to dry I trow;
> Thus paper streight it is, to write upon,
> As it were rubde and smoothde with slicking-stone.

After a century or so the enterprising Spilman family fell on
evil days; the last members were 'supported by the parish' and
in 1732 their ruined mill became a gunpowder factory. But
through them paper has established itself as a Kent industry.

## VI

How little after all in these pages I have written of Dartford! Nothing as yet of that strange fervent Evangelist, the
schoolmaster and curate of Clun, Vavassour Powell, who
was outlawed from wildest Shropshire for preaching unlawful
doctrines on the hill-sides, and, 'being indeed a fighting man',
joined the army and was called to Dartford. There he preached
again, in season and out; to Cromwell's soldiers encamped on
Dartford Heath; through plague-stricken days in the town,
when 'dead bodies were carried out by my chamber-wall-
window, yet it pleased God to preserve me and my Family.'
. . . Powell's biographer speaks of his fiery temperament, his

# INDEX OF PERSONS AND BOOKS

## INDEX OF PLACES